HOW WESTMINSTER WORKS . . . AND WHY IT DOESN'T

IAN DUNT

W&N
WEIDENFELD & NICOLSON

First published in Great Britain in 2023 by Weidenfeld & Nicolson,
an imprint of The Orion Publishing Group Ltd
Carmelite House, 50 Victoria Embankment
London EC4Y 0DZ

An Hachette UK Company

5 7 9 10 8 6

A CIP catalogue record for this book is available from the British Library.

ISBN (Hardback) 978 1 3996 0273 0
ISBN (eBook) 978 1 3996 0275 4
ISBN (Audio) 978 1 3996 0276 1

Typeset by Input Data Services Ltd, Bridgwater, Somerset

Printed in Great Britain by Clays Ltd, Elcograf S.p.A.

MIX
Paper from responsible sources
FSC® C104740

www.weidenfeldandnicolson.co.uk
www.orionbooks.co.uk

To Menissa Saleem
For reasons too vast to be put into words

CONTENTS

Introduction: Failure

Chris Grayling had to move quickly.

It was early 2013. After years climbing the Conservative party ranks, he'd finally secured a senior ministerial post. He was the secretary of state for justice. It was the kind of position from which anything was possible: home secretary, foreign secretary, even prime minister.

But to do that, he had to accomplish something eye-catching. It didn't strictly matter what it was. It didn't even really matter whether it worked or not. The project could fall apart in five years if needs be. By then, it would all be a distant memory, largely forgotten in the grandeur of a new department. What mattered was that it captured the prime minister's attention today.

The main imperative was that he acted swiftly. Ministers operate on a tight time frame. Typically they stay in position for around two years before they're shuffled off, either downwards towards the ministerial dead-end jobs, or upwards to the soaring heights of British public life. If they're lucky, they get three years; if they're unlucky, they get six months. Then the merry-go-round starts again. There was an election coming in 2015, so at most he had a couple of years.

But Grayling had a handicap. He suffered a particularly acute form of it, but it wasn't unique. It's a handicap faced by almost all ministers. The handicap was that he didn't know what he was doing.

He'd demonstrated no previous experience of the criminal justice system. He'd shown no evidence of having studied it, or worked in it or researched it. If he had any expertise at all, it was in TV and public relations, which he used to work in before running to be an MP. At no stage in his political career had anyone asked him to demonstrate deep subject knowledge in any area, let alone criminal justice. They hadn't asked for it when he ran to be selected as the local Tory candidate, or when he contested his seat at the general election, or when he was appointed to Cabinet.

So without any expertise or experience, Grayling made a decision. He would privatise probation. He would burn the existing probation model to the ground and start again from scratch, using market mechanisms.

In the years to come, this decision would cause misery and suffering on an extreme scale. People would die who might not otherwise have died. Probation workers would have their professional lives ruined. Hundreds of thousands of offenders would be released from jail without support or meaningful supervision. And a key section of the British state, tasked with keeping the public safe, would collapse into total chaos.

'He delivered,' says Richard Garside, director of the Centre for Crime and Justice Studies. 'He absolutely delivered on what he was going to do. And it was a complete disaster.'

No one talks much about probation. Many people don't know what it means. Most MPs have no idea how it works.

It doesn't trigger the same level of public interest as the NHS, or education, or policing. But it is one of the key pillars of criminal justice, dedicated to rehabilitating offenders and protecting the public.

The police exist to catch people who commit crimes. Probation exists to stop them committing further crimes.

After serving their jail sentences, offenders are subject to supervision. They have to attend meetings with probation services to make sure they're staying away from criminal activity. There might be other conditions too. They can be put under curfew with an electronic tag, or told they can't socialise with their former accomplices, or forced to attend drug treatment programmes.

Probation is often used for people who haven't gone to jail at all. Offenders who committed a low-level crime like theft are often given a community sentence, which means they're punished outside of the prison system; or a suspended sentence, which means it won't be enforced unless they reoffend. They'll be supervised by probation services and might be given an additional punishment, like unpaid work cleaning graffiti.

Probation is a strange mixture of empathy and severity. Its function is to support people so that they can stay away from crime but ring the alarm bells if it looks like they're falling back into it. That makes it sound simple, but in reality it's very complicated. Offenders typically lead messy, chaotic lives. 'I estimate that one in two will have been abused as a child, with about one in four taken into care,' Her Majesty's Inspector of Probation said in her 2019 annual report. 'A disproportionate number have special education needs or were expelled from school. A worrying number have become serious drug users or dependent on alcohol, or both, and many suffer with anxiety, depression or other mental health conditions.'

Effective rehabilitation of offenders therefore requires the bringing together of numerous social services: housing, mental health support, help with drug addiction, education, employment, benefits. It's hard, it's often unsuccessful, and it's almost completely unsung.

When Grayling became justice secretary, probation was working pretty well. The service was run by 35 probation trusts, every single one of which was rated either good or exceptional by the government. They'd managed to get reoffending rates down to 34.2 per cent after a decade of steady decline. The service had just won the British Quality Foundation Gold Award for Excellence. It was nothing spectacular, but a perfectly respectable record in a difficult area of policy.

Then everything changed. Grayling completely reinvented the system.

It was called Transforming Rehabilitation. He abolished the trusts and split the service in two. High-risk offenders would be dealt with by a publicly owned National Probation Service. Low- and medium-risk offenders would be dealt with by a network of privately owned community rehabilitation companies (CRCs).

The private companies would set up a suite of products that magistrates and judges could then use for sentencing. They would run unpaid work projects. They would manage accredited programmes, which are a form of structured intervention largely based on cognitive behavioural therapy. And these would all run alongside their supervision requirements – checking in with offenders regularly, making sure they were on the straight and narrow, working out what their risk level was. Whenever any of these initiatives was successfully completed, it would trigger a payment to the probation company.

There was also one further element. It was the crown jewels of the reforms, the core intellectual justification for what was taking place. It was called payment-by-results. After two years, when the reoffending data came in, the firms would be paid £4,000 for every offender who did not reoffend and £1,000 for every offence that had been avoided.

This payment would unleash the dynamism of the free market on the sclerotic world of criminal justice. It would bring innovation to the anaemic slumber of the public sector. The payments would encourage probation companies to experiment with different ideas. If they worked, they'd make lots of money. If they didn't, they'd be penalised.

On paper, it seemed ingenious. The National Probation Service would handle high-risk offenders and those who had committed violent or sexual crimes. The public would be assured that the most dangerous criminals would stay in the public sector under the ultimate responsibility of the government. But for lower-level criminals, the kind who rotate in and out of jail for minor offences like drugs and theft, the full possibilities of the market would be activated, with all sorts of different strategies to see if they could break the cycle.

There was a problem with Grayling's proposals. It was causation.

It manifested in two separate ways – on sentencing and on rehabilitation. He presumed that the number of sentences involving unpaid work or accredited programmes would remain fairly steady. The Ministry of Justice looked at the sentences being handed down under the existing system, worked out how much they'd need to pay for each one for the companies to make a profit, and then used that to write up the contracts.

But sentencing is not static. It responds to trends. Sometimes there are fewer people committing crimes. Sometimes police numbers fall, as they did when Grayling was justice secretary, so there are fewer people being caught committing crimes. And if either of those things happened, there would be fewer sentences, which meant there'd be fewer orders for probation services, which meant less income for the probation companies.

The same applies if different kinds of cases end up in court. If there were more serious sexual or violent crimes, the probation companies would make less money, because the offenders would come under the remit of the National Probation Service. And it would also apply if judges and magistrates happened to become sterner in their rulings. If they decided to send people to prison instead of issuing community sentences, another set of income streams would be cut off.

A similar problem applied to the back end of the probation experiment, through the payment-by-results model.

Grayling's system presumed that there would be a clear causal connection between the activity of the probation company and the rise or fall in reoffending. But in fact, prisoners reoffend for all sorts of reasons. Maybe they can't access benefits, or they become homeless, or they start taking drugs again. And that means that the cause of reoffending cannot be placed solely with probation. It's prompted by events happening in completely different parts of the system, run by completely different parts of government – the Department of Work and Pensions, the Ministry of Housing,

Communities and Local Government, the Department for Education, the Department of Health.

This had been well understood for years. In 2002, the Social Exclusion Unit concluded that 'the problems in prisoners' lives are often highly complicated and inter-related' and therefore required 'a co-ordinated multi-agency response'. In 2003, a government-commissioned report by Lord Carter found that rehabilitation reached its 'maximum effect' when 'programmes target a spectrum of risk factors – employment and education, along with behavioural or cognitive programmes'.

The payment-by-results model was therefore likely to be completely arbitrary. It would reward or punish companies on the basis of things that had nothing to do with them.

Years later, when everything had fallen apart, the Ministry of Justice would concede these arguments. 'Reoffending is really complicated and depends on factors like housing and access to benefits and so on,' Sir Richard Heaton, permanent secretary at the department, told MPs on the Public Accounts Committee in 2019. 'Looking back on it, we should have done differently.'

But by then it was too late.

The British public are supposed to be protected from poor ministerial decision-making by at least four separate institutions: the civil service, the Treasury, the press and Parliament. Before an idea can be implemented, they should step in to assess the evidence, evaluate the project, debate it, scrutinise it, test it and, finally, if needed, stop it. But in the months ahead, as Grayling pushed forward with his plan, each one of these institutions failed.

The warnings were issued, but no one listened to them. In early 2013, the Ministry of Justice launched a consultation about the plans. A huge range of expert contributions came in from those who worked in probation, inspected it or studied it. They were universally damning.

'The interface between the dynamic management of risk of harm and the payment-by-results model in our view creates an inherent tension,' HM Inspector of Probation said. 'We do not believe that this tension can be successfully managed within the framework proposed. Any lack of contractual or operational clarity between the public and private sector will, in our view, lead to systemic failure and an increased risk to the public.'

'Our overall response to the proposals in the consultation paper,' the Probation Chiefs Association and the Probation Association said in a joint submission, 'is that they will increase the risk of harm to the public.'

Those submissions were ignored. Grayling published a government response to the consultation that failed to mention any of the criticism and instead said: 'It is not a surprise, faced with stubbornly high reoffending rates, that there were important areas of consensus.'

The plan pressed ahead. Andrew Neilson, policy lead at the Howard League for Penal Reform, was at a debate on the proposals when he spotted Ed Boyd, who was working as a special adviser to the government with a focus on payment-by-results models. He approached him after the event, as he was getting on his bike to cycle back to the office.

'Don't you see?' Neilson said. 'This isn't going to work.' Boyd looked up the road and fastened his helmet. 'Oh, I'm sure it'll all come out in the wash,' he said, and cycled off.

Officials from Napo, the probation officers' trade union, made repeated requests for a meeting with Grayling, but they were all denied. Tania Bassett, a union official, finally caught sight of him at an event at the Tory conference and decided it was her one opportunity to speak to him.

She gulped down her wine, summoned her confidence and strode over to where he was standing. Once Grayling discovered which organisation she worked for, he started bellowing at her. 'I won't meet with you,' he shouted. 'You're histrionic. You're immature.' That was the only meeting the secretary of state had with the trade union of the service he was reforming.

Deep in the civil service, those warnings should have been listened to. Under the civil service code, officials are obliged to advise ministers 'on the basis of the evidence' and take 'due account of expert and professional advice'.

In fact, civil servants were to a large extent removed from the process. Transforming Rehabilitation was primarily the work of private sector consultants. Between 1 April 2013 and 31 April 2014, the Ministry of Justice spent £15.2 million on consultants working on privatising probation. Firms like Collinson Grant were charged with 'development of contract management functions', while Ernst and Young worked on 'development of the shadow bid and business readiness testing'.

Even so, civil servants could have spoken out. But most accounts from the Ministry of Justice at the time indicate that Grayling actively discouraged questions about the feasibility of the initiative.

'During the huge programme to outsource the probation service between 2012 and 2015,' the Institute for Government concluded, 'officials were not encouraged to highlight what many outside government identified as serious flaws in policy design.'

One civil servant had clearly had enough. In a last-gasp effort to force the government to change course, they started to leak internal information from the department. In December 2013, they sneaked out a Ministry of Justice risk register, which maps out the likelihood of things going wrong with a project.

It warned of a 'reduction in performance', 'service delivery failure' and 'operational confusion'. As a result, there would be a 'higher risk to the public' and 'poorer outcomes' for victims. The courts could 'lose confidence in the ability of the service to deliver sentences'.

That month, Grayling sat down to answer questions from the justice committee of MPs in Parliament. 'Your own risk assessment is that a score of 20 indicates significant detrimental effect and has roughly an 80 per cent chance of occurring,' Labour MP John McDonnell told him. 'They list a whole range of potential risks which have hit the 20 mark. One of them is a risk of an unacceptable drop in operational performance during the programme, leading to delivery failure and reputational damage. That means the general public could be put at risk.'

Grayling glanced up from his notes. 'It is not about scores,' he said. 'I will look you in the eye and say I have seen no evidence. I have not been provided with any warnings by my team that business as usual will not continue.' The leaked risk register was largely ignored.

After the civil service, the Treasury is supposed to provide a check against ministerial decision-making. This isn't really on the basis of social benefit, but value for money. It's tasked with protecting the taxpayer. But by virtue of that assessment, it is supposed to weigh up the potential risks of the plans and whether they are likely to satisfy their objectives.

Grayling's plan went straight through Treasury clearance and got the green light. It then went through a Major Projects review and was given another green light.

These two assessments significantly strengthened his hand. 'Mr McDonnell,' Grayling said, 'as you will know from the experience of your own party in government, the Treasury is quite assiduous in looking at things that are laid before it. The fact that it has approved the outline business case for the project suggests that the kind of things being highlighted as risks are not substantial ones and do not exist beyond the theory at the start of a project.'

Normally the press would succeed where the civil service might fail. It is meant to scrutinise power and shine a harsh light on the behaviour of ministers and the government. But probation is a policy backwater, with little public understanding or interest in what it does. It doesn't sell papers. It doesn't provoke comments from readers. It doesn't result in internet traffic. And it doesn't really interest journalists. To even begin to explain what the reforms entailed, journalists would first need to explain how probation worked, and that all sounds quite tedious and technical to a news editor.

Privatisation was therefore able to take place with barely a glimmer of coverage in the press. Only the *Guardian*'s home affairs editor, Alan Travis, made a sustained effort to assess the plans in a critical way. Throughout the entirety of 2013, just 24 articles were published in the whole of the British press mentioning the phrase 'Transforming Rehabilitation'. All but one of them was in a broadsheet newspaper.

Many of these articles focused on issues that were unconnected to the outsourcing of the service. Only a handful attempted to explain the core purpose of the initiative, and those that did were often supportive. The *Telegraph*, for instance, wrote a sympathetic article with the headline: 'Chris Grayling: Using same old probation services to cut reoffending is madness'.

Carol Hedderman and Alex Murphy, two criminologists with an interest in probation, carried out an extensive study of press coverage during this period. It did not make for reassuring reading. 'The level of privatisation is arguably the greatest change to the delivery of probation services since the Probation Act of 1907,' they said. 'However, the potential risks identified by probation professionals and academics received little attention.'

In fact, half of all the mentions of the word 'probation' in the press during 2012 and 2013 were in stories about the US, rather than the UK. They included the Mail Online pieces 'Liberace discarded me like a "piece of trash" after introducing me to drugs, says jailed ex-lover' and 'Lindsay Lohan "punched" glamorous blonde psychic palm reader in NYC club as she tried to woo boyband heartthrob'.

Projects at this scale would normally be expected to be piloted before they are rolled out nationally. This involves taking a local area and trialling the programme to see if the results are as expected. But instead, Grayling did the opposite. He took the various existing pilots operating in this area and scrapped them.

When he became justice secretary, pilot schemes on payment-by-results were taking place in Doncaster and Peterborough prisons. They weren't directly comparable to the probation reform, but they were operating in similar areas. And yet they were not due to report back until after the election, so Grayling simply ignored them. In 2014, they were wound up.

There were also ongoing pilots of private–public partnerships at probation trusts in Wales, Staffordshire and West Midlands, which had been set up in 2012. But Grayling cancelled them in his first week as justice secretary. Not only was the evidential basis for the policy ignored, any ongoing projects that could have informed it were actively dismantled.

Asked about his decision in the House of Commons, Grayling made clear that pilots were surplus to requirements. 'Sometimes,' he said, 'we just have to believe something is right and do it.'

The real problem of the pilots was their timescale. It requires patience to secure a viable evidence base for structural reform. By the time they would have reported back, the next ministerial reshuffle would have already taken place. Grayling would have lost his motivation for pursuing the reform in the first place.

'The aim was to deliver the programme prior to the election,' Michael Spurr, chief executive of HM Prisons and Probation Service, admitted to the Public Accounts Committee in 2019. 'There is no question about that. Our view was that we had enough evidence to be able to proceed at that point, and that those risks could be managed. We were wrong about that.'

The speed of implementation meant an entire pillar of the criminal justice system was overhauled without the data needed to ensure it would continue to function effectively. 'The Ministry designed and implemented its reforms too quickly and without sufficient testing,' the National Audit Office (NAO) concluded in 2019. 'Tight deadlines meant that the Ministry did not adequately test how the transformed system might work before letting contracts. It did not have a good understanding of probation trusts' delivery models, working practices and governance.'

That extended to the new private companies themselves, which had been encouraged to bid by ministers who were keen to see the project completed. 'Completing the procurement in a challenging timetable,' the NAO said, 'limited bidders' understanding of their exposure to business risk.'

One Tory MP with a close interest in justice policy looked on in amazement as Grayling drove the project through. 'It wasn't evidence based,' he says. 'It was driven by an almost theological belief in the effectiveness of market forces. There was a general lack of understanding of the complexity of it and a lack of understanding that probation is downstream of the problems that occur. It was a car crash. Everybody said it was going to happen. And the ministers carried on driving.'

The last defensive structure against the reforms was Parliament itself. It is supposed to hold the government to account. It can do this by amending or rejecting the legislation the government introduces.

But there was a problem. There was no legislation.

The Labour party, which sat on the opposition benches, was outraged. 'It is possible that the secretary of state is right and that the experts whom he believes are wrong are wrong,' Labour MP Toby Perkins said. 'However, surely in the interests of democratic accountability, a radical change of the sort he proposes should be debated properly in the House. Why is he so frightened of proper scrutiny of his policies?'

But Grayling had no need to subject himself to Parliament. During the course of the reforms in 2013, there were only three events in Parliament pertaining to them: a statement to the Commons outlining the plan on 9 January, an opposition day debate triggered by the Labour party on 30 October, and the justice committee hearing in which McDonnell challenged Grayling on 3 December. But none of these events involved a vote that could stop the justice secretary. MPs could talk about what was happening, but they could not do anything about it.

The reason for that lay not with Grayling, but with the Labour party. In 2007, when Labour was in government, it passed the Offender Management Act. It hadn't been intended to privatise probation – quite the opposite. The minister at the time said that trusts would be 'public sector based'. But the Act followed a pattern that dominated legislation under Labour and the various governments that followed it. It was extremely broad.

It served to massively increase the power of the government. It did not just allow the Labour minister of the time to do what they wanted at that moment without parliamentary involvement. It allowed any minister, at any time, to do whatever they wanted to do, at any moment. Section 3(2) of the Act contained the kill shot. 'The secretary of state,' it read, 'may make contractual or other arrangements with any other person for the making of the probation provision.'

Grayling could barely conceal his glee. 'I should thank the Labour party,' he said, as the blood drained from the faces of the MPs opposite him. 'It might not have been what Labour intended, but it is what the power does.'

In June 2014, the Ministry of Justice triggered the launch. The probation trusts were dissolved. The National Probation Service and the CRCs took over.

Probation staff were allocated to the private or public sector on the basis of a backdated time-freeze exercise. The government took a set date in the past and assigned points for the kinds of cases probation officers were working on at the time – lower points for low- and medium-risk cases and higher points for high-risk cases. Then they put the officers in a list, from low points to high, set the number of staff they needed, and copied and pasted the bottom of the list to the private sector.

It was as simple as that. There was no assessment of people's careers or their preferences. Instead, an otherwise innocuous day in the past defined the probation officer's future career. 'It made no sense,' says an officer working at the time, who was sent to the National Probation Service. 'It made no sense on any basis whatsoever. There was no way of rationalising what they were doing. The way they calculated who would go where was ridiculous.'

All of a sudden, from one day to the next, the country had a two-tier probation service. Teams who had worked together in the same office for years were suddenly split down the middle. Certain floors, wings or even rooms of the building were designated private or public. 'They put signs on the doors,' an officer says. 'They literally started labelling the kettles.'

None of this was technically planned. It was simply a second-order consequence of the fact that Grayling wanted to privatise probation but was worried about the public reaction to murderers and rapists being handled in the private sector. 'Lo and behold,' Heaton told the Public Accounts Committee, 'you then have a two-tier probation service. You have engineered a split. I do not think that anyone set out to design a two-tier probation service. It was a consequence.'

Eventually, the two sides of probation moved to different offices. And then things got worse.

The first problem was with the IT system. The Ministry of Justice said it would provide a so-called ICT gateway, which would allow different institutional networks to communicate with each other, by June 2015. In the end, it was delayed until September 2016, over two years after privatisation took place. Even by January 2019, only two of the private firms were using it. For long stretches, the firms were unable to share information between each other, the public service, or HM Prisons and Probation Service. The tiny pieces of intelligence that go to make up an offender's risk assessment – whether they've started drinking again, or were heard shouting at their partner, or failed a drugs test – began to fall through the cracks.

But the bigger problem came with a predictable cultural division between the two sides. National Audit Office investigators discovered that staff in the private companies thought the public sector officers were 'unduly critical and dismissive', while staff in the public sector thought private sector staff 'had become too focused on their commercial and contractual targets'.

Until now, the probation system had been based on the fluid assessment of risk. An offender might be considered low risk, but would be escalated to medium or high risk if they began to exhibit the behaviours that had once caused them to break the law. This was the approach that allowed probation officers to step in before an act of domestic violence or an assault on the street.

But now the risk assessment was split between different organisations. The service was segregated into 21 private contracts, 8 different companies, one public body, 41 police forces, the National Offender Management Service and countless individual prisons. The connections and local collaborative arrangements that had been in place for decades had been burned to the ground.

Worse, the regional structure of the new arrangements resisted any kind of rational assessment. The regions for the private and public sector probation services were only aligned in London and Wales, with the remaining five areas requiring the public sector services to work with two or three private sector groups.

The basic operating system of risk assessment information sharing started to completely break down. 'You had offenders that didn't know whether they were being supervised by the private sector or the public sector,' a probation officer said. 'You had different protocols for each private sector firm. So there were eight different companies that ran the twenty-one contracts, and each one of them had their own way of talking to children's services.'

And then, with alarming speed, it became clear that something had gone terribly wrong with the contracts.

As probation experts had warned, the Ministry of Justice had been unable to predict the kinds of sentences being handed down by judges and magistrates.

One of the problems was that recorded crime was falling. In normal circumstances, this would have been considered a good thing, but under privatisation it was a disaster. The expected workflow that all the financial calculations were based on had not materialised.

Those cases that were going to court were more likely to be serious crimes rather than the sort that would have triggered the probation services offered by the firms. There simply weren't enough sentences being passed down involving the kind of accredited programmes and light-touch initiatives the private sector made its money from.

'We were caught in the unfortunate position of not getting the forecast right,' Heaton said, 'and having a model that turned out to be inflexible and not having tested it.'

The National Probation Service was getting too much work. And the private sector was getting too little.

The wave struck the National Probation Service immediately and got worse from there. 'The first thing that hit was a massive increase in workload,' a probation officer from the time says. 'The first weeks were absolute chaos. There were people on 175 per cent capacity. And then the intensity of the caseload increased.'

The problem was not merely quantitative. It was qualitative. Until now, the probation officers had had a mixed caseload – some serious crimes and some less serious. Caseworkers went from having around 10 high-risk cases out of 30 to having 50 or so exclusively high-risk cases, predominantly involving violent or sexual crime. Those cases required substantial amounts of work. They needed parole reports, inter-agency organisational meetings, accommodation arrangements, child protection conferences, information assessment about changed circumstances, weekly meetings with the offender, regular reviews and extensive administrative requirements. But more than that, they had a greater emotional toll. Probation officers were no longer able to take a break from some of the most disturbing cases to deal with driving offences or theft. They had to embed themselves in the darkest areas of the human experience all day, every day.

This had three professional consequences. The first was that officers could not prioritise their workload. They were no longer able to set aside a less serious case because a high-risk offender had suddenly been put in custody. Now, any event that demanded their attention took them away from another event that also demanded their attention.

The second was a deterioration in their capacity to make professional assessments. 'If every case and situation you deal with is right at the top of the scale, you lose perspective,' a National Probation Service officer says. 'It can make officers view everything as more risky, or, more dangerously, it has the opposite effect, and makes officers more blasé about risk because they're living it every day. If you don't have those contrasts, that's a real issue. We saw that a lot.'

The third was exhaustion. The quantity and quality of the work was so severe that individual probation officers started to buckle underneath it. By August 2018, the public sector staff vacancy rate was 11 per cent, and as high as 20 per cent in London. 'They were burning out,' a probation officer says. 'That's what happened. The public sector group started burning out.'

While the public sector was struggling with too much work, the private sector was suffering from too little. During the bid for the probation contracts, the Ministry of Justice had only modelled the effect of a 2 per cent annual reduction in work for the private firms. That turned out to be hopelessly optimistic. In 2015–16, the actual volume of work going to the private sector was between 8 and 34 per cent less than originally anticipated, depending on the company. A year later, it was between 16 and 48 per cent lower.

Without a flow of cases coming in, revenue dried up. And then a depressingly predictable cycle emerged. The firms cut staff and reduced services in a desperate scramble to stay afloat.

Working Links, a company owned by the German venture capital firm Aurelius, which ran three of the private firms, announced substantial job losses, estimated by unions at 40 per cent of staff. 'After careful consideration,' the firm said, 'we are starting to streamline our support services.'

As the private firms went into decline, they started to operate on 'low contact models'. This allowed them to satisfy the terms of the contract and secure the payments, but without doing the meaningful work probation entailed.

Instead of sitting down for one-on-one interviews, some offenders were given group interviews with five or six people alongside a single probation officer. Others were asked to come to a reporting centre, where they gave their name, were asked if they had any issues, and were then ticked off a list. In some companies, probation officers were reduced to calling offenders on the phone, without any capacity to visibly assess their emotional state. Soon even this became impossible. At least one probation firm ran out of money to pay the phone bills, leaving officers with no way of making contact with offenders.

The private firms soon realised precisely what experts had warned of in 2013. Reoffending had too many causes to ever be put down to one single intervention. Even if they had thrown all their remaining money at a variety of rehabilitation programmes, it could all turn out to be for nothing if a reduction in housing led to more offenders committing crime. Eventually, even the Ministry of Justice came to accept the argument. 'There is a feeling now that reoffending is too random or arbitrary a rate to hold the community rehabilitation companies to,' the permanent secretary admitted in 2019, 'because it is affected by so many different factors.'

That created a grotesque inversion of the incentive system. Once the payments-by-results mechanism was found to be completely arbitrary, it became irrational for the companies to invest money in trying to achieve it. Instead, it made far more sense to cut investment, because that offered a guaranteed way to save money regardless of what happened with reoffending rates.

'Arguably the most important thing for keeping someone out of prison is a stable place to live,' Garside says. 'But the companies didn't really have control over that. There's no point spending money on teaching them basic literacy or getting them off drugs if they're sleeping in a cardboard box under Waterloo Bridge. So that's when the real private sector innovation came. They started selling off the corporate property they inherited, downsizing the workforce, getting rid of expensive staff, recruiting cheap staff and maximising the workloads.'

As the firms went into terminal decline, judges and magistrates began to lose confidence in them. 'We are not happy with the community rehabilitation companies for a variety of reasons,' one person involved in sentencing told researchers. 'Accredited programmes do not start on time and the enforcement of orders is poor. There is acceptance without rigour of non-compliance.' The split in the service meant private sector officers were not in court to report on their programmes, leading to a further decline in trust.

This meant that problems cascaded downwards towards total collapse. The original lack of work for the private firms dried up even further because many judges increasingly refused to impose any orders that might involve them. The basic failure of the system caused a crisis of confidence which led it to fail in an even more extreme way.

The Ministry of Justice desperately scrambled to try and salvage the programme. In July 2017, Grayling announced that the probation system had 'encountered unforeseen challenges' and said he would adjust the private sector contracts. He provided additional funding of £342 million for the firms, waived or ignored £5.5 million in financial penalties for poor performance and disregarded £9 million of taxpayers' money owed to the department.

But none of it helped. The private probation companies were in a death spiral.

The chief inspector of probation, Dame Glenys Stacey, found 80 per cent of them to be inadequate in at least one key quality area, and many of them in several. 'Probation is a complex social service, with professional judgement at its heart, but probation contracts treat it largely as a transactional business,' she concluded. 'Consequently, there has been a deplorable diminution of the probation profession and a widespread move away from good probation practice.'

An Inspectorate of Probation investigation report into the Dorset, Devon and Cornwall CRC found that 'workloads are unconscionable', 'leadership is inadequate', services were 'driven exclusively by financially linked contractual targets', professional ethics had been 'compromised' and 'immutable lines crossed because of business imperatives'. In London, the Inspectorate concluded: 'A combination of unmanageable caseloads, inexperienced officers, extremely poor oversight and a lack of senior management focus and control meant some service users were not seen for weeks or months, and some were lost in the system altogether.'

Between 2014/15 and 2016/17, serious further offences – when someone under probation supervision commits an extremely serious crime like murder or rape – increased by over 20 per cent.

In March 2015, 18-year-old Conner Marshall was beaten to death by David Braddon in South Wales. Braddon was being supervised by an inexperienced probation officer who assessed him as medium risk.

'The circumstance in which she found herself, a brand new probation officer, with woefully inadequate management and supervision structure, was not of her own making,' the coroner found. 'She was essentially left to her own devices, burdened as she was with a heavy and difficult caseload in an environment which was chaotic and stretched due to the impending implementation of the Transforming Rehabilitation programme.'

Outside the court, Marshall's mother, Nadine, made a statement. 'The coroner's findings have vindicated what we have always known to be true,' she said. 'This was a direct consequence of the chaos caused by the privatisation of probation services.'

On 14 October 2016, 27-year-old Michael Hoolickin was stabbed to death by Timothy Deakin outside a pub in Middleton, Greater Manchester. Hoolickin had tried to intervene to stop Deakin hitting a woman.

Deakin had been recorded as having a propensity to respond with extreme violence when faced with conflict, particularly after he had used cocaine. But for extended periods of time, including the weeks leading up to the attack, probation officers failed to make sure that he was subject to weekly testing.

'The court heard evidence as to the catastrophic impact the Transforming Rehabilitation programme had had on the staffing levels within the National Probation Service,' the coroner's report said. 'The court was satisfied this, in part, contributed to the failure to implement drug appointment and drug testing.'

In February 2019, Working Links, which owned three of the firms, went into administration. Interserve, which owned five of them, collapsed the following month.

David Gauke, who took over as justice secretary in January 2018, brought the privatisation experiment to an end. 'By the point I took it on it was clear it wasn't working,' he says. 'It wasn't providing the support needed. It didn't have the confidence of judges and magistrates. The companies were sustaining huge losses.'

But no one was punished for what took place. No one lost their job, or was penalised, or even rebuked. Quite the opposite. The civil service officials behind the programme won the 2015 Civil Service Award for Project and Programme Management. Antonia Romeo, the civil servant in charge of the project, was promoted to permanent secretary at the Ministry of Justice, the most senior position available.

Grayling was made leader of the House of the Commons in the next reshuffle, before being appointed transport secretary by then prime minister Theresa May. In that role, he awarded a £13.8 million contract to the firm Seaborne Freight to provide shipping capacity, despite the fact that it owned no ships, had never run a ferry service and copied-and-pasted its contract from a pizza delivery company. It is estimated that during his time at the department, he misspent a total of £2.7 billion of public funds.

While still an MP, he then secured a job advising Hutchison Ports, with a salary of £100,000 a year for seven hours' work a week.

The most remarkable thing about what happened in probation is how unremarkable it is. There is nothing remotely special about it. The same process takes place in department after department, policy area after policy area: health, education, defence.

Nor is there anything particularly remarkable about Grayling. Towards the end of his time on the front bench, he was dubbed 'Failing Grayling', but in fact this nickname was misplaced. The most harrowing thing about him is that he is a completely standard example of the quality of the ministerial class in Britain.

This country sees long-lasting, deep-set structural problems go permanently unresolved: social care, productivity, the state of the NHS, regional economic imbalance, an irrational tax system. The list could run for pages. At the same time, it is a frenzy of activity, much of it completely pointless, a lot of it positively harmful. The latest attempt by a minister, or prime minister, to look like they're doing something while accomplishing nothing at all or undoing that which has been accomplished previously.

The British political system rewards short-term tactics over long-term strategy, irrationality over reason, amateurism over seriousness, generalism over specialism and gut instinct over evidence. Probation is just one of countless stories about how successive governments in Britain have failed to operate with anything even approaching basic competence. They do not know what they are doing. They do not even attempt to know what they are doing. And then, when things go wrong, they do not learn from what happened.

This book is about how Westminster works. It is based on over 100 conversations with people across the political system, including ministers, civil servants, MPs, peers, academics, journalists and others, as well as countless books and reports from parliamentary experts, historians, think tanks, watchdogs and academics. We will follow a basic political timeline, from the general election to a new government's passing of legislation. And along the way, we'll assess every aspect of the system.

In the first chapter, we'll look at how the political parties pick the people they want to stand as MPs and on what basis they make that decision. We'll watch as the general election plays out and discover the strange iniquities and irrationalities of the electoral system. The second chapter will observe what happens to those candidates when they enter Parliament as MPs – the power of the Whips' Office, the pressures on their time and the crushing reality of what it takes to rebel against party discipline. The third chapter will then focus on the prime minister as they take their place in Downing Street, and how the strange broken architecture of the building impinges on their ability to deliver decent government.

In the fourth chapter, we'll look at the ministers the PM puts in place, from their work to their support staff, and the deadening sense of fear and short-termism that dominates their working lives. The fifth chapter will zoom in on the Treasury – the first-among-equals of government departments, which is supposed to operate as a check on the power of Downing Street but has been undermined by its own internal inconsistencies. In the sixth, we'll turn to the civil servants who support ministers, and find a world in which the inadequacies of the political system are replicated in their entirety right in the operational heart of the British state. The seventh chapter will then survey political journalism, from its nest in Parliament, and see whether the financial pressures that impinge on it have disabled its ability to challenge those in charge.

We'll then pause briefly for an interlude, and look at a case study: the withdrawal of British forces from Afghanistan. It's a heartbreaking story, in which the failures we have discovered in each part of the system conspired to humiliate Britain and betray its allies, showing once and for all the advanced state of decay in our constitutional arrangements.

Chapter 8 will look at the House of Commons, from the select committees to statutory instruments, and reveal a long-fought war between parliamentary scrutiny and heavy-handed government, in which the latter has the upper hand. Chapter 9 will go through every step of the legislative process, rooting out all the secret and little-known stages of a bill, and showing how little actual consideration is paid to the laws that impact on British citizens. And finally, we'll turn our attention to the House of Lords, where things are not as we might expect them to be.

We'll then finish with an epilogue, which lays out a series of possible solutions to our problems. Some of them are radical and far-reaching, some very minor. Hopefully, taken together, they offer a better way of doing things. There's also a glossary in the back if you come across any terms you are not familiar with.

We will strip the system down and lay it out in front of us, so that we can see exactly how the machine functions. This book is not about petty party-political squabbling, personalities or cheap point-scoring. We will ignore the empty calories we typically consume as political coverage. It is about systems and incentives: the basic operating mechanisms of the institutions that rule us.

They are rusty, corroded and splintered from misuse. But if we learn what's wrong with them, we can fix them.

We'll start with the one moment in British politics in which the public actually has a meaningful say: the election.

CHAPTER 1

The Vote

The most important moment in British democracy happens when no one's watching.

It's not the general election. The majority of votes at the election will be completely ignored. It comes long before that, in a room filled with party members, when they work out who is ultimately going to become an MP.

It's called selection, and it's the process by which candidates are picked to stand for a party at election time. It involves the headquarters of each political party – the Conservatives, Labour, the Liberal Democrats and others. And it involves their constituency parties – the local organisations and their memberships.

No one ever really talks about it. The British press spends far more time covering the Iowa caucus in the US than it does any of the pre-election procedures in the UK. But this moment decides who sits on the benches in the Commons or the chairs around the Cabinet table. It is the defining mechanism for establishing the talent pool in Westminster, from which everyone, up to and including the prime minister, will be chosen.

It happens behind closed doors, away from prying eyes, on the basis of a subsection of a subsection of a subsection of voters, with weak-to-non-existent democratic standards, according to a set of incentives that bear no relation to MPs' constitutional role.

For many members of Parliament, this is the most important contest of their career. That's because the majority of constituencies do not change hands. They stay the same, year after year, election after election, generation after generation. The fight for selection is therefore the only fight that really counts. 'Their achievement,' Tim Farron, former leader of the Liberal Democrats, says, 'was getting selected. Winning an election was almost a given.'

The experience of selection reflects the culture of each party. For the Conservatives it is a polite internal market, bulging with hypocrisy and thinly concealed political prejudice. For the Liberal Democrats, it is a unique combination of pragmatism and haplessness. For Labour, it is a factional bloodbath. But the fundamental process is extremely similar.

There are three stages. It starts with an initial screening process by party headquarters. This is followed by an interview with one or more committees of the local party. And it ends with a debate, called a 'hustings', where the final candidates perform in front of local party members before a vote. At each stage, candidates are whittled down until eventually only one is left.

Written down like that, it seems both democratic and thorough. In fact, it is neither. The screening process takes place according to the opaque machinations of party HQ. The interview stage involves senior figures of the local parties, operating according to standards that no one can evaluate and that probably do not exist. And even the final membership vote rests on a deeply unrepresentative slice of British public life.

In 1953, the Conservative party had a reported membership of 2.8 million and Labour over a million. Today, Labour has 432,000, the Conservatives 172,000, the Scottish National Party (SNP) has 104,000 and the Liberal

Democrats 74,000. Taken together, they constitute 1.1 per cent of the population. The National Trust has five times more members than all the political parties combined.

'Forty or fifty years ago, there were millions of people in these parties,' former Tory minister Johnny Mercer says. 'There's hardly anyone there now. They're sustained by huge donations by very small numbers of people. At times, they can have more in common with a trust fund rather than a political movement for change. You've got an increasingly small electorate of people who are choosing a Conservative candidate. It's smaller and smaller, and more purist and more purist, a kind of ever-decreasing circle.'

The MPs elected at a general election sit in the House of Commons, which is tasked with scrutinising the behaviour of the government. It is the single most important institution in the British constitutional system for the restraint of executive power. The entirety of our political culture hinges on the idea that the people who populate those green benches have the intention and the capability to hold the government to account.

But in reality, those qualities are never tested at any of the three selection stages. They're not even mentioned. Of the dozens of interviews with MPs and ministers conducted for this book, not one of them said they were asked about legislative scrutiny at any point in the process.

'The amount of knowledge anyone has in terms of the detail of parliamentary process is actually quite, quite low,' Tory MP Damian Collins says. 'If you said "you know, I think the government's got a terrible track record of moving negative statutory instruments and I'd be really hawkish praying against them", no one would even know what you're talking about. Most people in Parliament wouldn't know what you were talking about.'

*

The first stage of the selection process involves a sifting programme, in which potential candidates are assessed by party HQ to see if they are eligible. In the case of the Conservatives, this involves interviews and exercises with an assessment panel. Back in the 1990s, this was a bizarre ritual that involved going away to a hotel for several days and acting out role-play versions of the House of Commons or MPs' constituency surgeries. Now it is slightly more modern, with half a day of tests on political knowledge, team exercises, mock speeches and an interview. It's usually conducted by an MP and a senior member of the voluntary party.

One of the key traits the party looks for is the capacity to prioritise tasks, through elaborate fictional scenarios. 'You check your messages,' Anna Soubry, a former Tory minister, recalls of her approval exercise. 'The association chair has called to say they will have to scrap a big fundraising dinner because the star speaker has cancelled and the local paper has left a message claiming one of your councillors is about to defect to the Lib Dems. Which problem do you deal with first and how?' These are the kind of exercises they're given and those are the skills they're testing for – task prioritisation, presentational sensibility and common sense.

The Liberal Democrats use a similar approach. They hold parliamentary assessment days in which potential candidates write imaginary press releases, make speeches, do group exercises, show they can prioritise an in-tray, sit a policy exam and give a mock media interview. 'It's horribly artificial,' a senior Liberal Democrat official admits. 'There's a sense that those days are not as rigorous or effective as we'd like.'

On paper, Labour's process seems very similar, with potential candidates being screened by the National Executive

Committee (NEC). But the process is quite different and so are the underlying political dynamics playing out beneath it. Candidate approval, just like everything else in Labour, has been sucked into the gaping vortex of its perpetual civil war.

The Labour party has been fighting itself for as long as anyone can remember. It operates primarily on a right–left basis, with a socialist hard-line tendency, under various names and guises, fighting against the centre and right of the party. The names change – from Bevanites to Bennites to Blairites – but the basic principle remains largely the same.

'I don't know who said it, but there's a quotation,' says Neil Kinnock, former leader of the party. '"The Labour party will never want for enemies so long as there's a Labour party." The bloody thing is – it's a humorous, wry saying. But Christ, there's so much truth in it that it stops being funny really.'

The war is cyclical. Typically speaking, the hard left becomes so chaotic and offensive to voters that the party spends years in the electoral wilderness. Then the centre wrestles back control. It soon becomes deeply paranoid about what happened last time and begins to enforce an excessive degree of party discipline. This then alienates the hard left and their frustration spills over, making them more chaotic and offensive the next time they take over. One cycle spans from Michael Foot to Tony Blair, the next from Tony Blair to Jeremy Corbyn, then from Jeremy Corbyn to Keir Starmer. And so it goes on.

It is also to do with the unique psychology of those motivated by social justice. 'Democratic socialists are impatient,' Kinnock says. 'They are furious with the system that governs us, economically and politically. They want change. They want it radically and they want it quickly. And they're therefore prone to mistaking a resolution for a revolution and their personal enthusiasms for a gigantic popular surge. There are still quite a lot of people – decent people – who fail to take out personal insurance against those conditions.'

The NEC serves as the control centre of the party. It is, without question, its most important institution. It has therefore been the battleground for various frenzied clashes between its rival factions throughout its history. It's where they jostle with each other to establish dominion. It sets internal rules, has a key role establishing policy and, crucially, decides who can stand as an MP. It is composed of various elected representatives from different Labour groups, including the leadership, the front bench, the parliamentary party, local councillors and the trade unions.

Starmer got majority support on the NEC early on. He used it to give the NEC power to decide the longlist of candidates for every single free seat in the UK. They take the applications for a constituency and whittle them down to a minimum of six. Pro-Starmer NEC members are given a steer from the leadership about who they favour, who to put on the list and who not to. The leadership argued that this was so they could conduct due diligence. In reality, it was about political control.

Candidate approval highlights one of the chief differences between the Conservatives and Liberal Democrats on the one hand and Labour on the other. The Labour process is done on a seat-by-seat basis. The Conservative and Lib Dem processes are done nationally, thereby creating an internal market of approved candidates who can travel around the country trying to find a seat to contest. The process of finding a seat can take years and will usually involve several failed attempts. Typically speaking, a younger candidate would expect to be selected for a no-hope seat, will see if they can increase their vote share, and then be given a seat where victory is possible on their second or third attempt.

The second stage of the selection process involves interviews by one or more committees of the local party. This typically involves a grilling by a 'selection committee' composed of handpicked senior party members. For the Conservatives, it is often followed by an interview with the whole of the local association's executive committee. The process is designed to get the list down to around 5 or 6 people.

Many candidates have developed their own bag of tricks for these ordeals. 'Before I went for interview, I went around in a taxi for a day,' one Tory MP says. 'I'd say: "Take me to every single part of the constituency." And I'd stop and interview people while I was doing it, to find out what was going on. Because who knows a constituency better than a taxi driver?'

Fellow Tory MP and deputy Speaker Nigel Evans studied the local newspapers. 'I perched myself in the library and went through the last year of the *Advertiser and Times* and the *Longridge News*,' he says. 'I was abreast of all the local stories and all the councillors who had made a name for themselves on various issues. It helped.'

They'll be asked all sorts of questions: What do you think of specific government policies? What would you do to win the seat? What are your local credentials? What's your favourite book? What are your hobbies?

Not so long ago, they were also asked questions designed to establish whether a candidate was gay. There is a – probably apocryphal – story of a potential Tory candidate who was asked if he was married or engaged. He said no. He was asked if he was ever likely to get married. He replied: 'Well if that's the only thing that's putting you off, don't worry.

I shan't.' Nowadays, after a bit of pressure from headquarters, those questions are less likely to be asked.

For most potential candidates, this is a fraught time in which they are within touching distance of their most cherished ambition. But there is still space for gentlemanly behaviour. Peter Bottomley, the longest-serving MP in the Commons, once tried to secure the candidacy in North West Hampshire. Just ahead of him in the interview process was Sir George Young, whose wife was waiting outside. 'How's it going?' Bottomley asked her. 'Fine,' she replied, 'but not fine enough. He seems to be losing the audience.'

Bottomley was called in. 'You've got three minutes to say why you're the best person for us to choose,' the selection officer said. He replied: 'I'm not the best. I'm the second best. The best is Sir George Young. And, by the way, you aren't my first choice of constituency.' Young was subsequently selected.

But whether it's gentlemanly or not, the selection interview is a moment of supreme political importance. It's when the list of names is radically whittled down, from up to two dozen to the handful who will be presented to the local party membership. Ordinary members might cherish their ability to select candidates, but that choice is framed at the committee stage, when the range of available options is set down. 'They are all-powerful,' Evans says.

This is the point at which most potential MPs are eliminated from the process. But there are no set criteria for these decisions, or published standards, or even an agreed set of skills. There are just the prejudices and inclinations of the committee.

'I would like to say it's competence based, but it's obviously going to be ideological,' says Sienna Rodgers, who spent years covering Labour politics as the editor of the

Labour List website. 'Everything in the Labour party is factional. Each side will fight to the death for their people they want in. This is about choosing who has influence in the Labour party. It's fierce.'

Labour has the additional complication of its relationship with the trade unions. The three unions that matter are GMB, Unite and Unison. They attempt to influence selection at both ends of the process. At the top, they use their influence on the NEC, where the unions hold 13 of the 39 voting positions, to pack the longlists with their chosen candidates. At the bottom, they have a crucial advantage in the branch voting system. Constituency Labour parties are split into wards, which are represented by branches. To progress, candidates need to secure nominations from a certain number of branches. But each affiliated trade union also counts as a branch, meaning that union nominations allow candidates to sidestep local support, or at least minimise the need for it.

They also provide much-needed funds for a campaign. It's pricey to fight for selection. Simply printing and posting leaflets to local members is exorbitantly expensive, let alone additional expenditure on Facebook ad targeting, website creation or online video. Candidates will often spend thousands of pounds of their own money. But if they're connected to a union, it will often fund those costs. 'Being backed by a union is a massive advantage,' Rodgers says. 'You get costs paid for. You get their resources. It's huge.'

The last surviving candidates then go on to the third and final section of the process, in which they try to secure the nominations of local party members. It ends with a full hustings, after which they face the vote and discover their fate.

Even this stage of the contest, which is by far the most open and democratic, is a minority pursuit. We don't have full figures for how many party members vote in selection contests, but we can get a sense of them by looking at the figures we do have. Researchers Tim Bale, Paul Webb and Monica Poletti asked party members whether they had participated in the selection of either the party leader or their local candidate in 2017. Just 7.2 per cent of Conservatives, 9.5 per cent of Labour and 9.5 per cent of Liberal Democrat members had done so.

For Labour, hustings are often a bruising experience, with rival tribes trying to tear each other down. 'I'm so glad I'm at this end of my career and not the other,' says Margaret Beckett, who served as a minister from the Harold Wilson government to the Gordon Brown one. 'It must be a nightmare. The horror stories I hear from colleagues all over the country, in all sorts of places, about the knives and the fights and the ill-feeling.'

The Liberal Democrats are at the other end of the spectrum. Each candidate enters the room in turn, delivers a speech, answers questions and leaves. People very rarely ask difficult questions. There is no factionalism and hardly any rudeness. 'I'm sat there thinking there's this controversy about this person – why won't someone ask about it,' a senior Liberal Democrat official says. 'They're a bit wimpish. But that's partly as a result of Labour, of hearing what they're like, of not wanting to go down that road.'

The Conservatives are somewhere in the middle. Tories often talk of the great divisions of the past. They don't talk much about the great divisions of the present. 'The kind of divisions that people would have understood in the eighties,' Collins says, 'of "wets" and "dries", or people who were pro-Ted Heath or pro-Margaret Thatcher – that is all largely gone.' The same is true for Europe. No one ever says they preferred Heath to Thatcher. No one ever says they are pro-EU. The Conservative party membership has become fairly ideologically homogenous.

We know a fair amount about party members. We know that they are disproportionately older, middle class, male and white. The average age of a Conservative member is 57. For Labour it is 53, and for the Lib Dems 50. Just 30 per cent of Tory members are women, compared to 38 per cent in the Lib Dems and 48 per cent in Labour. White people make up 97 per cent of the Tory membership, and 96 per cent of the Labour and Liberal Democrat membership.

We also know quite a lot about how they think. And in this, they are all incredibly similar, regardless of which party they're in. The most common reason members of the three main parties give for joining is 'an attachment to the party's principles', followed by a desire 'to support the party's general policies or a specific policy that mattered greatly'.

They are more extreme politically than their party's supporters in the general public. Labour, Lib Dem, Green and SNP members are all more left-wing than party voters. Tories and UKIP members are more right-wing. Interestingly, they are all – right and left alike – more socially liberal than their party's supporters, including the Tories and UKIP. No one is entirely sure why, but it could be connected to a character type around those who like to participate.

Party members have one belief above all others that distinguishes them from the general public. They believe in the power to change the world. They are much more likely to say that individuals or organisations can make an impact on society. When asked to score their belief in personal ability to change the world on a scale of one to ten, the people who voted for these parties averaged just 4.18. But the people who joined them as members averaged 6.28. The scores for organisations' ability to change the world were 5.13 to 7.33.

In other words, they are campaigners and therefore believe that campaigning can be effective. Perhaps this is hardly surprising. After all, they're party members. They're unlikely to believe that everything they do is pointless. But it is worth remembering when we think about the decision-making process that goes into MP selection. These people are not constitutional theorists. They are not aloof, disinterested figures thinking about the maintenance of a checks-and-balances political system. They are not average members of the public. They are partisans. And that is the basis upon which they make their choices.

That partisanship is bolstered, in important but under-analysed ways, by the social arrangements around membership. The search for like-minded people forms a crucial part of why campaigners join political parties. And once there, many of them become deeply connected to the other people in the organisation.

'We have a lot of people whose whole social life and social interaction revolves around coming to our Labour club and meeting people,' a Labour MP told Bale, Webb and Poletti. 'It literally becomes their family. And it's combined with something to believe in and something to work towards. In many ways, it's like a sort of community or faith-based organisation with politics thrown in.'

There are three chief qualities local parties look for in candidates, regardless of whether they're Labour, Tory or Lib Dem: a capacity for campaigning, the look of a potential minister, and local roots.

'The predilections and prejudices of this very small group of 100 or 150 older people determines who you get as your MP,' says former Tory international development secretary

Rory Stewart. 'One of the reasons you end up with people who are good party campaigners and loyalists is that appeals to the party members, who themselves spend their weekends delivering leaflets. You also get lots of lawyers – hyper-articulate private-school-educated people – because Conservative associations have a tendency to think that's what they need in politicians.'

Local roots are arguably the most important quality of all. 'Local candidates have by far the best chance,' says Spencer Livermore, a senior Labour adviser on four general election campaigns. 'The nightmare scenario for anyone outside is someone who's been leader of the council for 20 years. They are by far and away the front-runner. Localism matters massively.'

This is borne out in the research. When Bale, Webb and Poletti asked party members what they wanted to see more of in candidates, local credentials were top of the pile. Some 71.5 per cent of Conservatives, 85 per cent of Lib Dems and 86.2 per cent of Labour members said they wanted more candidates from the local area.

For the small minority of the local party that takes part, the battle over selection is a hugely important process. In a safe seat, which will never change hands at a general election, it allows them to decide who will sit as the MP for the next 15 to 20 years. They face no real challenge from the public. The only challenge they face is from the party leadership.

Party HQ and local parties are in a constant tug-of-war over candidate selections. Party leaders – of all political persuasions, at all times – try to exercise control over the candidate selection process.

They do this for several reasons, some of which are perfectly noble. The Liberal Democrats managed to hugely expand their range of ethnic minority candidates through leadership interventions, as did the Conservatives. Labour conducted a similar, and highly successful, experiment using all-women shortlists. Some reasons are less noble, but understandable. Party leaders want to expand the talent pool from which they can form a frontbench team. The British system, unlike that of the US or most European countries, restricts ministerial or shadow-ministerial positions to those in Parliament. So there is a strong incentive for leaders to get impressive individuals into winnable constituencies.

'You can see it with Keir Starmer now,' says Ben Bradshaw, a former New Labour minister. 'He needs to get people selected in winnable seats who are ministerial material, because he hasn't got enough depth and strength in the parliamentary Labour party to run an effective and successful government.'

In other cases, it is about the brute reality of political narratives. By-elections – electoral contests in one seat outside of election time, which are usually triggered by an MP resigning or dying – are key political events for party leaders. Even though they are a tiny vote in a small area with no impact on who is in government, they have an outsized impact on the way the parties are perceived by the media. Opposition leaders in particular must win them in order to be seen as having forward momentum towards Downing Street.

All the parties therefore have a stripped-down process for candidate selection in by-elections, which typically allows them to take over the process. Sometimes they'll give the local party a list of two or three people to choose from, or they'll add an additional 'star chamber' element to the process, or they'll simply suspend the local party process altogether.

The same is true for snap elections, because of the radically shortened timetable available before polling day. This used to be a technical detail, but in recent years, snap elections have become almost the default setting for British politics. One took place in 2017 and another in 2019. Selections in these circumstances are heavily controlled by party HQ.

The primary class of people promoted by party leaders for selection are called special advisers, or 'spads' – an extraordinary new category of political animal that we'll look at in more detail later. They will have worked with ministers or shadow ministers, are deeply ingrained in the political and social circles of the leadership team, and want a clear route into a parliamentary career. 'The thing that central parties go for is people who've climbed up the greasy pole,' Livermore says. 'They've been a special adviser, or been in the party, and the leadership thinks this person would be useful in Parliament.'

Others come from friendly trade unions or think tanks, or are simply assiduous networkers, knowing who to connect with in the leader's office. 'It's all about aligning yourself with the leadership,' Rodgers says, 'making sure that you're known to them.'

The most obvious mechanism used by the leadership to control outcomes is the approved candidates list, or in Labour's case the NEC longlisting process. All parties have the power to prevent the names of those they don't like from getting on that list and to make sure that the names of those they do like feature prominently.

Sometimes leadership intervention takes the form of a phone call from head office – or even the leader in person – to the chairman of the local party, recommending a candidate and promising not to forget it if they find their way to selection. Most Tory chairmen insist they ignore such calls, or throw the letters in the bin without reading them. This is very unlikely to be true.

Often the leadership will simply pack the long- or short-list with their favoured candidates. Whoever wins, they win. Or they'll take an alternative route and stack the list with candidates so palpably inept that no one in their right mind could possibly vote for them, alongside their preferred alternative. 'It's an old trick,' Rodgers says. 'The one person they favour and then the rest are duds. They give that to the party and say: "Here is a lovely free vote for you to decide who you want." They don't really have any choice but to pick the one competent person.' Usually it works. Sometimes, either through ineptitude or stubborn resistance, the local party picks one of the duds.

Other times the leadership exercises control by shortening the timetable. In 2010, Brown had the NEC take over. It drew up the shortlists for individual local parties, handed each a piece of paper with four names on it and told them to hold a vote to decide the following Saturday. They bypassed the selection committee altogether. This was ostensibly so that Labour could reduce the number of careerists entering the parliamentary party and get a different kind of candidate in. 'It wasn't very successful,' one of Brown's allies at the time admits. 'In the end we ended up imposing lots of political insiders.'

Party leaders often have good reasons for wanting to control the selection system. It would be impossible not to, given how irrational many local decisions are and the pressures on them at the national level. But their heavy-handed attempts can often turn party members against them and result in MPs with no functioning relationship with their constituency party.

'I understand why they became quite excessive,' Kinnock says of the New Labour years, when central control reached dizzying heights. 'But you're only going to make it stick for any length of time if you ensure there is an element of democracy, which gives the decision real legitimacy. It's no good planting a candidate, getting them selected, and then having every member of the party hating their guts because they're a tosser or an actual twat.'

The pathway to success in selection is therefore twofold. If you make it through the local party, it is due to impressive campaigning skills, a confident manner or local roots. If you make it through party HQ, it is a result of spending years networking your way into the system. But neither approach even pretends to offer the kind of candidate you would need for a functioning legislative chamber. 'It's even more of a problem with the selectorate than with the candidates themselves,' Farron says. 'They don't realise what the job is.'

It is like a machine established for a completely different set of intended outcomes. The qualities evaluated in the selection process have no connection with the demands of life in Westminster. 'They're not the things that it takes to be an effective administrator or an effective policymaker,' a former senior Labour official says. 'So you get these people who work for a trade union for ten years, or work for the party for ten years, and then suddenly they are running our transport policy. Well, they don't know anything about that. If you were to select someone for that job based on their background, you would never pick that person.'

Who are the people who are selected? In 2017, the average age of an MP was 50.5. It's a remarkably constant figure historically – it was 49.6 in 1979. Twenty-nine per cent of MPs were privately educated, compared to 7 per cent of the population; 23 per cent went to Oxbridge, compared to 1 per cent of the population. Thirty-two per cent were women, compared to 51 per cent of the population. Eight per cent were ethnic minorities, compared to 18 per cent of the population. Nearly 7 per cent were openly LGBT, which is probably around the national average, although the figures are disputed. In 2015, 14.2 per cent had been lawyers and just over 30 per cent business people. Seventeen per cent were professional politicians – up from 3 per cent in 1979. Only 3 per cent had done manual jobs, compared to 16 per cent in 1979.

This much we can tell simply by looking at MPs or asking them basic questions. But it is much more difficult to get a sense of what they are like as people. What's their personality type? What's their emotional state? What kinds of things motivate them?

The chief reason for this difficulty is that they won't answer. And that's getting worse over time. In the early 1970s, the American political scientist Donald Searing managed to interview 83 per cent of the MPs in the Commons for a study of their motivations. It included all the biggest names of the time: Margaret Thatcher, Harold Wilson, Barbara Castle, Denis Healey, Michael Heseltine, Roy Hattersley, Michael Foot, Enoch Powell.

When researchers Michael Rush and Philip Giddings tried to conduct a similar study in the 1997–2001 parliament, the number of respondents dropped to 52 per cent. The Hansard Society – a well-respected institution with support across the political parties – tried another survey in 2010, in which only 25 per cent of MPs responded. In 2012, political scientists Rosie Campbell and Joni Lovenduski employed a corporate consultancy firm for their research and only secured 24 per cent of MPs, not a single one of them a frontbencher. They concluded that the tiny response rate created a research bias that made the results unreliable.

Things marginally improved in 2020, when James Weinberg, a lecturer in political behaviour, conducted surveys and interviews with 168 MPs according to a complex personality framework. The underlying data was still limited, at just 25 per cent of MPs, but the personality model he used was extremely thorough.

Aspects of his study were reassuring. It found that MPs were more motivated by equality, social justice and caring for others than the general population. It put the lie to the lazy assumptions about politicians that you'll hear in any pub across the country – that they're all in it for themselves or only entered politics for the money. These things have never been true and they're not true now. In fact, the MPs seemed to be motivated by wanting to help people, even if they disagreed on what that would entail.

'I mean, I've met literally thousands of politicians from all over the world in the course of my years,' a senior Conservative MP told Weinberg. 'They all believe that they're trying to do good and many of them are doing good and they're not in your party either, which is quite annoying.'

But there was also a darker finding. MPs were much more likely than the general population to be motivated by authority and social recognition. They prized so-called 'power' values above things like security, achievement and hedonism. 'They are significantly more orientated towards being in control of resources, assuming leadership positions and showcasing achievements according to social standards than the public they serve,' Weinberg says. 'These psychological drives are constantly at work in tandem with more benevolent predispositions.'

This is an important finding, because once MPs reach the Commons, the party enforcement operation will exploit precisely these attributes.

All of that will be a long way in the future for selected parliamentary candidates. First they have to win the election campaign. For most of them that will be either an impossible task or a predestined one. The majority will be campaigning in one of the UK's hundreds of safe seats, in which everyone already knows the result in advance. If they belong to the party which dominates the constituency, they can relax and enjoy the campaign without any fear of losing. If they do not, their aspirations are limited to increasing the size of their vote. That's particularly the case if they are a fresh young candidate looking to be given a winnable seat in the next election, or the one after that.

But for those in target seats, it's different. They will be funnelled resources. They will receive extra money and be bolstered by visits from high-profile frontbenchers. Most importantly, they will be sent an election organiser – a figure dispatched from head office to remorselessly exploit the data on local voting patterns.

For years before the election campaign itself, party activists knocking on doors will have been collecting information on voting habits. How did the people they spoke to vote at the last election? How did they vote at the local or mayoral elections? Are they strong party supporters, wavering party supporters or former party supporters? Are they friendly, hostile, a dedicated supporter of another party or do they simply never vote? All that information is fed into the local and central parties. By election day, they have a very detailed list of the people who promised to vote for them.

'The organiser knows what it takes to win,' Livermore

says. 'Every decent seat will have had five years of canvassing to know where your vote is. And the purpose of the short campaign is to contact your vote over and over to motivate them. We know, at a local level, that is the determining factor. We know that contact rates in a marginal contest make an enormous difference.'

This system translates into a punishing set of weekly voter contact targets for the candidate. 'It was a lot of pressure,' former Labour MP Paula Sherriff, who fought the highly marginal seat of Dewsbury, says. 'At one point it's "you must make this many thousands of contacts a week". If you didn't, they were quite unforgiving. It was really tough. Non-stop. Unrelenting.'

Meanwhile, party researchers are looking into the records of figures in opposing parties, to see what they can use against them. For their most prominent figures, it can even involve travelling to the British Library newspaper archive and trawling through microfiches.

Researchers also sneak into events where leading members of other parties are speaking to try to catch some offhand comment they can package up into an attack strategy. They particularly target rank-and-file events where frontbenchers will be relaxed and tempted to throw the foot soldiers some political red meat. Others are researching on Google or social media, looking for any comment that might have political impact.

'There'll be a bunch of stories that we collect up that will be of very little value until election time,' says Theo Bertram, a senior adviser to Tony Blair and Gordon Brown. 'Then at election time, by the law of economics, there are suddenly so many journalists who want a story. And all of this crap that you've had in your bottom drawer that you couldn't shift now looks like gold dust because there's literally ten times more journalists who are begging for something.'

The party attack machine will then bundle up stories on their opponents to offer to friendly newspapers. 'Our specialism was targeting Tories, but the Liberal Democrats were a nice snack between meals,' Bertram says. 'Ninety-nine per cent of the time no one is interested in the fact some junior councillor in Taunton is in favour of a reassessment of drugs, or a Liberal Democrat in Edinburgh thinks that we've gone too far prosecuting people on the sex register. But whatever, right? You're going to save those, write them up as the ten most bonkers Lib Dem ideas these people want to inflict on the country, and that's a *Mirror* story. That will get nice coverage. And if you're lucky, the Lib Dem leader will be forced to respond to it. And when he does, your own attack MP will be there on the radio saying it's outrageous what the Lib Dems want to do.'

Candidates will also be hounded by journalists throughout the campaign. Luciana Berger stood for Labour in Liverpool Wavertree in 2010. 'I got chased around by the *Mail on Sunday*,' she says. 'I got bundled out the back of a Tesco because they were following me with a long-lens camera. They planted a fake volunteer to snoop around in the campaign team. They went through my bins. They went into my dad's place of work. They turned up at my parents' front door.'

Meanwhile, candidates will be getting a first taste of the abuse they are likely to receive if they manage to secure a place in parliament. For Labour candidate Kim Leadbeater, whose sister Jo Cox had been murdered while serving as an MP, it came when she was campaigning in the Batley and Spen by-election. A grammar school in the area had shown an image of the prophet Muhammad during a religious education class, and independent candidate George Galloway had swept into the community, stoking the ensuing religious tension.

Leadbeater was confronted by a group of aggressive conservative Muslim men in the street, yelling about 'LGBT indoctrination'. As she tried to hurry away, they followed her, shouting: 'The colour of blood, the colour of blood is what you are.' A year later, the moment still haunted her. 'It was particularly bad,' she says. 'That felt quite dangerous. And what upset me about that was that my parents and my partner and my friends saw that play out on social media.'

Then, finally, election day arrives. To all appearances, this is a decisive moment in which the public voice replaces that of the politicians. The fate of the candidates hangs in the balance as everyone waits to discover the will of the voters. On television, breathless coverage will monitor every last second. The images of the evening, such as Michael Portillo losing his seat in 1997, will stay with people for the rest of their lives. If the government is kicked out, the removal vans will arrive the next morning at No. 10. No niceties, no politeness, just the brute decisiveness of British democracy.

And that drama will serve to conceal just how little influence most voters had on the process.

In the 2019 general election, 70.8 per cent of the votes cast had no impact whatsoever on the outcome of the election, totalling 22.6 million people. That figure is stable over time. It has barely budged since the 2010 general election, when 71 per cent of the votes cast had no impact, totalling 21 million people.

This is because the UK uses the first-past-the-post electoral system. The country is divided into single-member constituencies, and elections are held in each one to decide the local MP. Whoever gets the most votes wins. They can win by one vote, or by tens of thousands of them – it makes no difference to the outcome. There are no prizes for coming second and there is no representation for the people who voted for the losing candidates.

Hardly any other advanced democracy uses this system, except for the US and Canada. Over the course of the twentieth century, most gave up on it, from Australia in 1913 to New Zealand in 1993. No major democracy has ever adopted it after using a different system. Since 1945, only three newly democratic independent countries have made the conscious decision to adopt the system – Albania, Macedonia and Ukraine – and every single one of them has subsequently dropped it.

Even the UK rarely uses first-past-the-post outside of Westminster elections. The Scottish Parliament, Welsh Assembly and Northern Ireland Assembly all work to a different system, as do local authorities in Northern Ireland and Scotland and the Greater London Assembly. Elections for select committee chairs or the Speaker in Parliament do not use it either.

People tend to remember elections as seismic events of sudden political change. But in fact very few seats change hands. In 2010, when Labour was thrown out and the Tories entered coalition with the Liberal Democrats, just 117 out of 650 seats changed hands. In 2015, when the Conservatives secured a shock majority, just 111 did. In 2017, which saw the departure of leading figures like Nick Clegg and Ed Balls and the loss of the Tory majority, only 70 seats did. And in 2019, which was treated as a fundamental realignment in the basic assumptions of British politics, only 79 did. They accounted for just 12 per cent of the constituencies across the UK.

The reason so few constituencies change hands is because the majority of elections in the UK take place in safe seats. These are local contests in which one party is so powerful that there is no realistic prospect of it losing.

A third of the seats in the UK, comprising 14 million voters, have not changed hands since the Second World War. And that historical time frame actually makes them comparatively exciting hotbeds of political change. Some seats have not changed hands since the early years of Queen Victoria's reign. The constituency of East Devon, and its prior equivalents, has been in Conservative hands since 1835.

One of the core principles of democracy, and of the first-past-the-post voting system in particular, is supposed to be that it allows voters to 'throw the rascals out'. But in fact this is a theoretical right rather than a practical one. If anyone had noticed Chris Grayling's disastrous reform of probation and wanted to punish him for it in the election, they would have found it impossible to do so. The last time his seat changed hands was in 1874.

Under first-past-the-post, votes are wasted in two ways: through voting for anyone but the winner, or through voting for the winner after they have passed the finish line.

Any vote for a candidate who fails to secure the constituency is wasted. It did not elect the MP and it does nothing to get the party closer to power. It disappears into an electoral vacuum. This accounts for millions of voters, whose democratic wishes are ignored. In the 2019 election, 14.5 million people were disenfranchised in this way, amounting to 45.3 per cent of all voters.

Any vote cast for a winning candidate after they have defeated their opponent is also wasted. It does not contribute to the party's representation in Parliament. It simply piles up in a seat that has already been won. In 2019, there were 8.1 million surplus votes wasted, accounting for just over a quarter of all the votes cast.

At different points in history, this electoral system has favoured all the main parties. In 1906, it exaggerated Liberal support. Throughout the post-war period and right into the 1980s, it tended to favour the Conservatives. Then it favoured Labour until 2015, when it switched back and benefited the Conservatives again.

The reasons for it favouring one party over another at any given moment are a complex mixture of relative constituency size, turnout, and the efficiency of the party's vote distribution.

At the moment, Labour holds 20 of the 30 safest seats – overwhelmingly densely populated urban constituencies in places like Manchester, London and Merseyside. Hundreds of thousands of additional Labour votes pile up pointlessly without affecting the national election outcome. In Manchester's inner-city constituencies alone, Labour received enough surplus votes to win an additional four seats. They counted for nothing.

But regardless of whether they happen to be net winners or losers from the system at any given moment, the two main parties benefit from the general rule of how it operates. They have set concentrations of voters in given areas who will eventually hand them an electoral victory if they can target them appropriately. Generally for Labour it's the cities and for the Tories it's the rural areas.

The main losers are small parties with broad support across the country. In 2010, UKIP won 900,000 votes but did not secure a single seat, because its support was spread too thinly. In 2019, the Greens secured over 865,000 votes and only returned one MP.

Not all small parties lose out. Those who can concentrate their vote in specific regions can still win big. In Northern Ireland, this includes the DUP, Alliance, the SDLP and Sinn Féin. In Scotland it's the SNP and in Wales it's Plaid Cymru.

The breakdown of how many votes it takes to elect an

MP casts the situation in stark terms. In the 2015 general election it took just 23,033 votes to elect a DUP MP, but 3,881,099 people voted for UKIP without electing a single MP. In the 2017 election, it took just 27,931 votes to elect an SNP MP and 525,435 to elect a Green MP.

First-past-the-post has four main consequences – it reduces scrutiny, increases political tribalism, corrupts the policy-making process and allows the two main parties to amass complete executive power on the basis of a minority of the popular vote.

The scrutiny function is degraded by the simple fact that most voters cannot punish or reward a political party. If someone lives in a seat where a party has a majority of over 20 per cent, they cannot meaningfully register their dissent against it. Whichever way they vote, the end result will be the same. They are disenfranchised. Their capacity to influence politics through the ballot box has ceased to exist.

The increased tribalism is a result of the emphasis on local support. Parties with broad-based geographical support, regardless of their political position, are punished. This is why UKIP, which is far to the right, and the Green party, which is far to the left, are penalised in precisely the same electoral way. But parties that dig deep into regional or national identity, like the SNP in Scotland, or speak to values that are clustered in particular areas, like the Tories in rural England, are rewarded.

This is part of the reason that Britain has become increasingly divided along political lines, and in particular between rural areas and the cities. The geographical focus of the electoral system emphasises difference.

Those voters who do not fit the rudimentary geographic categories of first-past-the-post are erased from the political landscape. In reality, there is strong Tory support in many cities, just as there is strong Labour support in many rural areas. It's just mostly not enough to win. So over half of Conservative voters in London went unrepresented in 2019. In Scotland, 80 per cent of Conservative voters and 95 per cent of Labour voters went unrepresented.

Most other voting systems would represent those voters and show a country that was more diverse and eclectic in its political composition than the media narrative would suggest. But under the remorseless logic of first-past-the-post, minority opinion in an area is simply wiped out. London is Labour. Scotland is SNP. The countryside is Tory. This results in a political culture in which voters, and indeed whole swathes of the country, are converted into homogenous blocks, with one set of political characteristics. Urban voters are metropolitan liberal elitists. Rural voters are social and political conservatives. Scottish voters are progressive independence supporters.

In truth, a glance at opinion polls or the popular vote would disprove those ideas and show that these areas have as much that unites them as divides them. But by handing the victory to one party, and one party only, the area becomes monopolised by the winning group. People are stereotyped and classified without anything but the most superficial attention to their views. It is the great wallpapering of a plural national identity.

When MPs travel from their constituency to Westminster, this homogenisation translates into a system of constitutionalised machismo. They have been elected to represent an area that is painted in uniform primary colours. They therefore carry with them a boosted sense of frenzied tribalism that exists in addition to that demanded of them by the local party membership.

As we shall see, the culture of voters as homogenised blocks represented by MPs on a winner-takes-all-basis will go on to dominate nearly every aspect of the culture in Westminster.

First-past-the-post's third consequence is the corruption of the policy-making process. It does this by virtue of the incentives it builds into the political system. It makes it rational for governments to direct valuable resources, like health funding, to winnable seats rather than where they are most needed.

In 2019, the government announced a £3.6 billion towns fund intended to support areas suffering from high levels of inequality and deprivation. It was a multi-stage process. First, civil servants drew up a list of all the 1,082 towns in England. Then they tested them against a range of criteria, like income deprivation, skills and productivity. Finally, they came up with a list of 541 eligible towns, categorised into high-, medium- and low-priority groups, and handed it over to ministers to make a decision.

A few months later, the government unveiled a list of the 101 towns that were invited to bid for public support. Its contents were completely bizarre. Of the 101 towns, 12 were from the low-priority group and 49 from the medium-priority group. The list included Cheadle, a picturesque suburb in Greater Manchester, which was ranked 535th out of the 541 towns needing attention.

'We are not convinced by the rationales for selecting some towns and not others,' the Public Accounts Committee said. 'The justification offered by ministers for selecting individual towns is vague and based on sweeping assumptions. In some cases, towns were chosen by ministers despite being identified by officials as the very lowest priority.'

A few weeks later, Chris Hanretty, professor of politics at Royal Holloway, noticed the story in the newspaper and decided to do a bit of research. Instead of using need as the key variable, he used the size of the constituencies' majority. And suddenly a pattern emerged. Conservative-held towns were almost twice as likely to be selected as all other towns. Their success rate in the low-priority group was actually higher than the success rate for all other towns in the medium-priority group. But they were not all equal. Where the Conservative majority was very large, their success rate was more or less average. It was only when the lead was marginal that the success rate spiked. The same was true, to a lesser extent, in Conservative target seats where Labour or the Liberal Democrats had a majority of less than 5 per cent. These also had a higher success rate than Conservative towns with large majorities.

It's not just a Conservative problem. Similar patterns can be seen across governments and policy areas.

Academics at the Centre for Economic Performance at LSE looked at the relationship between marginal seats and hospital closures between 1997 and 2005, when New Labour was in power. They found that where Labour had a small majority, or was only slightly behind another party, there were over 20 per cent more hospitals than in safe seats, regardless of whether they were Labour-held or not. Hospitals in marginal constituencies were less likely to be closed down.

Tellingly, the same pattern did not hold for schools. Because unlike hospitals, school locations are not controlled by national politicians.

Living in a marginal constituency can quite literally save your life. The researchers found that because English counties with more marginal constituencies have more hospitals, they have a lower death rate from heart attacks.

*

First-past-the-post's final consequence is the most important, and the reason the system continues to be used despite the obviousness of its defects. It provides the winning party with an unprecedented degree of executive power. It does this through the creation of a strong majority in Parliament, which the winning party can use for the entirety of its time in office to force through whatever changes it wants.

There are periods in which the system fails to produce its intended outcome. Between 1970 and 1979, there were four general elections, four prime ministers and two minority governments. Then again, between 2010 and 2022, there were four general elections, five prime ministers, one coalition and one minority government. These are periods when the velocity of political change defeats the electoral system. But typically speaking, first-past-the-post is designed to try and rule them out.

Most other electoral systems provide proportional results in which parties must share power. They enter into negotiations, they see where they can work together, and then they try to form a governing programme. The British system is distinguished by giving one party total control of the country on a minority of the vote. Labour governed in 2005 with just 35.2 per cent of the vote. The Tories governed in 2019 with just 43.6 per cent.

This, ultimately, is what first-past-the-post does. It is what it is designed to do. It takes a minority vote, silences everyone else, and then hands the winning party total executive power, without anything to stand in its way.

There are all sorts of institutions, processes, incentives and personalities in Westminster. But it is this fact, more than any other, that defines what comes next.

CHAPTER 2

The Members of Parliament

The process of controlling MPs begins the moment they enter Parliament.

There's a quote by the philosophical father of conservatism, Edmund Burke, about the role of an MP that often does the rounds in Westminster. It's one of those lines that reliably pops up whenever there's some matter of constitutional importance being discussed. He made it in a speech to electors in Bristol in 1774, as he outlined what constituents should expect of their local MP.

'His unbiased opinion, his mature judgement, his enlightened conscience,' he said, 'he ought not to sacrifice to you, to any man, or to any set of men living. Your representative owes you, not his industry only, but his judgement; and he betrays, instead of serving you, if he sacrifices it to your opinion.'

It's a very nice quote, elegantly expressed. It is also hard to think of any vision of MPs that could be further removed from their current status. In reality, the Westminster system aims remorselessly to crush and eradicate independent judgement. Its ideal member of Parliament is ignorant, obedient, hyper-partisan and entirely reliant on the party authority structure to tell them what to do.

'It's a silent process,' former Labour health secretary Andy Burnham says. 'You arrive in Westminster. You're full of the joys of spring. And basically that is slowly sucked out of you. I woke up to that in 2016, after 16 years of being in Parliament: voting the way you're told to vote, taking the line you're told to take. I realised people's impression of me was not really me. It's that silent Westminster effect. It does it to everyone.'

The central mechanism for enforcing the compliance of MPs is the Whips' Office – the surveillance and disciplinary system for parliamentary votes. It threatens MPs who vote against their party, rewards those who vote with it and passes intelligence up to the leadership about any possible rebellions.

MPs feel its force immediately, because it's the Whips' Office that allocates them their parliamentary office when they arrive: spacious penthouses at the top of Portcullis House for favoured MPs and dark little cubbyhole basements for lowly ones.

Any MP who thought they were going to Parliament to plough their own furrow will have realised their error before they even uttered a word in the Commons Chamber. Ahead of their maiden speech – the first time they address Parliament – they are typically told by the whips what to say. Literally the first words out their mouth are often put there by the party's enforcement unit.

'I remember being sat down for my maiden speech,' Johnny Mercer says. 'I've never been to Westminster before. You get sat down by the whips and they're like: "Right, these are things you say in your maiden speech. You say thank you to George Osborne for his long-term economic plan." And I was like: Who the fuck is George Osborne? "You pay tribute to your predecessor." I was like: She was fucking horrible to me during the election, I'm not doing that.'

The word 'whip' actually refers to three things: an instruction, a person and a process.

It's the name of a document circulated to MPs on a weekly basis by the party, listing the business of the next fortnight and the expectation of when they'll vote. The importance of a vote was once communicated by how many times it had been underlined. A single-line whip was non-binding, a two-line whip was an instruction, with attendance required unless given prior permission, and a three-line whip was of the utmost seriousness, with failure to attend and vote as directed possibly leading to exclusion from the parliamentary party. If that happens, an MP is said to have 'lost the whip'. This means that they can sit in Parliament as an independent, but are no longer representing the party. Electorally, it is the kiss of death – independent candidates almost never succeed in elections.

Those terms remain in use today. Most government legislation involves a three-line whip to ensure it goes through, but the circumstances can become even more acute than that. In 2021, for instance, Tory MP Owen Paterson was found guilty by the Committee on Standards of an 'egregious case of paid advocacy', after he used his parliamentary position to promote two companies that hired him as a paid consultant. The committee recommended that he be suspended from the Commons for 30 days, but the government moved to protect him. It put MPs on a three-line whip to dismiss the committee report and scrap the existing standards system. Many Tory MPs were dismayed by what they were being asked to do. Thirteen rebelled against the whip. Others abstained, which means they refused to vote either way. But the party disciplinary system held together. It won the vote by 250 to 232.

There's a small army of people involved in the parliamentary whipping operation. On the government side you have the chief whip, who is appointed by the prime minister, along with three senior whips, six other whips and seven assistant whips. The opposition has a chief whip, a deputy and perhaps twelve or thirteen others.

In the middle of it all is one of the most interesting and under-discussed jobs in Westminster: the principal private secretary to the chief whip. You can tell how unusual it is by virtue of its stability. Since 1939, only four men have held the job, all of them subsequently given a knighthood. The first was Sir Charles Harris, who served between 1939 and 1961, and the last was Sir Roy Stone, who served between 2000 and 2021. In a political system defined by constant churn, the role is singularly resistant to change. And the reason for that is simple: this figure, more than any other, knows where the bodies are buried.

The principal private secretary is a civil servant with an acutely political role. They have to broker solutions between the parties on timetabling and legislation. This involves shuttling between the two and maintaining the trust of both, never revealing the secrets of one side to the other. It is a role that relies on absolute discretion and ambiguity. Whoever this person is, at any given time, they have the best intelligence in Westminster, because it extends across the House.

In the popular imagination, the whip's role is that of a bully and a blackmailer. It's referred to as the 'dark arts'. MPs who don't toe the line are threatened with punishment and humiliation – revealing their marital indiscretions to the press, freezing them out of a ministerial career, or simply shouting or even physically assaulting them. All those stories are perfectly true. They are also increasingly a thing of the past.

'It's changed enormously,' veteran Tory rebel Peter Bone says. 'When I first came in in 2005, it was very much "you've got to do what you're told". I remember being summoned in with Brian Binley by the senior deputy chief whip about some abstention we made and being talked to like we were schoolboys by the headmaster. They would threaten you with your career. I've been sworn at. All that sort of stuff.'

Various factors worked to reduce the ability of the whips to pursue these tactics. One of them was an increase in the space available on the parliamentary estate. The building of Portcullis House – which contains places for MPs to work, meet and socialise – reduced the scarcity of office space. Once upon a time, whips could tell MPs that they would exclude them from select committees, but now those roles are elected and outside of their control. Whip threats are also a double-edged sword. If they throw an MP out into the cold as soon as he or she votes against the party, they simply establish a permanent outsider who might vote against them again in future with more regularity.

But even though the whips are less brutal than they used to be, the basic enforcement mechanism remains in place. If you rebel, you will probably write yourself off from a ministerial position, at least under the current leadership. If you insist on assessing legislation on its own terms rather than simply voting as you're told, you will sabotage your political career. These incentives would be effective on most people, but they are particularly effective on MPs. As James Weinberg's psychological research showed, they are disproportionately likely to be motivated by authority and social recognition and to value leadership positions.

As well as enforcement, the whips deal in intelligence. One of their chief roles is to gather information on the mood of the parliamentary party and then pass it up to the leadership, so it can assess the threat of rebellion.

But information is also itself a form of enforcement. It is the whips who explain parliamentary procedure to MPs. When new members of Parliament enter the building, they are suddenly presented with an impossibly complex web of rules, conventions, precedents and demands that they have no experience of nor any training for.

Former spads have an advantage, in that they know how Westminster works and how to navigate it. Former lawyers do too, because they can at least read legislation. The rest have no experience of what is happening at all. The parties organise little training. MPs are given no instruction in how to scrutinise or even read legislation, let alone introduce it. Most remain largely ignorant of parliamentary procedure throughout their time in Parliament, no matter how long they're there. And this is not a failure by the political parties. It is a choice. If there is something they want, like support in a Commons vote, they make sure they get it. But it is simply not in their interests to tell MPs how Westminster works or what they're supposed to do. Because if MPs are ignorant, they will rely on the whips to explain everything to them – to tell them where they need to be and what they need to do.

The complexity of Parliament and the ignorance of its inhabitants are both part of a system of control. It is useful for the party leaderships that the situation should remain this way, so it does.

While the culture of the Whips' Office has become less explicitly bullying, the fundamental nature of the operation and the extent of its influence remains nearly as strong as ever. In almost every stage of the parliamentary process, as we will see, it acts to stifle debate, limit scrutiny, close down avenues of interrogation, reduce independent thought and strengthen the power of the political parties.

*

The rules of the Commons come from four sources: Acts of Parliament, practice, standing orders and rulings from the chair. Apart from Acts of Parliament, none of them have a solid objective meaning, the way a written constitution might. They can be changed, unchanged and rechanged as often as people like. The edifice is based on sand, with no firm grounding. It exists in so far as people choose to believe that it exists.

The one area of solid footing comes in the rules laid down in an Act of Parliament, because they are actual bona fide law which can, in theory at least, be enforced in a court of law. It's a very small part of the rules, but it does cover some crucial aspects of what the Commons does, not the least of which is statutory instruments – little hidden-away power mechanisms that turn ministers into mini parliaments. We'll come to those later. It won't be a pleasant experience.

Then there is practice. These are things that have been done for so long, and are therefore considered so obvious, that no one has bothered to write them down. Extraordinarily, they include some of the most basic elements of the day-to-day parliamentary process. Legislation, for instance, has three readings in the Commons. It would be unthinkable for any government to suddenly decide that there would now be only two readings. But this is simply habit. There is nothing to stop a government majority in the Commons voting to change it, either in one specific case or indefinitely.

'This is one of the things about the British system,' says Paul Evans, who worked as a clerk in the House of Commons from 1981 to 2019. 'The fact that we have three readings is purely invented. It's not written down anywhere. It's not an iron rule. It's just that we believe it to be true.'

Standing orders are rules of the House that have been passed by the Commons to govern its affairs. They are a product of the Victorian period, in which the government imposed ever more draconian measures to take control of the Commons Chamber. They're printed in a blue book and are available online. They currently stand at around 200 pages. This is about as strict as the rules get outside of an Act of Parliament, but they do not cover every situation, they can be suspended, and they are all open to the interpretation of the Speaker.

The Speaker is the chairman of proceedings in the Commons. They are elected by members of Parliament to preside over the proceedings in the Commons. You can spot them sitting on the large ornate chair in the centre of the Chamber, dressed in a robe, occasionally shouting at MPs to shut up. Their rulings are the fourth source of regulation. Decisions taken by the Speaker form a kind of parliamentary case law. They can be referred to afterwards by future Speakers about what to do in a given situation. They can become convention – a behaviour that everyone agrees should be followed. Or they can be simply ignored.

Conventions come in two forms: soft and hard. Soft conventions aren't written down. They've just grown over time as more and more people believe in them. Hard conventions are written down in a book called *Erskine May*. It was first produced in 1844 by a parliamentary librarian called Thomas Erskine May and is now on its twenty-fifth edition. It's here, for instance, that the rule against MPs calling each other liars comes from. It is not a rulebook. It is simply an account of how procedures have developed over time and the conventions that govern them. And yet they are treated as hard-and-fast rules by the Commons authorities.

Until recently, the book was not available to be read except by those who were prepared to spend hundreds of pounds for a hard copy. This changed in 2019 after a long

#FreeErskineMay campaign, and it is now available online. But that only goes some way towards improving its accessibility. The book is full of convoluted and archaic jargon describing an impossibly tangled web of rules going back centuries, which would be impenetrable to anyone but the most experienced MPs or parliamentary historian. A new member of Parliament would not be able to sit in a parliamentary debate and flip through it to find out what they can and cannot do.

Even if a convention features in Erskine May, it is not set in stone. It can be interpreted by the Speaker. Many are forgotten, some are paid forensic attention to.

The parliamentary rules are like gods: they exist as long as people believe in them. They are part of a process that turns subjective assumptions into objective requirements by virtue of the social consensus around their use. This allows someone in a position of authority to confidently tell a new MP that something is impossible because it is against the rules, while simultaneously allowing them to tell the new MP that what they are doing is permissible, despite being against the rules, because they are all open to interpretation. It is a system that strengthens the hand of those who have had the time and upbringing to understand it and its strange ephemeral ways.

Legislation operates on the same basis of impenetrability. It is first published as a bill and then becomes an Act when it receives royal assent and becomes part of statute law. Bills are divided into chapters, which are divided into parts, then clauses, then subsections, paragraphs and subparagraphs. The chief mystification of the legislative process involves the separating out of documents. Even if someone were to sit down with a government bill to read it, which no one ever does, it would be impossible to understand it on the basis of what it contains. This is because most bills amend previous Acts of Parliament.

Former home secretary Priti Patel's Police, Crime, Sentencing and Courts Bill, for instance, amended the Public Order Act 1986. The original legislation gave police officers the power to restrict protests if they risked 'serious public disorder, serious damage to property or serious disruption to the life of the community'. The new legislation added a number of new criteria, such as if the protest might 'result in serious disruption to the activities of an organisation'. But no part of the bill actually spelled that out. Instead, it said: 'Section 12 of the Public Order Act 1986 (imposing conditions on public processions) is amended as follows. In subsection (1) for the "or" at the end of paragraph (a) substitute "in the case of a procession in England and Wales, the noise generated by persons taking part in the procession may result in serious disruption to the activities of an organisation".'

This is a basic example. Many pieces of legislation amend numerous other pieces of legislation, meaning that an MP trying to scrutinise it would need to have several Acts of Parliament in front of them, all of which they had properly understood, in addition to the one they are trying to scrutinise.

Most parliaments dealt with this problem years ago. At bare minimum, they have something called Keeling schedules, which ensure that the relevant bit of text in the original legislation is printed out as it would be amended by the new law, so that people can understand it without needing multiple documents in front of them. Westminster does not.

In November 2013, Green MP Caroline Lucas tried to introduce a change where every amendment to legislation would require a 50-word explanatory statement, in plain

English, outlining the purpose of what it was doing. This had been the practice in the European Parliament when she was working there, and she was astonished to find that the same thing was not done in Britain. She found some support from the Conservative benches. Tory MP Zac Goldsmith rose to back her. 'There have been many occasions in the short time I have been in the House,' he said, 'when I have had to seek advice on votes I was being asked to cast. I have asked many backbenchers on both sides of the House and the whips but have still been unable to understand them or get any kind of clarity. I have had to abstain because I simply did not know what the amendments I was being asked to vote for were about.'

But it was a lonely voice. Lucas's initiative was defeated by 142 votes to 23. 'It was all to do with the power of the whips,' she says. 'They don't want MPs to know what they're voting on. You tell them which way to vote, but you don't give them any further information. There is a deliberate policy of keeping MPs in the dark.'

Even if legislation were written in a form MPs could readily understand, they would struggle to find the time to scrutinise it, because of their constituency work. As the Speaker's Conference on Parliamentary Representation said: 'An MP has a number of responsibilities. The main ones are: as a legislator, debating, making and reviewing laws and government policy within Parliament; and as an advocate for the constituency he or she represents.'

That seemingly simple description captures the great catch-22 of an MP's career. They do not have one job, but two. If they were to do the first job properly, they would not have time for the second, and if they were to do the second job properly, they would not have time for the first.

For most MPs, constituency casework takes precedence over scrutinising legislation. The Hansard Society found that 21 per cent of MPs' time is spent in the Chamber compared to 28 per cent on constituency casework and 21 per cent at constituency meetings and events. This is partly for basic electoral reasons. Constituency work puts you in a better position to win an election and legislative research will not. Your party will resent you for refusing to be docile and no one else will even notice.

It is also about where people find worth. The Commons is set up for MPs to fail. No matter how much they scrutinise a piece of legislation, the government's majority means it will go through anyway. They have been made utterly redundant. But in their constituency, they can make a difference. They can at least help with one case, solve one problem. And that is often a more satisfying way to spend their time.

Constituency work is typically done through surgeries, which might be held in the MP's office if they have a small constituency, or a succession of town and village halls if they have a large one. Strictly speaking, their role should be limited to matters for which ministers are responsible to Parliament – basically the activity of executive agencies or government departments. They should stay out of local council business – schools, housing, rubbish collection and so on.

Even that restriction leaves them dealing with huge numbers of problems, from immigration and asylum to social security, tax, child maintenance and farming subsidies. But in truth, it's never just restricted to the areas they are supposed to be dealing with. An MP who tells a constituent that they can't help will soon find themselves being attacked on social media for ignoring their concerns. And that applies even when the complaints are minor. Nearly every MP spoken to for this book had their own list of the trivial issues they were told to deal with, including a complaint to a department store because a constituent's toilet seat was the wrong size and a dispute over the delivery of the local paper.

'It's the same 20 people going with the same issues,' SNP MP Alyn Smith says. 'It's intractable payments or it's a long-running planning dispute to which there is no solution. If you say no, you look like a bastard. If you actually take it on, you're cheapening, demeaning and confusing the role that you're actually there to do.'

A survey of 40 surgeries in 2017 found housing was the issue that was most frequently raised, on 37 per cent, followed by immigration on 23 per cent and benefits on 13 per cent. Many members of Parliament report that the line between council and MP responsibility has completely broken down. 'Most of my work is council work,' a Tory MP says. 'Ninety per cent of my surgery work is council work that should be done by councils, but no one knows who their councillors are. So they think the MP can solve everything, from fixing the Sky telly to dealing with child support. We need to make a decision. Are we big top-level councillors or are we legislators? Because at the moment it's relentless. How much time do I have to start scrutinising everything that's going on here? It's impossible.'

There are some benefits to an MP's constituency casework. In many instances, people who would otherwise have been left helpless find themselves with a supporter who commands attention. This is particularly true in immigration cases, where an intervention from an MP can be decisive. Any authority receiving a letter on parliamentary notepaper demanding answers on what they're doing will take it seriously, offering an avenue of assistance to people who might otherwise have none.

The act of doing the casework can also inform the MP's role in Westminster. 'This morning we've spent a lot of time going to and fro with the Home Office about some Ukrainian refugees we're trying to bring here, in a social worker sort of way if you like,' Tim Farron says. 'But I'm also building up a much better picture. So the questions I can ask of the Home Office in Parliament will be a lot more informed, and a lot more real, based on my social work, than somebody who doesn't do that. And the same applies to nearly everything you do.'

A former clerk – basically a civil servant for the Commons – had the same experience when managing a parliamentary committee doing work on prisons. 'I'd underestimated, as a callow youth, how much MPs knew about this,' he says. 'They've all been to a prison, which most of the population haven't. Most of them have a local prison or have had to visit people in a local prison.'

But even if it's informative, MPs' constituency work often crosses a line that goes far beyond representing their constituents' interests. It involves the often arbitrary introduction of political heft to situations that should be dealt with equitably and fairly rather than because someone managed to get their local member of Parliament on side.

'I remember explaining to a Danish MEP what constituency cases were,' Smith says. 'And she looked with horror and said: "That's corruption. You intercede with the government on someone's behalf? That's corruption." And it's true. A letter from me going in on someone's behalf about her planning application should not trigger a response which isn't happening otherwise.'

In recent years, the volume of constituency casework that MPs deal with has been steadily rising. Many have now increased their surgeries to twice a week. They hurriedly make their way to their constituencies on Thursday afternoon and spend the entirety of their time working on local cases until Monday morning, when they return to Westminster. That is largely a result of policy failure at the national level – from the defects in a Ukrainian refugee programme or the failure of the Afghan evacuation initiative to breakdowns in the benefits system or the massive reduction in funding of local councils. Ultimately these problems wash up on MPs' shores through the constituency link.

'A hell of a lot of it comes back to MPs' offices, because we're the last port of call,' Lucas says. 'The Home Office is totally dysfunctional. If the Department of Work and Pensions managed to make more of its decisions properly in the first place, we wouldn't be involved in so many discussions about how you appeal and get the benefits that you are entitled to.'

It is a toxic feedback loop. The poor quality of unscrutinised legislation results in dysfunctional government programmes, whose victims then have to seek help from MPs, who are then so busy dealing with their cases that they do not have the time to scrutinise the next raft of legislation. And so the cycle continues.

The ceaseless work, and the atmosphere in which it takes place, can have a pulverising effect on MPs. Ashley Weinberg is an occupational psychologist who has been studying the working life of politicians for three decades. He has mapped out a range of areas in which they are subject to precisely the kinds of stresses that damage mental health. On a personal level, their work–life balance is a mess. The split in their lives between two locations through the week – often involving journey times of several hours – means that 75 per cent feel they do not spend enough time with their partner and 80 per cent feel they don't spend enough time with their children. This was particularly acute for those with young children whose constituency was more than 150 miles from London.

'For all the talk of moats and duck houses and the rest of it, the idea that it's some sort of luxury to live in two homes is risible,' former Labour MP Luciana Berger says. 'It's no surprise that there's lots of divorce and break-ups, because trying to maintain any sort of personal relationship is pretty tricky under those circumstances.'

MPs also experience a lack of control over their lives. Even if they perform to the best of their ability, they could lose their job at the next election. 'If somebody said to you that they were reviewing your position,' Weinberg says, 'and that you may not have a job in two months, you'd experience that in stress. They do too.' The prospect of the loss of their seat is viewed with morbid terror by many MPs. For a large number of them, it will be the end of a dream they have had their whole lives. Some will be able to go into the think tank world, or run a small charity, or enter the private sector. But many will not, even if they've been thrown out at middle age, with years to go until retirement.

The political parties offer little to no support. 'A forward-thinking organisation would give that thought,' Weinberg says. 'It would not leave them adrift. But at that moment you lose the election, you lose everything – your email, your status, everything has gone straight away. That's it.'

After leaving Parliament, some MPs report feeling 'emotional devastation and a profound sense of personal failure'. Some have experienced grief, others seem clinically depressed. One former politician told researchers: 'Of course, my life is over.' Eighteen per cent of those who lost their seats mentioned long-term problems such as exhaustion, depression, sleep deprivation, family issues and financial difficulties. This is combined with a sometimes savage sense of animosity and abuse, both inside Parliament and outside. The Committee on Standards in Public Life has investigated the emergence of an intensely aggressive online culture towards politicians. 'The scale and intensity of intimidation,' it concluded in December 2017, 'is now shaping public life in ways which are a serious issue.'

The simmering hatred in modern politics is not restricted to the online world, or even the world outside political parties. It can also take place inside them.

Berger was subject to a stream of antisemitic and misogynistic abuse from supporters of party leader Jeremy Corbyn and elements of the far right when she was a Labour MP. In 2018, when she was five months pregnant, a letter was hand-delivered to her constituency office telling her she was going to be raped and stabbed and have acid thrown at her. Shortly afterwards, two motions of no-confidence in her were submitted by her local party for being insufficiently supportive of the leader. She told local party members what she was going through. 'They sat there stony-faced at the end of it,' she says. 'There was zero humanity in that room. I never wanted to be in a room like that again. I walked down the aisle, collected my things at the back of the room and left. I vowed to myself I would never come back to a constituency party meeting.' A few months later, she left the Labour party.

Even outside of the abuse, the lack of control and the damage to their personal life, MPs are exhausted. The workload they are asked to manage is simply too much for any one individual to maintain.

'We're expecting an MP to be a constituency caseworker, a social campaigner, effective on the media, a lobbyist in

Parliament for their constituents, to somehow understand legislation, properly scrutinise it, and potentially be a policymaker,' Spencer Livermore says. 'What human being can do all of those things? It's absolutely preposterous.'

When the stress gets too much, MPs often have nowhere to turn. In any normal workplace, they might be able to confide in their colleagues. But in the cut-throat world of politics, that act carries with it a potential political risk.

James Weinberg was providing depression screening to MPs and councillors when he found that 10–20 per cent of his sample was suffering from moderate to severe depression. 'The follow-up interviews were quite eye-opening,' he says, 'because some of those politicians said very openly: "What can I do? I can't even go to the occupational health team, because if anyone finds out then that's political capital for them to use against me. We're in a job where we can't show any weakness."'

The strains put on MPs are typically treated as a personal matter. They are that, but they are a constitutional matter too. In 1992, former Tory health minister Edwina Currie laid out the problem to the Jopling Committee. The end result of the pressures MPs experience, she said, is a form of 'exhausted irrationality'. Quite simply, people who are this stressed or depressed are not capable of normal intellectual function.

'I've had it myself, if I'm honest with you,' a Tory MP says. 'I'm a different person to who I was in 2010. I've wanted to be an MP since I was 10 years old. But my health is worse. I've had all kinds of issues I've never had to deal with before. And then all the stuff on social media does take a toll on you. It's relentless.'

We have no studies to demonstrate this, for the simple reason that MPs will barely respond to academic research about their motivations, let alone speak openly about mental health issues. But researchers believe it is a credible postulation.

'What we can say is that in mass population studies, this range of common mental disorders causes a number of impairments in cognitive functioning,' James Weinberg says. 'Their attention to things, their memory of things, their ability to consider difficult problems are all much more negative. They're less able to have a large cognitive load of options in front of them and to weigh information in a balanced way and reach a rational decision. So we don't really want politicians who are suffering from those symptoms to be in the driving seat, so to speak, unless there is appropriate support in place.'

Probably the most depressing thing you can say about MPs' scrutiny function is that we are, in many ways, living in its golden age. As pitiful as that capacity appears, it is actually a considerable improvement from its historic state.

From the Victorian era right into the 1970s, there was a presumption that a government that lost a vote on an important matter would have to resign or dissolve itself and call an election. While that sounds as if it handed backbenchers power over the executive, in practice it entailed the opposite. They were shackled by the existential consequences of even a minor act of rebellion against the party.

'The choice for a private member on the government side,' wrote the constitutional theorist Ivor Jennings, 'is between support for the government, on the one hand, and, on the other, either a resignation or a dissolution.'

This view faded away in the 1970s. Ted Heath was defeated on his new immigration rules by a combination of the opposition and his own backbenchers. Labour leader Harold Wilson rose and said: 'I now ask the prime minister, since this is a matter of major constitutional importance – if he is not going to tender his resignation – to inform the House what the government intend to do in the circumstances of this vote.'

There was laughter in the Chamber. No one expected Heath to resign, and the thought did not cross his mind. 'The House has rejected two statements made in accordance with Acts passed by the House,' he said simply. 'Statements to replace them will be laid in due course.'

So finally there it was. The great catastrophic consequences of a defeat were a mirage. Governments would not resign unless there was a formal motion of no confidence, or perhaps if they lost a Budget or Queen's Speech. Backbenchers consequently lost some of their anxiety and every parliament since then has generally become more rebellious than the one that preceded it.

'Once you've voted against the government, it's so much easier to do it a second time,' says Philip Norton, a Conservative peer and one of the country's leading experts on backbench rebellions. 'So they developed a habit of doing it. And also they realised that they could vote against and, oh look, the world hasn't fallen in. They've not been deselected. There's no major constitutional consequence.'

Margaret Thatcher, despite her large majorities, was defeated on immigration rules in 1982, the Shops Bill in 1986 and the National Health Service and Community Care Bill in 1990. John Major was subject to numerous defeats. Tony Blair emerged unscathed from rebellions because of the size of his majority, but that only concealed the extent to which they took place. There were backbench Labour rebellions on issues like anti-terror legislation, banning the incitement of religious hatred, university top-up fees, faith schools, firefighters' pay and, of course, the Iraq invasion, when 139 Labour MPs voted against the whip.

In 2010–15, Conservative and Liberal Democrat MPs voted against the government in 35 per cent of divisions, although the coalition only actually lost two votes. Theresa May's Brexit deal was defeated on three occasions by her own MPs voting with opposition parties. Boris Johnson faced persistent backbench rebellions, primarily over COVID-19 regulations.

Backbench rebellions offer a very odd kind of scrutiny. They are, without doubt, the chief weakness of government. Backbench rebel MPs acting together have far more power than a junior minister or even most secretaries of state. In a system of strong Commons majorities, they are the one thing that can stop the ruling party from doing whatever it wants.

They take place in two ways. Either backbenchers rebel alongside the opposition party, or they rebel on their own.

The first case can defeat governments, but it is not consistent and it does not have an intellectually coherent posture. It simply operates wherever the main opposition party can bring itself to vote with the more extreme wing of the governing party in order to secure the superficial political triumph of embarrassing the government.

In March 2016, for instance, the coalition government set out plans to liberalise Sunday trading laws. Under the existing rules, large shops were limited to opening for a maximum of six hours, but ministers wanted to devolve responsibility to local councils in a bid to give them more leeway. Labour and the SNP watched with interest as various Conservative MPs expressed their disgruntlement at the plans.

The SNP's position was particularly telling. Shops in Scotland had already been able to open for longer on Sunday for years. And anyway, the rules would not even have affected their constituencies. They only applied to 353 councils in England and 22 in Wales. But the vote offered a tantalising opportunity to discomfit the government. They and Labour voted against, as did 27 Tory rebels. It was enough to inflict a defeat by 317 votes to 286. The plans were buried.

Backbenchers rebelling on their own, on the other hand, cannot defeat the government. They do not have the numbers to overturn a majority. But that doesn't necessarily matter. The sheer embarrassment of dozens of backbenchers voting against the party, or the unseemly spectacle of relying on the opposition to secure your legislation, means many prime ministers buckle to their demands.

'We went from a party that was absolutely Remain to one that elected a prime minister who was in favour of Brexit and that was because of years of rebellions,' Bone says of the Tories. 'That's the power of the rebellion. You don't have to win. You just have to have enough people with you to make the prime minister think: "hang on a minute".'

This type of approach is much less spectacular. It does not result in the government being defeated on the floor of the House. But it is in fact far more effective, because it forces the government to compromise before a vote is even taken. And that reveals something fundamental about the dynamic of backbench rebellions.

They do not encourage compromise at the centre of politics. They encourage compromise between the centre and the extreme, through the relationship between the leadership and the back benches.

The momentum for backbench rebellions comes from groups within Parliament, below the party level. They can be formal or informal, functional or social.

During Brexit, for instance, the European Research Group represented hard-line Eurosceptics, as did the more informal Spartans. The loose-knit cross-party group of MPs opposing Boris Johnson's approach to Brexit ended up being called the Gaukward Squad, because it included Tory MP David Gauke. Another group existed for those in Labour who broadly supported leaving the EU but were uneasy with the Tory attempt to do so, including MPs like Lisa Nandy, Caroline Flint and Gloria Di Piero. At various times all these groups were rebelling against their party leadership, whether it was Theresa May, Boris Johnson or Jeremy Corbyn.

Very little is written about the informal groups that operate in Parliament, but they are of pivotal importance. First and foremost, they provide a forum for MPs to plot. This is a strategic necessity – they are trying to organise a vote, usually with some degree of discipline, outside of the party whip structure.

'The group that I was involved in was only eight strong,' Bone says of his own Brexit outfit. 'We used to meet up regularly, every week, in one of the rooms in the House of Commons, in private. And many of the things that happened with Brexit came out of that room.'

But the function of the groups is also social and emotional. Rebelling against the party carries a heavy personal toll and often involves being ostracised by your colleagues. The groups give each other moral support.

'There wasn't really a very good space for people like me, Caroline and Gloria,' Nandy says. 'There wasn't really anywhere where you weren't getting it in the neck. We found a way to come together and sort of stick together a bit. It wasn't a very fun time. I remember one of the MPs saying to Gloria: "If you hadn't scooped me up, I don't know where

I'd be right now." People were cracking up. So those informal groups, and just the friendly face in the tearoom, that sort of thing became really, really important.'

The Commons tearoom is the birthplace of many backbench rebellions. Not so long ago, there were other locations that were just as important, like the smoking room and various bars on the parliamentary estate. But the ban on smoking made the former less pertinent, while the end of late-night votes did for the latter. The tearoom is a long room. The bottom end, which is more formal, is reserved for Conservative MPs, while the top end, which is more relaxed, is reserved for Labour. Other tables are reserved for the DUP, the Liberal Democrats and the SNP. The arrangement stays the same no matter who is in government. In the middle is a cafeteria.

It's fitting that a place called the tearoom should be pivotal to the way the British constitution operates. And that is not because it fits a national stereotype about what we drink. It is because the British system tends to push the business of politics away from the spotlight in the Commons and into private spaces.

'These buildings,' a Whitehall official says, 'were designed for plotting. They were designed to help MPs find other MPs who can put pressure on the government. That is happening all the time. But it's never talked about or known about.'

This is one of the core unspoken dynamics of Westminster. It is rarely acknowledged publicly by MPs or ministers. It is hardly ever looked at by academics, because it is so difficult to study. And it is only covered by journalists to the extent that they are told about it.

The moments of political challenge and conflict on the floor of the Commons are largely pointless or symbolic. If a rebellion has any real chance of success, it will secure its aims behind the scenes, away from prying eyes. By the time a dispute is being fought in public, it usually means that the rebels have exhausted all other avenues and already lost.

'It's a sign of failure that you've had to go public,' Norton says. 'The informal space in Parliament is where a lot of the work goes on. What happens on the floor is the public manifestation of a massive activity that's taking place away from the Chamber. But it's not observable. It's not measurable.'

Once whips realise there is a potential rebellion coming, they can take a range of actions. They will of course try to bully or seduce MPs into changing their vote, but if that fails, they have several possible stages of escalation. It starts with the chief whip, then other MPs, then the minister in charge of the legislation they're rebelling over, and then, finally, if necessary, the prime minister themselves.

Often getting the MP to sit down with other backbenchers is the most effective route. It triggers their natural desire to fall back in with their tribe. 'The whips would say: "Go to the tearoom, talk it through with X and Y",' Burnham says. 'That would often be what I was advised to do before I made a public statement on something.'

If that fails, rebels will often meet the minister in charge of the bill. As a last resort, they will be called into a meeting with the prime minister. The latter will often put serious thought into how they handle these meetings. Theresa May, for instance, used to sometimes hold them on a large table made from a tree trunk where the G8 had met, in a bid to convince the MP that she was taking them seriously. Other times, the rebel will be called into the prime minister's parliamentary office, near the Commons Chamber.

'What matters isn't actually what goes on on the floor of the House,' a former No. 10 civil servant says. 'It's the conversations behind closed doors. That is where the real meat of politics, of the concessions, takes place.'

But in truth, even these meetings often have a certain level of artificiality to them. With many bills, the government will have mapped out the concessions it is willing to make in advance and planned for when it will make them. 'It's about the timing of the concession,' a Whitehall official says. 'In an ideal world, a parliamentary handling strategy would have identified before it even starts the exact point where you would make a concession.'

In September 2020, the Johnson administration introduced the United Kingdom Internal Market Act. It provoked outrage because of clauses 42 and 45, which allowed ministers to make changes to trade provisions regardless of whether they were consistent with domestic or international law. Speaking in the Commons, Northern Ireland minister Brandon Lewis said that it would 'break international law in a specific and limited way'.

Jonathan Jones resigned his job as head of the Government Legal Department. Rehman Chishti resigned his position as the prime minister's special envoy on freedom of religion or belief. Richard Keen resigned his position as advocate general for Scotland. Amal Clooney resigned as the UK's special envoy on media freedom.

But in fact the provisions about breaking international law were a mirage. Later, they would be quietly dropped while the bill was in the Lords.

That was a pre-prepared concession the government had always intended to make. The real substance of the bill lay in what it did to the devolutionary settlement with Scotland and Wales.

A series of complex provisions in the bill ultimately put the power to pass laws on goods and trade in post-Brexit

Britain in the hands of ministers in Westminster, rather than the devolved assemblies. As Nicola McEwen, professor of territorial politics at Edinburgh University, said, it represented a 'significant recentralisation of power' from the devolved legislatures to Westminster.

'The substance of the bill was that regime, which now rides roughshod over the devolution settlement,' says a civil servant who was involved in the backstage discussions. 'But everyone was so concerned about the international law proposal that it took all the heat away from the substance of the bill. Quite a few people in government, including Jacob Rees-Mogg, who was leader of the House at the time, thought that was a brilliant wheeze. The focus was pulled and the government got what it wanted.'

If the concessions don't come, or they're not enough, MPs have to face the moment at which they rebel. Doing so will involve a mixture of discipline, military-style organisation, and often quite a lot of hiding. 'You always tell your whip that you're going to rebel,' Bone says, 'and then you hide. Literally hide. They can't get you on the phone, because you're not answering. They can't come around your office, because you're not in it. On the day, it's very useful if they can't get hold of you.'

Gauke found that his own resolve about rebelling was improved by the fact that he inadvertently had the rebellion named after him. 'I didn't agonise over it,' he says. 'I had a certain amount of righteous anger. But I found myself in a position of leadership by accident, really, because of the Gaukward Squad thing. I think it was Robert Peston who came up with it. A good pun did for me! If I wasn't prepared to be part of the Gaukward squad, then who was? So I think that that probably strengthened my position.'

For many MPs, the moment of rebellion is traumatic. 'It was horrible,' Nandy says. 'You're walking through the division lobby and your colleagues are swearing at you. These are people I'd been mates with.'

At this point, the whips will go into action. If the situation is desperate enough, they'll sometimes resort to trying to manhandle MPs into voting for the party line. 'I have literally seen people being physically pushed into the aye lobby or the no lobby,' Lucas says. 'They're still protesting, saying "I'm not sure if I want to vote this way." And the whip pushes them in, because once you're over the line, then the convention is you can't reverse out again.'

Sometimes MPs even find themselves being subjected to mild violence by former prime ministers. When Bone was standing in the lobby for a vote after the Brexit referendum, David Cameron punched him in the stomach. 'That was fair,' he says. 'He had every right to frustration. It wasn't in a vicious way. It was more than lightly, but it was in fun. I'm quite proud really.'

It's at this moment that the emotional bonds formed with other rebels in the informal groups become pivotal. MPs in this position have found themselves between parties – rebelling against one and yet still despised by the other. Everything relies on having support from your allies in the same position.

In 2011, the coalition government tried to sell off around 40,000 hectares of publicly owned forest in an ultimately aborted bid to save some extra money in the age of austerity. They thought they'd get around £100 million for it. It was put to a vote in the Commons. Conservative MP Caroline Nokes, who had only been in Parliament a year, walked through the no lobby alongside Zac Goldsmith and Julian Lewis. 'We were the only three Tories in that lobby,' she says. 'And it was terrifying. Labour were not welcoming and nice and warm and cuddly towards me. They were sort of hurling abuse. And eventually Zac reached out to me and said: "Come on, Caroline, we can do this."'

It's tempting to look at the drama of backbench rebellions and conclude that MPs have become freshly confident of challenging government and scrutinising legislation, no matter what pressures are brought to bear on them. But that is a mistake. Backbench rebellions might be on the rise, but they remain rare.

One of the reasons they're rare is because they're so traumatic. MPs are fundamentally tribal animals. Going against their team contradicts some of their most basic impulses. 'My loyalty to my party is one of the strongest emotions that I possess,' Earl Russell, the Victorian-era home secretary, said. 'It is a greater loyalty to a collective group of people than I ever believed myself capable of.'

They are selected as MPs by partisans to be partisan. Then they take part in an election that enhances homogenised tribal identity. And finally they arrive in the Commons to be told by the whips, and their own colleagues, that disobedience to the party is a form of social and professional death.

This process naturally produces individuals who are extremely susceptible to toeing the line. 'It is not to Britain,' one MP told the researcher Emma Crewe when asked about her sense of loyalty, 'not the abstract idea of the Labour party, or to beneficiaries, it is to party members – party people. It would be very difficult to be disloyal to party people. I can't bring myself to go into the division lobby with the enemy.'

This is one of the key reasons why so few MPs are prepared to fully scrutinise legislation and then vote according to their judgement, instead of renting out their intellectual autonomy to the whips. It is to do with social shame. All of the incentives point the same way. Their moral sense, their social sense, their electoral sense and their own rational calculations for career advancement operate in one direction: towards doing what they're told.

'You're humiliated by the whips, who force you to vote on the party line day in, day out,' Rory Stewart says. 'There's barely any point reading the legislation. It becomes clear your promotion has nothing to do with expertise. It's about loyalty and defending the indefensible. The culture in the tearoom is very gossipy and trivialising. You can't earnestly grab someone in the corridor and try to talk seriously about a policy issue. It's not the done thing. It's a very unserious culture. It doesn't reward earnestness in any way.'

As the MPs are getting accustomed to this culture in the House of Commons, the new prime minister is getting used to their new home in Downing Street. And it's there that we'll turn next.

CHAPTER 3

The Power

After the election, the new prime minister will stand outside the doorway of No. 10, make a speech and then walk into the building.

We all remember those speeches. Margaret Thatcher saying: 'Where there is discord, may we bring harmony.' Tony Blair saying: 'A new dawn has broken, has it not?' But we don't see what happens afterwards, when the door closes behind them. That's what this chapter is about.

The euphoria over their victory doesn't last long. As soon as the new prime minister is inside, the civil service sits them down for a harrowing conversation. First they're asked to write a letter of last resort to the commanding officers of the four British ballistic missile submarines, outlining what action to take if a nuclear strike has destroyed the British government. Then they're given a briefing on current terror threats. Finally they're told that they can no longer use their mobile phone.

'We have terrible trouble with prime ministers and mobile phones,' says Gus O'Donnell, former Cabinet secretary and the man who delivered the introductory conversation to Gordon Brown and David Cameron. 'You just have to confront them with the facts. They tend to have a rather naive view about what can be intercepted and don't realise how much of private conversations can end up in the public domain.'

There is then one final element that sobers prime ministers up. According to the constitutional literature, this is the moment they realise they don't have much power.

It's called the theory of the weak centre. In truth, it's barely a theory at all. For Westminster types, it's considered a fact. Civil servants assume it. Politicians dwell on it. Political theorists investigate it. Read any book on the UK's governance structure or its constitutional history and it is one of the first points it will make.

It goes something like this. The prime minister has two distinct problems. The first is that they have a very small staff. Lord Egremont, who served as private secretary to Harold Macmillan, said that 'the prime minister had only four young men on whom to depend'. Ferdinand Mount, head of the No. 10 Policy Unit under Thatcher, complained that she had a 'tiny staff, considerably less than the staff at the disposal of the mayor of a major German city'. Almost all Westminster-model countries have a larger prime ministerial department, as do most European countries. Canada has the Privy Council Office. Australia and New Zealand have the Department of the Prime Minister and Cabinet. Germany has the Bundeskanzleramt. Britain doesn't have a Department of the Prime Minister at all, let alone many people in it.

The second problem is that the prime minister can't actually do much by themselves. They can't prepare their own legislation or even initiate a public consultation. Everything must go through government departments, which have their own views about the wisdom of what the centre wants. And unlike the centre, they have huge resources – big budgets, thousands of civil servants and a greater level of granular detail about the subject area.

So prime ministers are trapped, with too few people to achieve anything by themselves and surrounded on all sides by organisations with much greater resources than they have. The weak centre theory is popular because it is grounded in these basic facts and is profoundly counter-intuitive. It runs counter to the mainstream perspective on politics and therefore appeals to clever people who have done further reading. The problem with the theory is that it is false.

Far from being weak, British prime ministers are notable for the sheer magnitude of their power. There are hardly any leaders in the free world with fewer limitations on what they can do.

The prime minister is not limited by any real division of constitutional functions. Unlike the US, where the president faces an independent Congress with a monopoly on law-making powers, there is no meaningful separation of power between the executive and the legislature. The government controls Parliament.

Within England, the prime minister is not restricted by any local power centres. Unlike the US or Germany, there is no state government that passes its own laws.

Nor are they limited by having to bargain with other parties. Unlike almost any country in Europe, the prime minister can govern on their own without a coalition partner as a result of the first-past-the-post electoral system.

They can create or dismantle ministries at will. They can select whoever they want from parliament for their Cabinet and get rid of them whenever they please. There is nothing to stop them doing anything they like. There are almost no constitutional restraints on their actions whatsoever. Nothing stands in their way.

'There was a lack of checks and balances about how central authority is wielded in the UK, which for me was more important than the fact that the levers can be a bit rusty and indirect,' Nick Clegg says of his time as deputy prime minister. 'You would have weekly meetings where Cameron and I would sit and literally just between the two of us make decisions which would then immediately percolate into changes in the tax system or the benefit system. You wouldn't have that in the US. You wouldn't have that in Germany or Italy. If anything, I thought: "Wow, that's a bit random. I'm sitting here, just trying to work it out as we go along."'

The problem with the centre is not that it is weak. The problem with the centre is that it's dysfunctional.

The dysfunction starts with the architecture.

For reasons no one can rationally explain, the nerve centre of government is based in a house.

The buildings in Downing Street were constructed between 1682 and 1684 by a duplicitous penny-pincher called George Downing. He was an ally of Oliver Cromwell during England's experiment with republicanism, then switched sides and worked for Charles II when monarchy returned. He sent his former allies for trial and execution, before later being imprisoned in the Tower of London for running away in the face of danger.

He was, as Samuel Pepys described him, a 'perfidious rogue'. But his various political power plays did secure him one crucial historical achievement: a patch of marshy land around Westminster, upon which he decided to erect a row of fifteen houses. Unsurprisingly for a man whose own mother called him a cheapskate, he did so as economically as possible. The properties were 'shaky and lightly built',

Winston Churchill said nearly 300 years later, 'by the profiteering contractor whose name they bear'.

In 1732, George II presented part of what became No. 10 to Robert Walpole, the first prime minister – or, to use the official designation, First Lord of the Treasury. Walpole said he would only accept it if it was received in his official political capacity. Maybe it was an act of humility. Or maybe he knew that it would need a lot of work and preferred that the taxpayer foot the bill.

No. 10 was joined to a much grander house at its back and absorbed a small cottage to its side. Walpole got his architect, William Kent, to gut the interior and join the properties together, with a magnificent staircase as the centrepiece. The work was attractive, but superficial. As historian R. J. Minney said, in what would make a good constitutional metaphor if it wasn't so on the nose: 'The money had been spent lavishly. A delightful home, spacious and decorated with taste, had been provided for the king's first minister. But neither Kent nor Downing had given much thought to the foundations. It was inevitable that the timber would rot and that the house should be in need of constant and costly attention.'

A few other early prime ministers occupied the house with their families, but for long stretches, including most of the nineteenth century, it was surrounded by brothels and gin parlours, so most chose to live elsewhere. It wasn't until Arthur Balfour in 1902–5 that a prime minister opted to make it his home again. This was largely a question of habit. He'd been living there while serving as leader of the Commons, and simply continued doing so when he secured the premiership. But because of that decision, and through the random whims of the British fetish for precedent, Downing Street has now been the home of every prime minister since, at some point or other.

There have been regular changes to the building throughout, but they're always incremental. It has never been redesigned from the ground up to make it suitable for governing, or indeed for working on any kind of serious project at all. In 1960–3 there was a reconstruction that offered the opportunity of a complete redesign, but conservationism won the day.

'I am sure that if you were starting from fresh, you wouldn't start with No. 10,' said Robert Armstrong, principal private secretary to Edward Heath and Harold Wilson. 'But you aren't starting afresh. I think a conscious decision has been made – and made repeatedly – that the right thing to do is to preserve No. 10 in its eighteenth-century form and live with that.'

The only really spacious area is the Cabinet Room, but that feels cramped because it has a massive table in it. To one side of it there's a room for the prime minister's most senior private secretaries – the uppermost position in the Downing Street civil service hierarchy – and another for more junior private secretaries. At the other end are a couple more rooms, usually used by political advisers. This network of quarters is typically the operational centre.

Off from these rooms and up a short flight of stairs there are some more tiny offices, called the Wiggery. They were originally a wardrobe but have been converted into working cubbyholes by an assortment of assistant private secretaries, press secretaries, policy advisers and chiefs of staff throughout the modern period.

Upstairs there is a study, which used to be a bedroom but has since been converted into an office. In it, there is a painting of Margaret Thatcher that was commissioned by Gordon Brown. There's some additional working space above that, and then the flat, where prime ministers and their families are expected to reside, although sometimes they swap it out for the larger domestic quarters in No. 11, particularly if they have children.

Harold Wilson, Ted Heath and Thatcher used the first-floor study to work. Clement Attlee, Anthoney Eden and John Major used the Cabinet Room. Tony Blair set up in one of the rooms off the Cabinet Room, but found it embarrassingly dark and cramped when fellow world leaders were visiting, so he moved to the senior private secretaries' room. That then forced them out to the more junior private secretaries' room, which forced the junior secretaries upstairs to the Wiggery. This has now become the default office set-up for prime ministers for the time being. Theresa May and Boris Johnson both used it. 'Out of the offices available,' says Nikki da Costa, director of legislative affairs during both their tenures, 'it is probably the most effective place.'

The most famous space in Downing Street, apart from the front door, is the grand staircase, which holds the portrait of every prime minister since Walpole. It is the heart of the building structurally, but also emotionally, because it captures why it remains the place of government. It is steeped in history. It speaks to the British sense of continuity with the past. Those portraits are like ghosts watching over the current occupant.

'It is a heritage which every prime minister guards with care and affection,' Thatcher said. 'The feeling of Britain's historic greatness which pervades every nook and cranny of this complicated and meandering old building.' Jack Brown, who became the first ever researcher in residence at No. 10, said: 'It truly is a house like no other, its air so thick with accumulated history that for the unfortunate it can become suffocating.'

And all of that may well be true. But what it describes is a museum, not the operating centre for a nation's government. The fact that it is impossible to work effectively in Downing Street has been accepted by nearly every one of its modern occupants and those who worked alongside them.

Marcia Williams, Wilson's personal and political secretary, said: 'Its designers have not succeeded in making it either an efficient office or a comfortable home. It seems to exude an air of condescending contempt for both roles.' Douglas Hurd, Heath's political secretary, said: 'It is hard to imagine anyone governing anything substantial from Number Ten.' Jonathan Powell, Blair's chief of staff, said it was 'extraordinarily ill-suited to be the headquarters of a modern government'.

There are no open-plan spaces for teams to work together. There are nowhere near enough basic meeting rooms. There are no places for staff to socialise. It's cramped, badly organised and irrationally structured. And it suffers from the irreducible and unfixable problem that it does not have the room for the kind of staff capacity required of modern government.

The continued use of Downing Street is an act of pathological national sentimentality, the product of a country that has come to value tradition over function and its past over its future.

Various attempts have been made to reform it, but they all came to nothing. Powell tried to convince Blair to swap it for open-plan space in the nearby Queen Elizabeth II conference centre, but was twice defeated. In August 2008, Gordon Brown set up a horseshoe-shaped work centre in the chief whip's office in No. 12 Downing Street. Cameron dropped it as soon as he entered government. Dominic Cummings, chief adviser to Boris Johnson, moved to

70 Whitehall to create a kind of space station information nerve centre, but the project died when he was sacked.

Instead, the British government has simply made do with a physical structure that prohibits it from working effectively.

Most prime ministers start their week with a meeting with their official spokesperson to look at what's been in the media over the weekend and how to respond to it. On Tuesday morning they'll meet with their Cabinet. On Wednesday evening they have an audience with the monarch. Most weeks there'll also be National Security Council conferences with the heads of the intelligence agencies, and appointments with the home secretary, police and MI5 on terror threats.

This will all take place alongside visits from heads of foreign governments, global trips, international summits, statements to the Commons, charity receptions and party political events. Their time will also be stuffed with policy submissions, intelligence reports and draft speeches, with anything left over crammed into a red box, which will be given to them to work on overnight or over the weekend.

Beyond all that there is the basic conveyor belt of political punishment: a remorseless daily diet of crisis, scandal and outrage, the frenzied day-to-day battle over whichever story is dominating the press. Something has gone wrong in a department, a minister has said something offensive, rebels on the back benches are getting restless, an MP has been caught breaking lobbying rules; or there's been a terror attack, or an inflationary surge, or a war, or a banking crisis. Events from outside the building will dominate the time of every occupant of Downing Street, regardless of how effective they are at working inside it.

The vast majority spend their time in No. 10 on the back foot, firefighting chaos as it threatens to subsume them. Quite often it does.

The configuration of No. 10 moulds itself to the prime minister. It is a house that rearranges itself around them, both physically and socially. There is no set place for departmental communication, legislative work, research, party political management and the like. Instead, like the endless makeshift restructuring of the building, everything moves continually, from year to year, administration to administration, party to party. The one constant is the importance of face time.

Everyone in the building is like a planet orbiting the sun. Every administration, no matter what its politics or overall culture, follows this pattern. Status is based on face time with the prime minister. The more face time you have, the more senior you are. This is the only real currency, the primary source of authority.

It therefore follows that proximity is the most important resource. And the key battle, in almost any political memoir you read or interview you conduct, is about the desperate scramble to secure space close to wherever the prime minister happens to be working. 'In No. 10, as in love, proximity is everything,' Harold Evans, press secretary to Harold Macmillan, said. 'That and the instinct that takes you to the right place at the right time.'

All the other usual social signifiers fade away. The size of an office, its view, the amount of light it has, the ornate furniture within it – all the things that might be considered indicative of success in any other working environment – become irrelevant. 'I very rapidly gave up my big office to someone much more junior,' recounted Andrew Adonis, head of the No. 10 Policy Unit under Tony Blair, 'and moved downstairs into this tiny cubbyhole, so small that you could barely get a desk and a chair in. I could only have a visitor if they stood. But I chose to have that room because it put me right next to the prime minister. I would rather have a tiny cubbyhole than a room ten times the size a few more metres away.'

As those who want face time crowd in, those unable to secure it are pushed aside, further outward from the sun, or upstairs into the chilly isolation of deep space. In the worst-case scenario, they find themselves in the Cabinet Office. This is located in 70 Whitehall, but is connected to No. 10 by a single door. It functions as a definitive marker of who is in and who is out. 'Certain Cabinet Office officials have a link door pass,' a Cabinet Office civil servant says. 'Most don't. It's a big deal if you can get into No. 10.'

The combination of face time and limited space means that teams are constantly moved around and split up. It is not unusual to find that groups of people who are meant to be working together on projects central to the government's agenda are operating from multiple different rooms on multiple different floors of the building.

Those close to the prime minister then start thinking about how they can use their proximity to prevent others from securing their own face time. The best possible office is one close to the prime minister that also allows you to stop other people being able to go in to see them.

'My desk was immediately outside the door of the prime minister's office,' Gavin Barwell, chief of staff to Theresa May, said in his memoirs. 'This had one big advantage: it made me a literal gatekeeper. Provided I was at my post, no one could pop in to see the prime minister without me knowing about it.'

The emphasis on face time is a natural consequence of a political culture grounded in machismo. The electoral system operates on the principle of winner-takes-all and creates a majority for a single party leader who can then do whatever they like. This translates into a primitive emperor-like structure that values base demonstrations of political virility over rational communication arrangements.

It is also a consequence of the building's structure. Knowledge confers power in any political culture. If someone can demonstrate an understanding of the current mood in government, or the views of the prime minister, or awareness of an upcoming policy direction, they prove themselves to be a reliable indicator of what is really going on. That elevates their status inside and outside the building. But since the working environment has not changed since the days of the American War of Independence, this information is most likely to be gleaned by virtue of physical proximity.

'I was very grateful because my office was right below the Private Office,' a former Downing Street official says. 'So I could pop in a lot, ask the odd question about what else is going on and glean some information. If you get pushback in Whitehall you'll go: "That issue was addressed and this was the feeling from the prime minister, therefore I'm content that we are going in the right direction." But to make that something you take satisfaction in is a sign of dysfunction. It means your effectiveness basically depends on your ability to loiter.'

In that fraught situation, prime ministerial consistency becomes absolutely essential. Being able to secure accurate information means nothing if things might change as soon as you walk out the door. 'My relationship with Blair was important,' says Michael Barber, who worked in No. 10 during the New Labour years. 'Lots of people around

Whitehall who talk about "what the prime minister thinks" don't really know. But he really did trust me, so I could say, "the prime minister thinks" and people would listen.'

Prime ministers who regularly change their mind therefore find themselves inadvertently sabotaging the status of those who are closest to them. 'Boris was very bad,' a Downing Street official during the Johnson administration says. 'He'd say one thing, then a secretary of state would text him and Boris would go: "Oh yes, you're right." So he'd reverse it and then suddenly he's just basically cut the legs out of his entire operation.'

Downing Street has four main structures to communicate with government departments: the Cabinet, the Cabinet Office, the Private Office and the Policy Unit. These are the forums the centre uses to liaise with the departmental silos and make sure they're doing what they are supposed to be doing.

The traditional metaphor that's used for this process is a lever. The prime minister wants to do something – ban upskirting photos, say, or reduce A&E waiting times. So they pull the lever. What happens next? Something or nothing, or perhaps a messy combination of both.

If the process is very simple, like a ban on upskirting photos, it can usually be done fairly easily. The relevant department writes up the legislation, it passes through Parliament, and then it's on the statute book.

If the process is complicated, like A&E waiting times, it's more difficult. It's about trying to find out the various reasons something is happening and addressing them, from NHS staffing levels to pay to resource management. And that will require a much greater degree of sustained attention, long-lasting cross-departmental cooperation and political muscle. You have to find all the various objects that have got stuck in the lever and remove them, so that it functions.

This is the point where prime ministers typically fail. They find it easy to pass a law banning something. But complex change involving broad inputs and a long lead-in time tends to get lost in the dysfunction of Downing Street, or it's slowly relegated until it becomes an afterthought under the daily firefighting of political life.

And yet, as we shall see, it is possible to use these levers. It requires a clear idea of what you want to do and a credible process for how you will accomplish it. The problem is that there have been very few prime ministers with the ability to satisfy those requirements.

In the popular imagination, the Cabinet table is where this process takes place. The prime minister sits down with the people they have selected to run government departments, they debate what they're going to do in each area, and then they decide how to pursue it. Indeed, this is the historic origin of our entire system of modern government. But in fact it hasn't worked this way for decades and arguably never did.

Successive prime ministers have reduced the role of Cabinet to what is effectively a rubber-stamping operation. The big break came with Thatcher. She maintained the formality of Cabinet discussion while diligently working to eradicate its content. 'Margaret Thatcher was going to be leader in Cabinet,' Nicholas Ridley, one of her close allies, wrote. 'She knew what she wanted to do and she was not going to have faint hearts in her Cabinet stopping her.'

Blair watched this from opposition and replicated it in government. Cabinet meetings still took place, but they were brief, rambling and without any kind of decision-making input. 'I met somebody at a Labour party function once, fairly early on in the life of the government,' Margaret Beckett says. 'He was passionate to know why we weren't building more council houses. He kept asking me what had been said about it in Cabinet. I thought: "He is a nice man. He is really enthusiastic. He feels passionately about housing. I cannot tell him that the Cabinet does not discuss it." It's just not like that. [Former deputy prime minister] John Prescott will discuss it with Tony, and then tell us what they've decided.'

Occasionally the Cabinet has a bit more power. Typically this is when a prime minister starts to feel their political strength slipping away and needs to shore up the support of their colleagues. James Callaghan experienced it, as did Major and Brown. But the far more functional element of Cabinet is the Cabinet subcommittees. These range across policy platforms, from national security to domestic and economic strategy. These smaller meetings, with select secretaries of state looking at specific areas of policy, are typically more substantial and meaningful affairs, especially if they're chaired by the prime minister or one of their key allies.

The second organisation mediating the relationship between the centre and the departments is the Cabinet Office, based in 70 Whitehall and connected to No. 10 through that crucial doorway. The doorway acts as a symbol not just of who is in or out of the inner circle, but also of the Cabinet Office's mercurial constitutional status. Technically it is responsible for serving Cabinet as a whole. In reality, it's primarily responsible for serving Downing Street.

'The conventional role of the Cabinet Office,' Callaghan said, 'is to serve all the members of the Cabinet, but if the prime minister chooses, as nearly all of them do, to work closely with the secretary to the Cabinet, then it becomes an instrument to serve him above all the others.'

Compared to most departments, it has a relatively small staff, of around 2,050 people. But it still provides an important additional resource for an effective prime minister.

'No. 10 is like a gearstick and the Cabinet Office is the transmission,' Jonathan Powell, Blair's chief of staff, says. 'If departments have different wheels going at different speeds and different directions, the car's not driving so well. So you want some transmission between the gearstick and different departments.'

The Cabinet Office is pure undiluted bureaucracy, so it provides additional resources for the prime minister to designate towards his favoured projects.

In 2021, for instance, Andrea Leadsom was tasked with conducting a review into early-years development for children – a project that took in education, health, social services, benefits and various other elements. She was assigned a team from within the Cabinet Office's Economic and Domestic Affairs Secretariat to do so.

The third body mediating the centre and the departments is the Private Office. It is composed of around seven senior civil servants who work directly for the prime minister. At the top is the principal private secretary, who works more closely with the prime minister than any other official. Their key task is the management of information flow – organising papers into what needs to be read or decided now and what can be read or decided later. They'll also be writing notes on alternative views and recommendations for various options. They are effectively quality control, 'the key instruments filtering the world and making it manageable' for the prime minister, in the words of historian Anthony Seldon and political analyst Dennis Kavanagh.

Underneath the principal private secretary, there will be a handful of other private secretaries with specialities in various areas who are sent in from their respective departments for two or three years – one each from the Home Office, the Foreign Office, the Department of Health and so on.

Among other things, they function as the grandest minute-keepers in the country. If a prime minister has a meeting with a secretary of state, the relevant private secretary will send a readout to their department afterwards on what was agreed. If a secretary of state sends Downing Street a note looking for approval for a policy, a private secretary will collate views in No. 10 and then send on the submission to the prime minister. It's a web of correspondence between the centre and the departments. But because it is from the civil service, it is functional rather than political. It is a skeleton without the circulatory system.

The final and most significant piece of the puzzle is the Policy Unit. Of all the institutions within Downing Street, this is arguably the most important. When it works well, the government has a fighting chance of success. When it fades into obscurity, the government typically falls into disarray.

The story of the Policy Unit is about the relationship between politics and expertise.

When the Policy Unit first emerged, it seemed like a logical solution to the central problem undermining the British political system: the lack of specialist knowledge about the world. There had always been a few external experts advising government. David Lloyd George established a secretariat of such advisers during the First World War. Churchill had a statistical section of economists attached to his office during the Second World War, led by Professor Frederick Lindemann. The economist John Maynard Keynes was recalled to the Treasury in 1940 and remained there until his death. William Beveridge, the designer of the benefit system, was a temporary civil servant.

Those who were concerned about the general lack of expertise in the system started to advocate for a more regular use of these outsiders in the late 1950s and 1960s. Among them was Thomas Balogh, a Hungarian academic who secured British citizenship in 1938. He was brought into No. 10 by Harold Wilson in 1964. Specialist appointments, Balogh argued, could bring 'expert knowledge in the policy-making machine' and 'enforce adequate consideration and positive elaboration of policies from the point of view of the government of the day'. He was joined by the economists Nicholas Kaldor and Robert Neild in the Treasury and the social welfare expert Brian Abel-Smith at the Department of Health and Social Security. At this point no more than a dozen external figures had been appointed.

In 1974, when Wilson started his second term, he added a small seven-person team to Downing Street, headed by former LSE academic Bernard Donoughue. It was the birth of the Policy Unit. 'The purpose of the Policy Unit,' Wilson said, 'is not only to bring in experts to extend the range of policy options from which the government – and in particular the prime minister – has to choose. The Policy Unit was set up, and its members were selected, to provide a team with strong political commitments to advise on, propose and pursue policies to further the government's political goals.'

Notice how Balogh and Wilson formulated the idea in the same way. This was not expertise for its own sake. It was expertise that fitted the prime minister's agenda and would help them pursue their party's goals. Nevertheless: the expertise came first, the politics second.

The Policy Unit lay at the centre of a wider pattern of development towards a new type of figure in the British political system: the special adviser. They are distinct from normal civil servants, in that they are hired directly by the government and can therefore operate politically, outside of the civil service's requirements of impartiality.

Callaghan kept the Policy Unit, as did Thatcher, who considered scrapping it as part of her small government initiative but then ended up enlarging it to ten people. It expanded to thirteen when Blair came to power and a variety of new units were added: the Strategic Communications Unit, the Research and Information Unit, the Social Exclusion Unit, the Performance and Innovation Unit and, after the 2001 election, the Strategy Unit and the Delivery Unit.

Suddenly the centre wasn't so weak any more. It still had nowhere near as many staff members as a typical government department, but it had grown significantly in size from Macmillan's 'four young men'.

Meanwhile, special advisers began to spread across government departments. The Thatcher administration employed around 30 of them, Major around 40. Under Blair, when they became known simply as 'spads', there were typically 70 to 80 of them in any given year. They were put in every department – most employed two, some more.

They became the recruiting ground for the next generation of politicians. Ed Balls and David Miliband were spads. Ed Miliband, the Labour leader after the party fell out of power, had been a spad, as had David Cameron, the man he faced across the dispatch box. It started to feel as if the spad system was effectively a fast stream into political leadership.

When the coalition government came to power, it pledged to reduce the number of spads but it did not last. By 2013, there were just under a hundred. As we'll see, they are now a permanent, and increasingly disturbing, part of the political system.

The Policy Unit has some civil servants in it and nearly always has done. They're there because they understand Whitehall. They can take the party political thinking and provide it with the institutional know-how to get things done. But it is primarily composed, and always has been, of spads. The mix on the Policy Unit is usually around two thirds spads to one third civil servants. When Thatcher left No. 10, she had six spads and two civil servants. When Blair left, there were six spads and four civil servants. When Brown departed, there were eleven spads and five civil servants.

The Policy Unit can be whatever the prime minister wants it to be. Indeed, the chief thing to remember about terms like 'spad' and 'Policy Unit' and 'chief of staff' is that they don't actually mean anything. They are just buckets into which the prime minister can dump whatever functions they like. Sometimes the unit is tasked with coming up with medium- and long-term policy assessments. Often it is deployed to marshal research for briefings with the prime minister when they engage in discussions with a secretary of state. But typically it operates as a politicised version of the Private Office, with spads mapped onto its departmental structure – covering health, education and so on. It adds the circulatory system to the skeletal system of the civil service.

'Within our Policy Unit, there would be people that were shadowing government departments,' Alastair Campbell, Blair's press secretary, says. 'That was about coordination – we all needed to know what people were doing.'

At one stage, New Labour even tried melding the Private Office and the Policy Unit together, effectively absorbing the civil service process into the party political process. 'It didn't work,' Powell admits. 'We split it back into Policy Unit and Private Office and no one's tried to put it back again since. It was a mistake.'

Somewhere over the course of this evolution, the idea that spads should be experts faded into irrelevance. Balogh and Wilson's idea that they would bring outside specialism into government slowly disintegrated. While the expertise aspect disappeared, the party political element consolidated.

But then something interesting happened. An expert did find their way into Downing Street. And they demonstrated just what could be accomplished if people set their minds to it.

His name was Michael Barber. He'd started working for the government in the Department for Education alongside education secretary David Blunkett, education minister Estelle Morris and spads like Conor Ryan.

In Labour's first term, an education white paper called Excellence in Schools was published, with a vast collection of detailed ambitions: maximum class sizes of 30 for children under 7; national targets for 80 per cent of 11-year-olds to achieve 'expected standard' in English and 75 per cent in maths; programmes for a structured hour every day in school on literacy; the creation of a numeracy task force.

Barber set up a Standards and Effectiveness Unit in the department. Spads in No. 10 and the Department of Education acted as transmission agents for the daily communication needed to make the changes happen. The day-to-day decision-making process flowed through Blair, Barber, the education private secretary in No. 10, the principal private secretary in the Department for Education, the spads in the department and Blunkett himself. 'They were all aligned,' Powell says. 'They were all going in the same direction.'

This was strengthened by a clear demonstration from the prime minister that the reforms were at the forefront of the government's agenda, through his 'education, education, education' mantra. 'That slogan was the leader sending a signal,' Campbell says. 'That got the Treasury thinking "education is going to be up there". But it also gave power within the government system to Blunkett to say: "I have got the number one priority."'

It proved powerfully effective, providing verifiable improvements in numeracy, literacy and class sizes. So in 2001, after Labour had secured a second term, Blair asked Barber to set up something new. It was called the Delivery Unit. This would be part of a new three-unit system operating in Downing Street.

The Policy Unit was tasked with liaising and coordinating between No. 10 and the departments on immediate issues, operating according to an articulable narrative and political agenda set by the prime minister. The Strategy Unit was tasked with long-term policy thinking, looking ahead four or five years. 'It was allowed to do blue skies thinking,' O'Donnell says. 'What if we legalise drugs? What if we changed the way we tax business? They were told to think the unthinkable.'

The Delivery Unit, on the other hand, was involved in the business end of policy: the point at which it translates into real-world results. It took Barber's approach to education and expanded it to four departments – the Home Office, Health, Transport and Education – in line with Labour's second-term election manifesto. It set aspirations, like an improvement in A&E waiting times. Then it set a target that would reflect that goal, like a maximum four-hour wait. Then it set progress reviews to provide data on departmental performance towards the target.

Departments reported every two months for a stocktake meeting. Barber asked Blair for 100 hours of his time every year, comprising two hours a week. Apart from that, he said, the unit could be left alone and would get on with securing the goals.

The introduction of independent expertise to the Downing Street machine, with its own remit to construct a unit and run it, provided three key advantages.

The first was a defensive wall against distraction. Many administrations become entirely reactive in the face of crises and scandals. They do not have the organisational barriers to protect the part of the government that is working to fulfil complex objectives from the day-to-day political firefighting. But no matter what happened, the Delivery Unit was allowed to get on with its work.

After 9/11, Barber turned to Blair and said: 'Whatever you have to go and do in the world, I will never be distracted from this. We are going to get these targets met. We are undistractable.' That proved essential to the unit's ability to deliver. It was why the targets could be met despite the firestorm of controversy over Iraq.

The second advantage was curiosity, of an academic sort. The standard approach of Westminster is to project answers, typically with a sense of tribal confidence. The Delivery Unit took a different approach – it asked questions. Those questions provided interesting results. Barber asked the Department for Transport, for instance, why railway performance was so poor in October. They were told the same thing that commuters are always told, as they sit shivering on a platform waiting for a delayed train. There were leaves on the line. 'Oh yes,' he replied. 'We know that leaves fall off the trees. What we want to know is why that takes you by surprise.'

The problem with leaves on the track is that they make trains slide when it rains, so that they miss the station. Drivers therefore go slower and the schedule is delayed. The

Delivery Unit prompted the Department for Transport to look at other countries to see who had found a solution to the problem. Canada had, but it involved chopping down all the trees near the line, something that was possible in a big, expansive country but not in Britain. Poland, however, had a better idea. It used a machine to put resin on the track before the leaves fell, which created enough friction to counteract the moisture. This was the approach adopted in Britain. Between 2003 and 2013, train performance in October improved consistently.

The third advantage of the Delivery Unit was a lack of Westminster aggression. 'Very early on, I spoke to people who'd previously run units at the centre,' Barber says. 'I got their advice and I did the opposite. The classic character who you see over and over again in Downing Street is going around yelling at people, saying: "The prime minister is incandescent about this, he's totally frustrated, what the hell are you doing." You know, all that stuff. Well, we didn't do that.'

Delivery Unit staff were trained in how to negotiate, based on research from Harvard University. They were shown how to talk constructively but honestly to senior figures, including secretaries of state and top civil servants. The goal of a conversation was to deliver a message in a plain-speaking fashion but leave the room at the end of the meeting with the relationship stronger than when they went in. They made sure departments could take the credit for work they had helped them achieve. They pledged to never ask departments for research unless they thought they themselves needed it for the proper functioning of their policy area.

'You can spend prime ministerial power by going around yelling at people,' Barber says, 'and you will get some stuff done, in the short term. But you're not actually enhancing the power of the prime minister. You're spending it. You're using up his power. Whereas we were investing it.'

The Delivery Unit experiment didn't survive. Brown did not give it the consistent focus it had enjoyed under Blair, and it subsequently went into decline. Under various governments since then it has simply become irrelevant.

The Policy Unit has survived, but it flickers in and out of pertinence. It has never had the defined role it did during the New Labour period. Sometimes it was about the lack of a clear organising principle from the leadership. Sometimes it was about the person put in charge of it.

James Marshall, for instance, who was made head of the Policy Unit under May, had no background or interest in policy but was given the role as a consolation prize after he failed to secure another post he wanted. Unsurprisingly, that did not prove a very effective way of selecting the big brain of a government operation.

Sometimes it is to do with the quality of the staff, or their background, or the instruction they are given. 'We've seen recent episodes where it just doesn't work,' O'Donnell says. 'They've tried to fill it entirely with special advisers and left the civil service out of it. Or sometimes they've got the wrong kind of special advisers and they just don't know how to make the system operate.'

The Policy Unit would be moved around, usually on the second or third floor of No. 10, sometimes split into different rooms. There was a small glimmer of hope when Dominic Cummings moved core elements into 70 Whitehall in 2020. They found themselves in an open-plan office with the Cabinet Office's Economic and Domestic Affairs Secretariat, which oversees the legislative portfolio. Suddenly a degree of communication was possible that could never be achieved in Downing Street itself.

But eventually, the core architectural dysfunction of Downing Street asserted itself. 'If they had completed that move, I think it would have been fantastic,' da Costa says. 'People started to talk to each other, you had more policy debates and there was greater coordination. But what ended up happening was that they made the Policy Unit and legislative affairs a satellite of No. 10, just because of the geographic distance. It's no good saying it's only five minutes to sprint down the corridor. That five minutes is a huge operational difference.'

And so government after government has retreated back into the claustrophobic power-play asylum of No. 10, with its broken incentive system of face time and professionalised loitering.

Without the Delivery Unit to provide a space away from the day-to-day firefighting, successive administrations found that they were constantly on the back foot, unable to focus on their core political mission, or even really remember what it was, because of the remorseless battery of news and crises. Without the Strategy Unit, they were unable to develop any kind of long-term ideas about where the country was heading and what the government's response to it was, let alone what it could do now to alleviate or exploit those future conditions. And without an effective Policy Unit, meaningful political communication between the centre and the departments started to break down. The levers got all bunged up again. Prime ministers would pull them, notice they weren't working, and curse the various imagined enemies that were responsible for it.

Key indicators of public service performance went into decline. In the early 2000s, the government introduced a four-hour standard for A&E, with a target of 98 per cent of patients being either discharged, admitted or transferred by that deadline. This was relaxed in 2010 to 95 per cent.

Over the ensuing years, the numbers got worse and worse. The NHS has not met the four-hour standard at a national level in any year since 2013–14. It's been missed every month since July 2015. That year, the percentage of people being seen within four hours hit 90 per cent. By November 2019, just before COVID hit, it had fallen to 80 per cent. After the pandemic, the decline continued. By March 2022, just 72 per cent of patients were being dealt with within four hours. A&E waiting rooms are now in an advanced state of disarray. Figures coming from the Royal College of Emergency Medicine show that an average of 1,047 people a day are waiting more than twelve hours in A&E.

This happened for a number of reasons. COVID hit the health service like a bulldozer. It came after a decade of austerity-led funding settlements that failed to increase financial support in line with demand. There was growing pressure on the NHS, in both A&E and general admissions, from an ageing population. Lack of capacity in other parts of the system, such as social care, meant delays in discharging patients who were fit to leave hospital, with knock-on effects in A&E departments. And there were long-standing challenges in recruiting and retaining staff.

But it was precisely these sorts of complex disparate causal links, playing out against an advanced time horizon, that the post-2001 Downing Street unit system was designed to address. As it went into decline, governments lost their advance warnings of what was coming, the ability to centrally assess it and the political clear-sightedness to deal with it.

Perhaps in those moments, when the prime minister tried to pull the lever again and discovered that nothing happened, they concluded that the constitutional textbooks were right, and the centre was weak. But in fact that was nonsense. They were as strong as any leader in the free world. What they lacked was a functional approach to governance.

That lack of a functional approach then emits out, from No. 10 to the government departments, through the prime minister's selection of ministers. And it's this process we'll look at next.

CHAPTER 4

The Ministers

The prime minister's power over the key personnel in government is extremely simple. They can hire them and they can fire them.

This seems perfectly intuitive from a British perspective, but it is comparatively rare internationally. The coalitions formed by proportional representation electoral systems abroad mean it is much harder for the prime minister to get rid of Cabinet figures, because their placement is the result of careful negotiation between the parties. In the UK, on the other hand, it is as natural as breathing. Barely a month passes without rumours of a Cabinet reshuffle.

It is this power, perhaps more than any other, that gives the centre control over the departments. But it also has a secondary effect. It mangles up British governance so that nothing meaningful can ever be done, because no one is ever in place long enough to achieve it. And even if something meaningful were done, it would soon be changed by the person who comes along next. It's the reason why Chris Grayling woke up one morning with a burning need to privatise probation at lightning speed, without pilots, or an established evidence base, or a proper trial period.

In almost any other part of society, from medicine to finance, promotions involve putting the people with the most knowledge, skill and experience into the positions where they can most capably deploy them. But in government that hardly ever happens.

One of the core features of the British system, at every level, is that no one knows what they're talking about. And if by accident someone who does know what they're talking about finds themselves in a senior position, they're quickly moved on.

Julian Smith, for example, proved a highly accomplished Conservative secretary of state for Northern Ireland. After three years without a devolved government in Stormont, he succeeded in restoring the power-sharing agreement in January 2020, winning the respect of figures across the political divide, including the Unionist First Minister Arlene Foster and the Irish Taoiseach Leo Varadkar. And then, after 204 days in the role, he was sacked.

The chief criterion by which someone finds themselves in a particular ministerial position is whether it consolidates the prime minister's short-term tactics for maintaining power. That can take different forms – removing rivals, rewarding loyalists, or balancing competing wings of the party. But whichever form it takes, it is the primary concern.

Often the simple rumour of a reshuffle will do the job. A prime minister will let it be known for months ahead of time that one is coming, even without it being considered at all, so that potentially rebellious ministers stay on their toes. This is typically the point at which progress in a government department stalls, as ministers become transfixed by what's going on in Westminster and their civil servants start to wonder who'll be running the department next.

'A reshuffle is effective, but the rumour of a reshuffle is much more effective,' a Downing Street civil servant says. 'You want to extend that period for as long as possible because it genuinely does affect everything. Sometimes that can lead to paralysis. But sometimes it just keeps them behaving themselves.'

Rumours are useful because reshuffles are a degrading power. They're the prime minister's ultimate sanction, but each time they use it they become a little weaker. Those flung out of the ministerial ranks onto the back benches become potential enemies. And those who remain on the back benches having been passed over for promotion start to get a sense that they will not succeed under this administration, so their personal incentives change.

'Every time a prime minister reshuffles their government, the pool of people who have a grudge against them grows,' Gavin Barwell said in his memoirs of the May administration, 'bringing the end of their time in Downing Street closer.'

The reshuffle starts with a whiteboard, typically provided by the propriety and ethics team in the Cabinet Office. The government is broken down by department, with magnetic names in place for each minister. The prime minister and their team get rid of those who are going to be sacked or moved, then pick up the list of people considered for promotion and see where they can fit them in. There is a cursory bit of discussion about relative performance and skill sets. Civil servants around the prime minister will sometimes try to focus the conversation on candidates' qualities. It's not completely irrelevant, but it is a second-order priority.

'Let's say the secretary of state is a great communicator but isn't really very good on detail,' Gus O'Donnell says. 'You'd advise the prime minister to put them alongside a junior minister who's really into detail. You try to do those things. But you're only one voice, you know. So then the chief whip comes in and says: "Well, sod all that, you've got to reward all these people and you can't possibly give jobs to these other people."'

Parliamentary support is consolidated by rewarding those who have been supportive, penalising those who have not and finding face-saving positions further down the ministerial chain for those who have to be moved but could turn into a problem on the back benches.

On the day of the reshuffle, prime ministers start by calling in the people who are being let go. Sometimes this can be fairly genteel. When Peter Bottomley was sacked as Northern Ireland minister by Thatcher, he opened the door into her office and said: 'You didn't need to see me.' She replied: 'It's good form.' He stayed for 45 minutes so that the press would not think they'd had a row. Then when he left, he heard her say to her private secretary: 'He's actually quite interesting isn't he.'

But things are usually less civilised and more chaotic. Theresa May's winter 2017 reshuffle broke down when health secretary Jeremy Hunt simply refused to resign. Then Justine Greening, who had been serving as education secretary, turned down the role of work and pensions secretary and said she'd rather go to the back benches. That left May having to put Esther McVey, who was originally going to get immigration, in the work and pensions job. Caroline Nokes, who was next in line, was slotted into immigration instead. Here we see a decent illustration of why ministers end up in a particular post. It starts with a prime minister's grand plan for maintaining support and often ends with a Rubik's Cube of inadvertent knock-on effects in which names and job titles are put together seemingly at random. But the one thing it has nothing to do with is expertise. That is simply not a criterion.

'I worked in the European Parliament for 10 years, so there was absolutely no danger of me being sent to the Brexit department,' Nokes says. 'I represent a huge rural constituency, was married for about 17 years to a farmer and ran an animal welfare charity, but I'm not going to be sent to the Department for the Environment, Food and Rural Affairs. I spent 12 years as a local councillor, so the obvious place to send me was the Department for Communities and Local Government. These were all places where I could have added value. But instead they sent me to immigration. I knew nothing – nothing – about immigration.'

In some cases, there's a bit of luck and the right person happens to land in the right role. David Gauke, who ended up reversing Grayling's privatisation of probation, was made justice secretary in the same 2017 reshuffle. Other times, the minister is of sufficiently high calibre that they end up picking up what needs doing at their department quite quickly. But more often than not, the reshuffle process ends up putting in place people who do not understand the subject matter and do not have the skills to learn about it.

Partly this is due to the pool of candidates from which prime ministers can form a Cabinet. As we've seen, the selection process for MPs prioritises networking and campaigning rather than deep subject expertise or the capacity to run an effective administration. In other European countries or the US, leaders have the option of selecting ministers from outside of the legislature. In the UK, the only way the prime minister can do this is by putting them in the House of Lords.

'Parliament is a limited gene pool and you select around 100 ministers out of 300 MPs,' Rory Stewart says. 'Most of those MPs are people who are increasingly professional politicians, made a reputation as local councillors, are very active campaigners, and know their patches well. They haven't had much exposure to subjects. In the US, a defence secretary can be someone like Lloyd James Austin, a four-star general and vice chief of staff for the army. In the UK, we get Gavin Williamson.'

The bigger problem, which far exceeds that of the talent pool, is about a fundamental lack of seriousness in the appointments. Expertise is not just an irrelevance. It is often considered a handicap, because a minister who knows the subject matter will be harder to subjugate to the prime minister's will.

'We have this system where a minister can one day be defence and the next day health, so they're not going to be subject experts,' O'Donnell says. 'You need them to be good at making decisions because they are the number one decision maker. Yet how many have been taught about decision making, or how to assess evidence or even basic stats?'

The primary drivers to the allocation of individuals within government are loyalty and reward. This results in people being appointed who simply do not have the intellectual capacity to understand good government, let alone the background knowledge of the subject area that might allow them to deliver it.

'There are rewards for being useless,' a former Cabinet minister says. 'People who should have been sacked, who are utterly fucking shite, have hung around for years. A good number across government, you just look at and think: What the fuck?'

Most Whitehall departments, such as the Home Office, have around four or five ministers. At the top is the secretary of state, who is the political head of the department. In the Home Office, this is the home secretary. The next rank down are the ministers of state, who take responsibility for one of the portfolios in the department, like crime or security. And the rank after that are the parliamentary undersecretaries, who are given responsibilities over small policy areas, like illegal immigration. Over the whole of the government there are about 20 secretaries of state and around 100 ministerial positions underneath them.

Beneath those three ranks are around 50 parliamentary private secretaries, usually referred to as PPSs. The only time they're ever mentioned is when they resign, at which point journalists will say that there has been a ministerial resignation over some controversy or other. In fact, they're not ministers at all. They are ostensibly the link between a minister and the back benches, operating as a liaison between MPs and the department and passing on messages from civil servants to the minister when they are speaking in Parliament. In practice, just like spads or the chief of staff, it is a newly created role that can be whatever people say it is.

Sometimes it is a useful way of providing promising MPs with an apprenticeship in ministerial duties. They will spend a year or two sitting behind the minister in a delegated legislation committee or a select committee hearing, learning the tricks of the trade and hopefully picking up what is required to operate effectively. But more often than not, it is a redundant position in which the PPS is given nothing to do. 'To be perfectly honest, I think some ministers probably find they don't really need their PPS,' Ben Bradshaw says. 'I mean, I didn't really use my PPS very much, because I didn't really see the need or the function for them.' This is by far the most common experience of the PPS system, both from ministers and the PPSs themselves. 'It was fluff,' a former PPS says. 'There was no work. There was no involvement. There was nothing. I was just a person to sit behind him in debates in Westminster Hall. And I did nothing. I mean literally nothing.'

The real function of the PPS is to increase the strength of the government. Being given the job title indicates to the MP that they're going places and might secure a junior ministerial post at the next reshuffle. That encourages them to keep their nose clean and toe the government line. It also gives the whips a pool of recruits to deploy at will. These are the figures who stand up to speak in backbench or opposition day debates when a normal backbencher will find something better to do with their time. They're often the ones who ask a question that exactly replicates the government's preferred language and talking points on the issue at hand. These are called lines-to-take and are often written for them in their entirety by the whips. They are a bank of deployable parliamentary support for tasks that are beneath ministers and of little interest to backbenchers.

The inclusion of the PPSs significantly increases the size of the payroll vote. This refers to the group of people who are paid a government salary and must therefore abide by collective responsibility – the joint agreement on the public support of government policy regardless of your personal conviction. In actual fact, PPSs are not paid anything above their MP salary, but they are treated as if bound by this commitment to vote with the government.

Taken together, the payroll vote typically adds up to around 170 people. For a government with no majority, like May's after 2017, that accounts for 53 per cent of its MPs. Even for one with a big majority, like Boris Johnson's after 2019, it accounts for 46 per cent. It is a means of ensuring that around half of the parliamentary party must vote for the government. 'Basically,' a former PPS says, 'it gives you cannon fodder.'

*

Ministers have a Private Office in their department, just like the one working for the prime minister in Downing Street. It'll have perhaps six or seven senior civil servants in it, including private secretaries who report up the information coming from the department and transmit down the information coming from Downing Street. As in No. 10, they shadow the various portfolios in the department. So in the Home Office, it would perhaps be crime, security and immigration, although they change according to the initiatives of the government at the time.

Most importantly, there will be the principal private secretary. This figure acts as the overall interface between the secretary of state and the department. They accompany them to departmental meetings, go with them on trips and work as the office manager. As at No. 10, they are responsible for overseeing the flow of information to the minister.

Junior ministers will also have their own Private Office, which functions the same way as that of the secretary of state. This is the default model, from Downing Street on down.

Outside of the Private Office is the permanent secretary, effectively the chief executive of the department. They appoint officials, oversee changes and are in charge of overall management.

For many civil servants, a job in a Private Office is a key ambition. 'It's considered the top place to work,' a former civil servant says. 'Working for a minister is the glory role. You get to see more of everything. It's the pinnacle for loads of civil servants.'

For ministers, the relationship can sometimes be more complicated. Sometimes they build a decent working relationship with their Private Office, the principal private secretary and the permanent secretary. Sometimes there is a problem with one of them, or some of them, or all of them. They might find them obstructive, or ineffective, or simply not get on.

Ministers can petition the prime minister and the Cabinet secretary, the most senior figure in the civil service, to get rid of a permanent secretary, but this is rare. Instead, they are usually bypassed by the minister working exclusively through the Private Office and keeping them out of the loop. Douglas Wass, the permanent secretary to the Treasury, made the mistake of warning against a doubling of VAT when the Tories returned to government in 1979. 'He was allowed to stay in post for another couple of years,' a civil servant working at the department at the time says, 'but he was never involved in any serious decision after that.'

Occasionally they are removed. Gordon Brown squeezed out his first permanent secretary at the Treasury, Terry Burns, because he was sceptical about Brown's plans to take banking supervision away from the Bank of England. In a far more brutal manoeuvre, Treasury permanent secretary Tom Scholar was sacked within days of Kwasi Kwarteng becoming chancellor during the short-lived Liz Truss administration. This degree of public aggression, without even trying to make the new relationship work, caused shock and outrage throughout the civil service and the knock-on effects proved catastrophic, reducing market confidence in the government and contributing to a sustained burst of panic in the bond markets.

It's easier for ministers to change personnel in the Private Office. They can ask the permanent secretary to move staff around and they'll usually be keen to do it if things aren't working. But civil servants have a few limited defences. They're technically appointed on merit, so they can protest vexatious claims. And more pertinently, such a move also carries reputational risk to the minister. 'It's unrealistic for you to come into a job in a department and clear out your whole Private Office on day one,' says a former secretary of state, who struggled with his own office. 'If you suddenly clear out everyone from the office, how is that going to feel in the department? You want to try to develop a good relationship with civil servants and not immediately get a reputation as someone who can't manage people.'

The question about how far ministers can control the civil service positions around them has never really been conclusively addressed. And that's because the relationship between ministers and civil servants in general is not defined with any specificity. Are ministers setting policy direction and civil servants managing the organisation that delivers it? Or do ministers want to have a role in managing the organisation while civil servants want a voice in policymaking? There's never been a clear delineation of these roles. It's all left to the generalised smudge of British constitutional thoughtlessness.

'Does the minister get a choice of permanent secretary or is he going to work with someone he doesn't like?' Jonathan Powell says. 'Likewise the private secretary. Do you really want someone in your life 24 hours a day who you can't stand, or are you allowed to change them? Usually, the system can fudge its way through those issues, but they're automatically contentious. If you're someone like Priti Patel and you come in and think you're going to run the Home Office – you're not, you can't, and you're never going to be able to.'

There is an additional problem, which applies even if, by some miracle, a department secures a highly competent minister with a decent understanding of the policy area. The problem is that the vast majority of them have no experience of management. 'It's hard for ministers to deliver policy through an organisation they're not actually technically in charge of,' Powell says, 'especially when they've generally speaking never run anything in their lives. They have no idea how to run something.'

For years, this was the model by which ministers interacted with their departments. But then it changed.

The arrival of the spad fundamentally altered the relationship between government and civil service. They emerged under Wilson, were retained under Thatcher, formalised under Blair, and then took on an aggressive new form under Johnson. They now constitute an entirely new layer of power in the British political system. The standard formulation since the New Labour years is that a department will have at least two spads – one for policy and one for media – and sometimes more than that.

Spads were originally meant to bring expertise into government. It was accepted that they would be political and that the knowledge they brought would be harnessed by a government with an agenda, but the expertise came first and the agenda came second. Somewhere along the line, that changed. There have been a handful of genuine experts – Tom Burke on climate change, Michael Barber on education, Paul Gregg on job markets, Peter Levene on defence equipment, Alan Walters on economics, Douglas McNeill on finance markets – but they are notable for their rarity. Instead, the party political element of Wilson's formulation increased in size and the expertise element dwindled.

We know a fair amount about spads. They're mostly male. Between 1979 and 2013, only 28.4 per cent were women. This barely changed as the years went by. When researchers assessed the composition of the spad workforce during the Johnson administration, they found that 71 out of 109 were men. Spads are also mostly young – the median age for appointment to government is 33. And they're mostly humanities students – typically history, politics or the classic political career entry point of politics, philosophy and economics at Oxbridge. If they had a previous career, it is overwhelmingly likely to have been in politics – as a parliamentary researcher, perhaps, or central party staff – although occasionally they come from consultancies, banks, PR firms or think tanks.

Spads are hired by their minister and they expire with their minister. Their average professional lifespan corresponds to how long ministers are generally kept in a position – typically two to three years. The number who last longer decreases year after year past that point. Almost no one serves as a spad for more than ten years. After that, they go on to run for selection as a party candidate, or work in a charity or NGO, or enter a public relations firm. It's a stressful, badly paid and insecure job, but it is seen for what it is: an exciting thing to do in your twenties and early thirties, which will give you invaluable professional experience of government and look impressive on your CV.

The reason successive governments have maintained or grown the spad workforce is quite simple. It is because spads are extremely useful to them. They have created a job category that has no definition. There is a special adviser code, which governs their behaviour and gives an idea of the kind of things they can do, but no firm definition of what they should do or what they're for. There isn't even an open recruitment process. Most spad positions are never advertised to the public. They're secured through the informal networks of the party.

At the start, there was quite a strong degree of opposition to the spads from the civil service, but it quickly became untenable. 'In my early years,' wrote Daniel Greenberg, from the Parliamentary Counsel's office, 'I attended one meeting on a bill of enormous political significance where special advisers were present. A superb civil service lawyer of the old school objected to their presence, and at one point refused to continue unless they were asked to leave. He won, and the meeting continued without them. Today, I doubt if many civil service lawyers or administrators could still be found who appreciate, and care about, the theoretical limitations on the role of specialist advisers sufficiently to insist upon their leaving a meeting in similar circumstances.'

Spads quickly became a part of life, as natural to the business of government as either the minister or the civil servant. They've ended up doing all sorts of things. They take on meetings, carry out preliminary sifts of policy options, manage the diary, keep their eye on social media, construct a communication strategy, maintain a network of press contacts, feed in intel from the parliamentary and constituency party, keep departmental officials focused on the minister's priorities, insert political elements into departmental communication projects, act as a sounding board, work on the party manifesto and plan parliamentary tactics.

But their core functions, the ones ministers end up relying on most of all, are smaller in number.

Firstly, and perhaps most importantly, they're someone who is on the minister's side. It's a lonely job being a minister, in which you are surrounded by people with distinct sets of interests. The prime minister can get rid of you at any moment, regardless of your performance. The press might come after you tomorrow. Your junior ministers were chosen by the prime minister, rather than yourself, and therefore owe no direct loyalty to you. The officials at the department will be there long after you're gone. But the spad is joined to you at the hip. You pick them. You keep them. And their professional fate is conjoined with yours.

'From a minister's point of view it's nice to have someone with more skin in the game,' a former senior civil servant at the Treasury says. 'Officials won't lose their job. But spads are more invested. They feel the jeopardy. And therefore they think differently.'

Ministers probably spend more time with their spad than with any other human being on earth – certainly much more than their family, who they'll rarely see, given the workload and the need to be away from their constituency during the week. 'You become very close,' Ben Bradshaw says. 'You know each other very well. You share all your innermost secrets with your special adviser – dilemmas over policies, things you don't agree with the government over, reshuffles and so on. It's a very close relationship and probably quite a unique one in politics.'

Spads bring one undeniable and important benefit to the political process – they can, if they are good, maximise the use of ministerial time. At their best, they function as a primary node in the information flow within a department. Ministers are often drowning in the work they receive. They can be unavailable to officials for long stretches of time. But if the spad knows their minister well, they can operate as an outsourced version of their brain – giving the go-ahead to explore something further, or discouraging an idea the minister won't accept. It improves the fluidity of internal communication and decision-making.

'They were like a kind of second me,' Bradshaw says, 'because the civil service quite quickly discovered that if my spad said something, it was because they knew exactly what my views on something would be. And that's really useful for a department.'

Sam Freedman worked with spads closely when he was acting as a policy adviser to Michael Gove as education secretary. 'A really effective spad essentially operates as an extension of the minister and is able to therefore expand their capacity effectively,' he says. 'It's a function of a good minister, who will appoint a good spad, who will then follow what they're doing. If you're doing that, then the system works quite effectively.'

But even in this best-case scenario, any real sense of subject specialism has been jettisoned. Instead, the knowledge the spad brings with them is of the party and its dogmas. 'I bring a particular expertise,' a spad told Institute for Government researchers Ben Yong and Robert Hazell. 'A knowledge of the party, the wider movement. You may produce a wonderful policy and I might say: "You know what? That is all very interesting but it is never going to fly so don't waste your time on it."'

What spads really provide is the politicisation of expertise, a filter that interrogates the impartial advice from the civil service to make sure that it is in the interest of the governing party rather than simply objectively true or socially beneficial. This has always been possible through the behaviour of the minister, but the spad increases their capacity. Policies developed by officials are killed or saved by virtue of their party political implications. Those that survive are given a political gloss. Other ideas are stillborn, unable to get a hearing.

In a way, it was inevitable. The role of the spad had no real definition. So it was moulded to the things Westminster found important: party politics and media handling.

Often the spad forms a cocoon around the minister, forcing all communication to go through them and preventing civil service officials from being able to secure access themselves. They turn into an impenetrable party political membrane, blocking out inconvenient or unvetted information from the real world. Sometimes this is due to their own initiative. Sometimes it is because the minister prefers it that way.

'Looking back,' a former civil servant says, 'I was often irritated. They get in the way. Occasionally they're so political they're just really difficult to work with.'

Then another persistent dynamic in Westminster began to mould the role: the centralisation of power. Spads started to be absorbed into Downing Street's control capacity.

No. 10 always had quite a considerable degree of control over spad appointments. It could set the overall number. It could act as a feeder for potential recruits. It could decide whether a junior minister got one. And it had a veto power over appointments. Initially, this was rarely used. Thatcher only deployed her veto on a handful of occasions. Blair used it six times. But under Johnson, the number of vetoes shot up and so did the number of direct appointments from the centre.

The change came predominantly because of Dominic Cummings. He had been a departmental spad himself, working for Gove at the Department for Education when Cameron was prime minister. 'He loathed No. 10,' says Freedman, who worked alongside him. 'He tried to do everything to undermine them and not do anything they wanted him to do. But I think because of that, when he then entered No. 10 with Johnson, he knew how dangerous that could be. And so he tried to impose much more central control.'

The Johnson government pursued what was essentially a spadification policy over British politics. Some of the most prominent people in the administration, like Cummings, and David Frost, the prime minister's chief negotiator with the EU, were spads, or started out as one. The number of spads in No. 10 doubled from where they were in 2010. By 2019, 44 of them – a third of the overall total – were working for the prime minister. They also spread through the departments.

Spads had to attend a weekly meeting in No. 10 headed by Cummings. This in itself was not unusual – such meetings had been a feature of previous administrations. But those previous meetings were primarily to do with information sharing about political priorities. Under Cummings, their purpose was to set explicit demands from Downing Street and maintain discipline. Attendants reported that Cummings would threaten their jobs and angrily dress down those who hadn't complied with his instructions.

Other spads were hired to split their time between the departments and No. 10. They effectively acted as a surveillance network against ministers, feeding in information to Cummings.

In August 2019, Sonia Khan, an adviser to chancellor Sajid Javid, was fired by Cummings without him even bothering to inform her minister. She was marched out of Downing Street by armed police officers. In February 2020, Javid resigned rather than accept the prime minister's demand that he fire all his spads and accept a new joint unit that would allow Cummings to spy on him. 'A chancellor,' he said, 'like all Cabinet ministers, has to be able to give candid advice to a prime minister so that he is speaking truth to power. I believe that the arrangement proposed would significantly inhibit that.' His successor, Rishi Sunak, accepted the joint unit.

The same month, the justice secretary's spad, Peter Cardwell, left his position and stated that the decision had been made by No. 10. Then the defence secretary's spad, Lynn Davidson, also left after criticising Cummings' treatment of her colleagues.

New Labour had used spads as a means of facilitating communication between No. 10 and the departments through the No. 10 unit system, but that had involved working with the civil service. Cummings and Johnson's approach effectively replaced the civil service with a completely spadified system, controlled entirely from No. 10. They had adopted it as a way of sidestepping civil service independence from the party and No. 10.

The Cummings approach continued after he left government, albeit with less zeal. What will happen to spads in future remains uncertain, but it is telling that no one in the system – whether they're a politician or a civil servant, a critic or a supporter – believes they can be removed. And yet the dynamics that operate on spads give an indication of how they will evolve. Their chief quality is their lack of definition. They will therefore likely continue to be moulded by the priorities under which Westminster operates: central control, party politics and media management.

Even if ministers came into a department with a wealth of subject specific knowledge and the full armoury of modern management skills, they would still find it almost impossible to operate effectively. And that is because the professional, social and political pressures on them are configured in such a way as to make fruitful work impossible.

Before they've even had a chance to get to grips with their department or their staff, they will be hit by an avalanche of work. And that workflow will not stop, or let up, at any stage. It will pile pitilessly upon them, until they either find a way of managing it or drown underneath it.

The worst part is the box work – the red box of papers that ministers are given to take home and work on overnight or over the weekend. It will contain an assortment of decisions that have to be taken: who will be on the board of a museum, which buildings are listed, which schools get funding, what should be done in an immigration case, who has a warrant issued against them. Some of the work is fiendishly complicated and technical, covering things like potential funding systems for public service initiatives. There is often no straightforward way to present it so that it is easy to follow or gives the whole picture. It is far more suited to a meeting, with visual presentation, than it is to pieces of paper in a box. But the rigidity of the system means it must come in the form of a submission from civil servants, at which point it will typically baffle and frustrate a minister, who will then have to hold a meeting on it anyway.

'You could be making 30, 40, maybe 50 decisions a day,' says David Lammy, who served in various ministerial positions under Blair and Brown. 'There's something about that system that's creaking. There's something almost about the human capacity to absorb the material. There's something that really feels like this isn't humanly possible.'

Worst of all, the structure of a ministerial day means the box work is most likely to be approached just when ministers are least capable of properly addressing it. 'The box system is completely crazy,' says Freedman, who has reviewed his fair share of submissions. 'Ministers very rarely get into their box work until after dinner, so they're knackered when they open it. It's actually mad when you think about it. Can you imagine a big company working on the basis that they get all the decisions, put them in a box, and give it to the CEO to make when they're hammered at eleven at night. It's just cognitively stupid.'

The reason ministers can't approach the box until late at night is because every other moment in the day has already been eaten up, whether it's with meetings, public events or legislation. Departmental question time in the Commons, at which they face questions from MPs and their opposite number on the shadow front bench, also demands a lot of time, including training sessions with civil servants for every possible question that might be asked of them.

'You're briefed on every hour of your day, every minute,' says Lynne Featherstone, who served as a Home Office minister in the coalition. 'You're diarised, all the time. It's possible to have 20 meetings a day.' The cascade of work often robs a minister of their independent judgement. In an effort to get through all the papers, they start to just agree to whatever is being presented to them by the civil service. 'It's a massive machine,' a former civil servant says. 'You come into this machine and one of the things you can do is just sit back and trust the civil service. Just follow their recommendations.'

Sometimes the civil service knows what it is doing. It has seen a procession of junior ministers and secretaries of state come and go. It knows that the ones currently in place will not last. So it manages the information flow to constrict the decisions they are likely to make. This can involve creating lists of options that are completely outlandish and then one that it wants the minister to take.

'I had a briefing with the civil service four weeks after I went in,' says Johnny Mercer, who served as veterans minister in Johnson's government. 'I said: "You're configured for me to basically just sit here and have a heartbeat. You're configured for really shit ministers. You're going to box me in, so all decisions come up here and I literally can only make one choice." The system could work without me. If they could get a stamp with my signature, they could have worked without me.'

The boxing-in approach can be quite dangerous. As with the attempts of party leaders to pack the selection list of candidates with obviously unsuitable individuals, there is always a danger that the object of your tactic actually picks one of the lunatic options. Several civil servants say they learned not to try to box a minister in with crazed options when they found that they would often actually select them. 'Liz Truss did it all the time,' Freedman says. 'Truss would always choose the maddest option, just by default.'

But the framing and volume of the work is not always an attempt to control ministers. Sometimes it is simply an inadvertent product of the civil service's own culture. Decisions that could easily be taken at a lower level are passed up out of an institutional aversion to risk. No one wants to be held responsible for the decision, so it flows ever upwards, landing eventually in the minister's box.

In December 2010, for instance, a civil servant sent out a letter to a charity called BookTrust, which provides free books for children, cancelling their grant. It turned into a media firestorm that played out over Christmas, ruining everyone's roast turkey and mulled wine. Leading authors and poets, including Philip Pullman, Carol Ann Duffy, Ian McEwan and Sir Andrew Motion, orchestrated a campaign against the government.

But ministers at that stage had no idea that the decision had been made, let alone that the letter had been sent out. It's events like these that make civil servants extremely cautious and encourage them to always double-check everything with ministers.

Politicians repeatedly criticise their officials for this nervousness, but it is a perfectly rational response to the environment they find themselves in, in which a seemingly innocuous decision can have brutal political implications for ministers if it comes at the wrong time or is executed in the wrong way.

The same happens with briefings or preparations for question time. 'They're so scared of getting something wrong or leaving something out that your briefings are immeasurably long and can take hours,' Featherstone says. 'But they're very scared that the minister will be cross if they didn't put something in on that and she gets asked a question. So there's this unending terror on the civil service of leaving anything out.'

While trying to breathe under their workload, ministers will also be facing the full range of day-to-day political pressures: hostile media interviews, attacks from the opposition, protests against them, abuse on social media, and threats to their position from rivals within the party. Somewhere along the line, they find that they've started speaking in a completely new voice. Whenever they do media interviews, they adopt the language of the professional politician. It is managerial, vague, riddled with meaningless stock phrases and composed almost entirely of jargon – 'deliver for working families', 'standing up for the British people', 'take no lectures'.

'It's partly a protective device,' says Lisa Nandy, shadow minister for levelling up. 'The pauses all being in the wrong place – it's because you're trying to give your brain the chance to catch up with your mouth on a live interview. And the stock phrases pop out because you don't really know what you want to say.' Most people presume this style of conversation is the result of media training, but in fact ministers receive very little help with dealing with the media. Most of it is learned by watching those around them.

Sometimes politicians are forced into this style of speaking by the contortions required of their party's underlying policy position. 'I was once sent out to simultaneously argue for and against a policy,' a frontbench politician says. 'We had to put somebody up because they were running a whole thing on us not having a policy position on it. But the thing is: we didn't. I was dispatched because I was very junior and all the more senior people had point-blank refused to do it. So out I went with two completely contradictory briefing sheets and spent twelve minutes banging the table and saying: "Excuse me, but I make no apology for listening to the public." I think I got away with it. Although I don't think it was my finest moment.'

The main reason the managerial style has developed is because ministers don't want to make a mistake. They are aware, on some level, that they are speaking to the audience of voters at home. But the most important object of their interview is the team in Downing Street watching on TV. 'When you're a minister,' says Andy Burnham, health secretary in Brown's government, 'your first objective in an interview is to come off not having created a problem.'

More than anything, they do not want to commit the supreme political crime of creating inadvertent news. They don't want to accidentally trigger a story by admitting something they shouldn't or speaking too informally. So instead they resort to political management speak.

The effect of this manner of speaking is another reduction in scrutiny, this time from the public at large. It is simply impossible for a voter to assess what frontbench politicians are saying because they are not saying anything at all. There is no specificity or falsifiability to their statements. There is, in a very real sense, no meaning to them. So the basic function of judging politicians on their words, and the extent to which those words reflect their actions, becomes that much harder. Everyone is forced to become a Kremlinologist, parsing the significance of something from coded language.

'There is a word that sums up the approach that ministers often take,' Lammy says. 'That word is fear. Ministers fear getting it wrong, they fear saying the wrong thing, they fear committing their government to spending, they fear the columnists and the journalists, they fear going downwards and not upwards in the next reshuffle, they fear the advisers around the prime minister's office or indeed around their own secretary of state. And eventually they fear saying anything at all.'

The intensity of the pressure and the remorselessness of the workload has a deadening effect on ministers. They are under-slept, over-stressed and emotionally drained. 'The thing that's often ignored is how the political class is chronically and universally knackered,' Nick Clegg says. 'There is a level of physical exhaustion in politics that is quite unusual and quite unexpected. You are basically operating pretty sleeplessly. But whatever it is – three, four, five hours' sleep a night – you are constantly on display. You're constantly physically having to show through your demeanour that you're composed and in control.'

After a while, many ministers start to feel like a falsified version of themselves. Their decision-making is often outsourced to the civil service, their public utterances have no connection to their internal judgement, and the ceaseless grind of box work makes them suspect that they aren't actually achieving anything, even now that they have secured their life goal of entering government.

'It makes a fraud out of you,' Burnham says. 'It makes frauds out of people.'

If a minister is to have any chance of mastering their brief and their department, let alone accomplishing something meaningful, they need time. Nokes puts it at 18 months. 'Your first six months, you're borderline useless, however brilliant you are,' she says. 'You're adding nothing. For your second six months, you're constructive. And for my third six months, I knew everything. Absolutely everything.'

The trouble is that ministers are rarely kept in post for much longer than that. Many of them don't even make it that long. The strong incentive for a reshuffle at the prime ministerial level means that ministerial positions are in a constant state of churn.

Between 1979 and 2010, there were 13 home secretaries, 13 education secretaries and 14 Cabinet ministers with responsibility for pensions. In each case, they had an average tenure of just over two years. Between 2001 and 2010 alone, there were six transport secretaries.

Things improved somewhat during the coalition, because the internal dynamics of multi-party government make it harder to rearrange the ministerial ranks. But when single-party government started again, the process reasserted itself. In the two years of the May administration between the 2017 election and her resignation, only 17 of the 27 ministers who attended Cabinet served continuously.

The problem is getting worse rather than better. Since the year 2000, there have been 22 housing ministers – approximately one for every year. Grant Shapps holds the distinction of the longest time in the post since 2010, managing to survive for just over two years. Seven housing ministers since 2010 lasted nine months or fewer. This is an area of acute policy failure, where soaring costs have caused personal hardship, broken dreams and national economic harm. And yet, for nearly a quarter of a century, no one has been left in place long enough to implement a consistent policy on it.

In recent years, the speed of ministerial turnover has reached preposterous levels, which makes the era of New Labour look like an oasis of stability. Between September 2021 and September 2022, there were five education secretaries. That was extreme, but not unrepresentative. During the same one-year period, there were three health secretaries.

Certain positions are more prone to churn than others. The role of leader of the House changes at a high velocity, for instance, as does the position of justice secretary. This is because they are often seen as a ministerial consolation prize: junior enough to give to someone in a demotion but senior enough to save their blushes.

'The leader of the House is representing Parliament within the government,' Tory MP Peter Bone says. 'So I really hate the fact that the leader of the House has come down to: "Right we've got to keep this bloke in the Cabinet and we can't put them on the back bench – I know, we'll make him leader of the House." And you've seen that happen a lot of the time.'

In the case of the leader of the House, it is constitutional vandalism. But in the case of justice, it is a disaster for the public interest. After the Conservatives came to power in 2010, not one justice secretary served for a full three years. David Lidington served for just six months and twenty-eight days.

Over the 12 years between 2010 and 2022, the policy direction of the Ministry of Justice swung several times between a liberal approach to criminal justice and an authoritarian one. Ken Clarke was a liberal for two years and three months. He was followed by Grayling, who was an authoritarian for two years and eight months. He was followed by Michael Gove, who was a liberal for one year and two months, who was followed by Liz Truss, who was an authoritarian for ten months and twenty-eight days, who was followed by Lidington, David Gauke and Robert Buckland, who were more liberal, and were then followed by Dominic Raab, who swung back to authoritarianism.

Even with one party in power, the political direction veered wildly at a whim over and over again. During this period, there simply was no long-term criminal justice policy. Perhaps the authoritarians were right and a tough 'prison works' attitude would reduce crime. Perhaps the liberals were right and a focus on rehabilitation and reducing short-term sentences would. No one will ever know, because neither approach was given the opportunity to bed in. Over this period, the rates of self-harm, assault and deaths in prison rose to unprecedented levels. Prison education provision went into long-term decline, with a consequent reduction in adult prisoners trying to get a qualification. Staffing levels fell, as did staff retention and experience. 'I was there for 18 months,' Gauke says. 'I really felt I stopped doing the job in the middle of things, without being able to see the consequences of anything that I previously announced.'

The constant churn of ministers creates a powerful incentive. It means it is logical for the minister to try and do something quickly. It doesn't exactly matter what it is, except that it is eye-catching and can be delivered within a short time frame. As we know, this is where ideas like the privatisation of probation come from. There are countless others: identity cards, the Millennium Dome, countless reorganisations of the NHS, innumerable failed IT systems, a seemingly endless history of school reforms, the construction of two aircraft carriers with no aircraft to launch off them, bridges to Northern Ireland. The list could run for hundreds of pages.

'Ministers come in and they've got this desire to do something,' O'Donnell says. 'They want 100 free schools, or 20,000 policemen, or however many thousand more doctors. What you try to do is get them to express their wishes in terms of desired outcomes such as better educational or health outcomes. Then you can discuss what the evidence tells us about the best way to achieve those outcomes. Unfortunately some ministers just want to be able to say we built more hospitals or recruited more police as these "results" are more tangible.'

These plans will often be key for a minister's continued professional advancement. If they can carve out some space from the box work and get a handle on their department, they need to aim for one project – just one – that can secure headlines and catch the attention of the people that matter.

'You have this endless flying-in of ministers,' Clegg says, 'all of them pompously thinking, "I am going to reinvent this policy area, I am going to do what none of my predecessors have done before", and then giving these portentous interviews about how they are going to change direction on immigration, change direction on schooling, or God knows what else.'

There are no corresponding incentives for the minister to work on a long-term project that might provide benefits in a decade, or dedicate themselves to improving an existing programme that is starting to produce decent results now, or even to leave well alone when previous policies need time to bed in. And even if there were, there'd be no guarantee that the person who came along in 18 months' time wouldn't just undo all their work in their own search for glory. The perpetual system of reshuffles creates a structural disincentive to long-term national strategy and a structural incentive towards short-term personal tactics. This is part of the reason why the volume of legislation has driven remorselessly upwards. There was an average of 1,645 pages per year in the 1980s, 1,803 in the 90s, and 2,804 in the 2000s – an increase of 70 per cent over three decades.

Nor are ministers ever held to account for the short-term decisions they make. There is a myth in British politics that ministers function according to an honour system where they resign as a result of failed policy. It was cemented in place in 1982, when Lord Carrington resigned as foreign secretary over the failure to foresee the invasion of the Falklands. It is not true and never has been. Ministers resign over all sorts of things – sex scandals, criminal activity, breaking lobbying rules, misleading the House, losing government data, security breaches and so on. But they never resign over a failed policy. By the time the failure of their headline-grabbing experiments takes place, they have usually moved on to another position, or perhaps the one after that, reshuffled away from the scene of the crime.

'A friend of mine who's a teacher told me something recently,' a former civil servant says. 'He said he would absolutely love a secretary of state for education to come in and say: "I'm doing nothing for four years." Just let the previous shit go. They come in, divvy up the shit again, create no real change, no real outputs, and then go off and someone else comes in with the same vision. Just to have one of them come in and say: "These four years, nothing's going to happen."'

But it will happen, because it must do. Even if the perfect education policy were put in place today, it would be reinvented within a few years, because it would never be in the new education secretary's interests to leave it. And so the cycle will begin again, spinning on and on, going nowhere.

There is, however, one government department that is tasked with assessing what the others are doing and working out if it at least provides value for money. This is where we'll turn to next.

CHAPTER 5

The Treasury

There is a government department that seems to address many of the problems in the British system. It challenges the centre and provides an effective scrutiny function against ministerial short-termism. It contains an outspoken and self-confident intellectual culture whose persistent questioning demands intellectual depth from those who run it. And it regularly offshores bits of its own function so that they are independently assessed without party political interference.

It is the Treasury. The first among equals of government departments, the one that monitors all the others. But the Treasury has a dark secret. It does not impose on itself the scrutiny it applies to others. And because it fails to do so, its own area of policy has fallen into total disrepair.

The most extraordinary quality of the Treasury is the sheer extent of its power. There is no other body in the country, including the monarch or Parliament, with a greater ability to stand up to the prime minister. It is the primary organisational check on the power of No. 10 – the only other institution with the might and the incentives to scrutinise what it does, and the only department to keep all other departments in line too.

This is because it controls the money, and once you control the money, all the other constitutional arrangements will shape themselves around you. That is, in many ways, the story of British democracy. It was Parliament's power over taxation that allowed it to steadily secure more and more independence from the monarchy through the seventeenth and eighteenth centuries. And now that process has transferred to the Treasury.

You can see the extent of this power in the movement of civil service personnel. For decades, until the administration of Theresa May, the Treasury effectively had a lock on Downing Street's civil service hierarchy. It provided the individual who would occupy the post of Cabinet secretary – the most senior position in the civil service. And it provided the individual who would occupy the post of principal private secretary in No. 10 – the official who works most closely with the prime minister.

The big names in the civil service during the post-war period, who occupied one or both of these roles, were all Treasury men: Norman Brooke, Burke Trend, Robin Butler, Alan Turnbull, Gus O'Donnell, Jeremy Heywood. The Treasury was the training ground for the civil service vanguard, the people whose hand rested on the shoulder of the prime minister. 'If you're in No. 10, you want to make things happen,' says O'Donnell, who left his position as permanent secretary in the Treasury to become Cabinet secretary in 2005. 'What's the biggest barrier? It's the Treasury. So working with the Treasury is really, really important, because that's where the money is. And money brings with it power.'

The Treasury also exports a lot of its senior people to run other departments – a process that only really works one way. In fact, Treasury officials sometimes treat the idea of running another ministry as a kind of alternative career path if they fail to make it to the top of the Treasury. But people from other departments never come in to run the Treasury. Liz Truss tried to bring in Antonia Romeo, who presided over the disaster of Grayling's probation reforms, as permanent secretary to the Treasury in 2022 following the sacking of Tom Scholar, but the move was killed at the last moment. James Bowler, a 20-year Treasury man, was put in instead. The Treasury likes being run by its own people, and it likes other departments to be run by them too.

It is well aware of how much power it has and how pivotal a role it plays in the political life of the country. 'It's quite a political department,' a former civil servant in the Treasury says. 'People there will pride themselves on understanding the politics of this game.'

The chancellor is the second most powerful politician in the country. Unlike most secretaries of state, they are typically in post for a long time. In the 48 years since Denis Healey took office, there have only been 15 chancellors, and even that figure is inflated by the rapid turnover in the position between 2020 and 2022, when 5 individuals cycled through the post.

The Treasury is the only department with two very powerful ministers – the chancellor and the chief secretary to the Treasury. It is also the only department where the junior ministers have formalised job titles – financial secretary, economic secretary and so on. There's more churn in these positions, but it's noticeable how reliably they churn upwards. The economic and financial secretaries often move up to the chief secretary position. The chief secretary often moves up to the chancellorship. This was the case for John Major, Norman Lamont and Alistair Darling. Liz Truss and Rishi Sunak eventually cycled up all the way to prime minister.

The centre has long recognised the bulging power of the Treasury and tried to cut it down to size.

After his 1964 election victory, Wilson attempted to shatter the Treasury's monopoly on economic policy by creating a Department for Economic Affairs. The Treasury successfully sidelined it, and it was mothballed in 1969.

The fraught relationship between the centre and the Treasury reached its nadir under Blair and Brown, where the pair functioned almost as a kind of executive duumvirate, with two warring fiefdoms defining a government psychodrama that lasted a decade. At one stage, Blair considered trying to undermine Brown's department from under him by asking John Birt, former director of the BBC, to come up with a plan to reform the Treasury. He proposed splitting it in two, with the assessment of departmental spending extracted from macroeconomic and tax issues and put in the Cabinet Office. Again, it came to nothing.

'All that came out of Lord Birt's review,' Brown would later write in his memoirs, clearly savouring the memory, 'was the renaming of the Department of Trade and Industry as the Department for Productivity, Energy and Industry, but that plan also went wrong. Within days of taking office it was revoked by the new minister, Alan Johnson, when we realised that the initials could be pronounced Dippy.'

During Blair's time in power, the chief secretary role had generally been given to someone from the Blairite faction so they could keep Brown under surveillance. When Brown entered No. 10, he used it in the same way to keep watch over his successor as chancellor. During Budget preparation, there were therefore two separate internal circulation lists – a more secretive one that excluded the chief secretary and a more public one that included them.

There was another attack on the Treasury when Theresa May became prime minister. Her chief of staff, Nick Timothy, was outraged that chancellor Philip Hammond favoured a soft Brexit, and anyway thought his austerity instincts were antithetical to his own planned new era of high-spending working-class Toryism. He plotted a return to Wilson's plan, with a Department for Economic Affairs being based in the Department for Business, Energy and Industrial Strategy and the Treasury's functions being split in two. When Treasury officials asked to see a draft, they were denied access. Hammond was resigned to his fate. Once May won the 2017 election, he concluded, she'd turf him out and carve up his department. But it wasn't to be. The election was a disaster, May lost her authority and Timothy resigned. The threat faded.

A couple of years later, there was another attempt, this time led by Downing Street chief adviser Dominic Cummings. He attempted to enhance the strength of the centre through the spadification of the political system and installed a spy unit alongside the chancellor. But soon enough Cummings was himself packing his bags and leaving Downing Street, as Timothy had before him. The threat receded once more.

A final salvo took place when Liz Truss became prime minister. She'd spent the preceding Tory leadership race promising to challenge 'Treasury orthodoxy' and aggressively struck out at the department once she was installed in No. 10, not least by dramatically removing the permanent secretary. The experiment was a disaster, helping to trigger a brutal market reaction against her Budget, and saw her become the shortest-lived prime minister in British history. After 45 days, she'd been forced to resign and the might of the Treasury was, if anything, significantly strengthened.

The only organisation that has ever really succeeded in reducing the power of the Treasury is the Treasury itself. At two key moments, in 1997 and 2010 – both, tellingly, upon the election of a new government – it separated out a core decision-making function and placed it in independent hands.

The first was when Brown became chancellor. Until then, the Treasury still made the ultimate decision on interest rates. The Bank of England, the UK's central bank, would advise the chancellor publicly, but the chancellor made the final call. It was known as the Ken and Eddie show, after chancellor Ken Clarke and Bank of England governor Eddie George.

'They were civilised encounters,' said Howard Davies, a Treasury man who had also chaired the internal bank committee that prepared the draft advice, 'but sometimes with an element of Whitehall farce. On occasions, faced with a carefully worded letter, representing thousands of hours of work by the bank's economists leading to a considered recommendation of a quarter-point rise, Ken Clarke would open the meeting by saying cheerily: "Well there's obviously no chance of a rise this month." He then asked for our views, but only on how long we needed to stay before the bank team drove out of the Treasury courtyard.'

Labour swept the ludicrous theatre away. They offshored the interest rate decision, making the Bank of England independent. It was instrumental independence rather than full-blown autonomy. The Treasury would still set the inflation target regime with the bank controlling short-term interest rates, but it was independence nonetheless. It was also extremely effective. Brown exercised an impressive self-denying ordinance, making sure he never discussed interest rates. His successors, from whichever party, did the same.

The next change came when George Osborne became chancellor in 2010. He'd had five years in opposition to dream up what he'd do if he secured power. One of his ideas was to create an Office for Budget Responsibility (OBR). It would provide the economic and public finance forecasts that had previously been written by the Treasury. The capacity for a chancellor to try to present his own record in the best possible light was now significantly reduced.

The OBR's economic and fiscal outlook doesn't just assess the state of the economy. It also provides commentary on whether Treasury costings are reasonable. Its three heads to date – Alan Budd, Robert Chote and Richard Hughes – have managed to stay within remit while maintaining their independence. It has been described by the Organisation for Economic Co-operation and Development (OECD) and the International Monetary Fund (IMF) as a model for independent fiscal institutions around the world.

Its effect is most noticeable when OBR forecasts are published alongside the chancellor's statements after important Treasury events. In the November 2020 spending review, for instance, Sunak did not mention Brexit once in his speech in the Commons, despite it being set to take place just 37 days later. The chancellor was a Leave campaigner, and it was anyway not in the interest of the government to raise any of the possible negative consequences of its central political ambition. But the OBR's economic and fiscal outlook told a different story, warning of 'heightened uncertainty', 'tighter credit conditions' and lower business investment. It was therefore unsurprising that Sunak started railing against the OBR in 2022, with government sources – either Sunak himself or someone acting under his authorisation – telling *The Times* that he 'absolutely viscerally hates' it for making 'policy judgements' that overshadowed his spring statement.

Those attacks were stepped up again when Truss became leader, with her chancellor, Kwasi Kwarteng, sidelining the OBR altogether for his mini Budget. The negative market reaction, which subsequently brought down the administration, was partly due to investor nervousness over a government marking its own homework. As Truss's regime fell apart, the OBR emerged strengthened.

The Treasury also enjoys an independent assessment of its work more subtly, through an organisation called the Institute for Fiscal Studies (IFS). It is perhaps the only think tank in the country whose name is always preceded by the words 'highly respected'. It could rename itself with the prefix and it would make no difference to the copy journalists write when covering its pronouncements. Its judgements on the chancellor's decisions are received like stone tablets from on high, and typically form the consensus around each Budget.

The IFS is an independent research institute. It does not look like a Treasury body. In fact, quite the opposite. It looks like a persistent threat to the Treasury's reputation. But Treasury civil servants rely on it extensively to control their own ministers. 'The Treasury uses the IFS a lot,' says O'Donnell, who is now IFS president, 'in the sense of saying: "Well, minister, you may want to do this tax change, but the IFS will point out publicly that this benefits the top 1 per cent and does nothing for everybody else." And that can help you persuade ministers to make better decisions.'

This relationship is not entirely an accident of fate. The IFS is partly sustained by the Treasury itself. Its largest single donor is the Economic and Social Research Council (ESRC), which is funded by the government using public money. 'One of the reasons that the Treasury funnels through the ESRC to the IFS,' a former Treasury civil servant says, 'is so they can say to ministers: "Well, if you do that, the IFS will say this." It's much easier than saying it yourself.'

The unique position of the Treasury in the political system has given it a distinctive corporate culture. No other government department has a firmer sense of its identity. Those who work there consider themselves part of an elite corps. They are the defenders of the taxpayer against the short-termist profligacy of other government departments.

'The institutional power is fantastic,' says Jill Rutter, who worked at the Treasury between 1978 and 1997. 'When I was a little baby Treasury official, I had to go to a meeting at the Foreign Office. It was all very serious. All these very earnest people in the Foreign Office saying "we've got to bail these exporters out who are suffering from the sanctions we've placed on Iran". And I said: "I'm sorry, we don't agree." One of the Foreign Office people whispered: "Who is she?" And another one replied: "She's the Treasury." There was nothing they could do. There's me, a year out of university, the most junior person in the room by a mile – other people at my grade in these departments weren't even getting to watch, let alone take minutes. And there was me saying: "You want to do this? Well we're saying no."'

The Treasury has softened slightly in recent years, but it is not a cuddly place, or a fun one. One former official describes it as having 'the emotional intelligence of a doughnut'. And yet it is surprisingly egalitarian in its intellectual climate. Under even the big-beast chancellors of old, like Lawson, Howe or Clarke, officials would sit around a large table and debate the decision facing the department, with even junior officials encouraged to take part.

'One good thing about the Treasury compared to some other departments,' John Kingman, former second permanent secretary to the Treasury, said during a Q&A in 2020, 'is it's always been a place that exposes arguments between officials to the chancellor. The chancellors I've worked with have really valued that, and because they valued it, it tended to happen – including things that would be unthinkable in some other departments, like junior officials arguing with their bosses in front of the chancellor of the exchequer.'

That all came to a stop when Brown entered the Treasury. 'We assumed he was another big beast – self-confident, intellectual,' Rutter says. 'That's what we were used to. We'd had a Nigel Lawson and we'd had a Ken Clarke, and they loved all this to-and-fro. So the first meeting he comes in and sits there. The Treasury officials start going hammer and tongs at each other. He was like a rabbit in front of the headlights. And only then did we realise that he'd never take a decision in a big meeting in front of us.'

Instead, the large Treasury debates were replaced by a tiny group of loyal spads. Officials at the department transmitted their views to him through the Two Eds – Balls and Miliband. And then they were told what was going to happen, without any need for debate. They also faced the rather more unpleasant experience of having to negotiate his thug enforcement unit of Ian Austin, Charlie Whelan and Damian McBride.

Things recovered somewhat with Darling, Osborne and Sunak, but never quite reached the intellectual freedom of the pre-Brown years again.

The Treasury's control over other departments operates in two ways: spending decisions and business cases. The first decides their overall budget, the second assesses ministers' bright new ideas for individual projects.

The chief secretary to the Treasury works as a financial enforcer. They will sit down for bilaterals with the secretary of state for each department, buttressed by additional meetings between the Treasury spending team and the departmental finance directors. 'The key skill,' Davies said in his book on the department, 'is to beat up Cabinet colleagues, leaving the minimum visible bruising.'

The budgetary process has a strong policy element, which informs the financial one. David Gauke, for instance, was known as a liberal justice secretary – challenging the use of short prison sentences and the broader 'prison works' agenda on the right of the Conservative party. But that was not strictly a result of ideology. It was a result of his years as chief secretary to the Treasury, looking at the evidence on reoffending.

'The easy thing, if you are the secretary of state in the Ministry of Justice, is to do the whole "bang them up, put them in prison, throw away the key" thing,' Gauke says. 'You know: rah rah rah. Goes down nicely with the tabloids. The Conservative base likes it. But it's really expensive and it's really bad value for money. If you're looking to reduce crime, it's not what you would do. So I had this reputation of being a very liberal justice secretary. But you could say that I was actually just the man from the Treasury.'

Departments have three ways of responding to the Treasury. The first is to be a teacher's pet – lay out a very detailed and modest description of what you want to do and how much it will cost, accept the commands that come back and stick to the requirements.

The second is to try to get No. 10 onside. If a department can't secure agreement with the chief secretary, it engages the chancellor. And if that doesn't work, it'll engage the prime minister, although it'll try desperately to avoid reaching that point.

The third is to try and get the public onside through carefully coordinated leaks and ministerial interventions. This is easier to do if you're the health, defence or transport secretary, where there is instinctive public sympathy with your case, than if you are in charge of things like prisons, where there is not. Typically speaking, the extent to which you can successfully follow the second course will depend on how successful you were following the third. Public support significantly increases your chances of prime ministerial support.

This work is necessary and is broadly well done. 'If you want to run a serious country, you have to have a finance function that is composed of people whose job it is to scrutinise departmental spending plans and keep them under control,' says Jonathan Portes, former chief economist at the Department for Work and Pensions and the Cabinet Office. 'That's a core part of the job and you can't get around it.'

The Treasury is also the first and last line of defence protecting the public from the short-termism of ministers across government, who are desperate to secure get-rich-quick headline-grabbing projects regardless of their efficacy or cost. It's accused by those in other ministries of being the department that 'just says no': entirely negative, terminally cynical, with few ideas of its own except how to dismiss those of others. And this, for many of the people who work there, is a badge of honour. 'It's a criticism made by people who lost the argument,' one former senior civil servant at the Treasury says. 'Ministers are too short term. Politicians' time horizon is the next election. But our problems are long term.'

The Treasury's standard institutional response to questions around the strenuousness of its assessment is to lay the blame with politicians. The department's position, articulated consistently by permanent secretaries like Andrew Turnbull and Nick Macpherson, is that Britain wants to have Scandinavian levels of public services with US levels of taxation. They correctly point out that since at least Thatcher, and possibly earlier, politicians have not been prepared to have an honest conversation with the public about taxation.

The Thatcher and Major administrations viewed tax cuts as a core outcome of their political mission. New Labour, on the other hand, raised several taxes and invented others, but it was mostly done by stealth, without getting voters onside with the principle. The coalition refused to significantly raise taxes even when driving through an aggressive austerity programme.

When Johnson and Sunak finally did announce a tax rise through National Insurance in September 2021, all hell broke loose. It triggered backbench rebellions and contributed in part to the crisis of confidence in the Tory parliamentary party that swept the prime minister from office. The Tory leadership race that followed was dominated by a debate over tax cuts, and Truss's victory was grounded in a promise to implement it. Even after Sunak replaced her as prime minister, the demands for tax cuts continued.

Treasury officials insist that they must be draconian in their approach to departmental spending precisely because politicians aren't prepared to make the case to the public for tax rises. These are considered politically impossible, therefore there must be someone, somewhere, making sure the sums add up. 'There is absolutely zero sense that we have the political appetite to pay loads more in taxes,' one says. 'And until we do that, we have to bear down on everything.'

The Treasury argument is true, on its own terms. But the quality of its departmental decision-making is open to question. Plenty of extremely poor evidence-free initiatives do get past the Treasury, such as the privatisation of probation. And many more sensible projects do not.

The Treasury's assessment of projects is subject to two chief weaknesses: space and time. It is poor at recognising the value of investment outside London. And it has a weak track record on authorising investment that requires a large outlay in the present to save money in future.

There has historically been very little recognition from the Treasury that money might be spent to address regional inequalities. Instead, spending decisions are reduced to isolated cost–benefit analyses on the basis of existing productivity patterns in the country. If London is more productive, for instance, it makes economic sense to build more transport infrastructure there, rather than trying to alleviate national imbalances by building it elsewhere. This tendency has improved recently, with updates to the Treasury's Green Book, which offers staff guidance on how to appraise projects, but so far to little effect. As with the argument on tax, the Treasury blames politicians, in this case for failing to see the opportunities.

The department is also almost pathologically sceptical of the argument for long-term investment. 'Its philosophy about how the economy operates was always short-termist,' says Diane Coyle, a former economist at the Treasury. 'But in the context of new technology, the need for energy transition, levelling up and the requirement for wider growth spatially, it's become particularly damaging.'

In the department, this translates into a fiercely critical perspective of anyone making the case for long-term investment. And that goes much further than just overexcitable ministers trying to establish a political legacy.

'Imagine a health secretary who came to the Treasury and said: "I want to do a massive investment in prevention and it will repay because there'll be less demand for NHS services in the future",' Rutter says. "Give me £6 billion now and down the line it will reduce the pressure on the health service." The Treasury reflex will be: "Well, I can see that I write you a cheque for £6 billion now, but actually I don't think that your successor plus four will be asking for a single penny less."'

Sometimes the Treasury is right to be cautious about ministerial initiatives. But sometimes it exhibits a sense of institutional inflexibility that goes directly against the evidence base.

The problem can be seen in the response to the COVID-19 pandemic. On the one hand, the Treasury broke all its rules during this period, authorising astonishing levels of public expenditure over furlough and maintaining the British economy almost single-handedly. But once the emergency was over, it reverted to its traditional way of doing things. And yet the after-effects of the pandemic are long-lasting, particularly when it comes to children's education.

By the time lockdowns were over, most children in the UK had lost over half a year of in-person schooling. This accounts for roughly 5 per cent of their entire time in school. Virtual learning systems were set up, but there was only so much they could do. Teachers reported covering less of their curriculum, pupils doing less work, and reduced engagement. These effects were not equal. The more disadvantaged a pupil was, the worse the effects were.

Absence from school, even for a relatively short time, can have a severe impact on cognitive ability. The effect was seen almost instantly by researchers. Despite the Netherlands having some of the best digital infrastructure in the world for home learning, empirical studies there showed that primary school pupils were scoring significantly lower in tests than previous cohorts after eight weeks of school closures. The magnitude was almost exactly equivalent to eight weeks of normal educational progress.

Research from other countries on teachers' strikes and the impact of extreme weather events offered a strong evidential base for the likely impact on future earnings. Reviews have found that a year of schooling increases individuals' earnings by 8 per cent per year. Analysts estimated that the reduction in earning potential over a pupil's life from school closures is therefore around 2.5 per cent.

On a human level, this gap in education is a disaster, and on an economic level it is no better. The impact of reduced earnings adds up to an average of £40,000 in lost income over a pupil's lifetime. It affects 13 year groups, comprising 8.7 million schoolchildren, resulting in a potential £350 billion in lost lifetime earnings across the UK, thus triggering a reduction of £100 billion in tax revenue for the exchequer.

From the mid 2030s, all workers in their twenties would have lower skills than they would otherwise have. And for the 50 years after that, roughly a quarter of the entire workforce would have lower skills, leading to lower economic growth. The Education Recovery Commissioner recommended a £15 billion investment in school catch-up to make up for the lost education of the COVID years. IFS researchers made the case for a recovery package in the tens of billions. The US spent £1,600 per pupil. The Netherlands spent £2,500.

And yet the Treasury held out. It refused to commit to a large expenditure in case it became difficult to cancel in future. In total, over several drip-feed announcements, the Treasury authorised just £5 billion in education catch-up funding for England, equating to about £500 per child.

It was, in the eyes of almost all experts, a short-sighted, self-defeating and economically illiterate way to behave. 'The vast majority of microeconomists and education economists would say this is a no-brainer,' Portes says. 'The idea that there are significant long-term impacts to the economy without a lot of investment in catch-up is common sense and supported by the research. There's a large margin of error about what those benefits will be, but that doesn't mean that you can justify not doing it.'

The Treasury's single greatest failing is over its policy area. And the reason for that failure is the same as that which applies across Westminster: lack of scrutiny.

For all the vivaciousness of the Treasury's internal culture, it is not open to outside questioning. In fact, it operates with a degree of secrecy that is unheard of in any other part of government, except for perhaps the security services.

The ostensible reason for this secrecy is that it prevents market-sensitive information from leaking out, or people playing around with their income in advance of tax changes. The argument is perfectly reasonable, but the privilege has been stretched beyond any credible limit. It has also been made a mockery of by the fact that chancellors regularly leak almost the entire contents of their Budget days before it is delivered. Many Treasury decisions that are not market-sensitive and do not involve any forestalling risk are anyway kept secret.

The real reason for the secrecy is that it strengthens the chancellor's political hand.

Policy from outside the Treasury is subject to a variety of processes that, while weak, at least hold out the possibility of improvement. Other departments must bid for a slot in the legislative programme, something the Treasury has no need to do. They face some degree of scrutiny in the Lords and the Commons, whereas the Treasury faces none in the Lords, which is largely excluded from participating in economic matters, and very little in the Commons, where MPs exhibit a complete lack of economic literacy. Most importantly, other departments are scrutinised harshly by the Treasury, an approach that becomes functionally non-existent when it comes to its own proposals.

As we've seen, departmental spending is subject to high-pressure, maximum intensity bilateral conversations with the Treasury imposing fierce demands on projects such as road building, hospital construction or science funding. But the Treasury makes policy decisions with long term implications — like freezing fuel duty, cutting beer duty or providing bungs to entrepreneurs — on the basis of no scrutiny at all and under severe last-minute deadlines.

The consequence of this lack of scrutiny is that the Treasury presides over one of the most egregious failures of policy in the entirety of the British political landscape.

Part of the problem lies with the Budget event itself, which is a monstrous combination of base politics and technical economics.

In private, or after they've left office, chancellors are perfectly open about the disparity between these elements. Conservative chancellor Norman Lamont, for instance, introduced a low rate of income tax in 1992 in order to undermine Labour ahead of the election that year, and then brought in a series of phased increases in tax in 1993, once the Conservatives had secured another term in office. 'It was not a very good Budget,' he said of the 1992 effort, 'but it did help us to win the 1992 election. My next Budget helped to lose the 1997 election for the Conservatives, but it was definitely my best Budget.'

After he left office, Labour chancellor Alistair Darling laid it out plainly. 'The Budget statement isn't just like a company annual report or announcing your housekeeping measures for the next year,' he said. 'It is a political statement of what the government is about.'

There are also more acute political incentives at play. The Budget does not just contribute to the fortunes of the party; it can define the fortunes of the individual chancellor. So there is a very strong push towards turning it into a set-piece spectacle that wrong-foots the opposition and boosts their personal standing within the party.

The Budget therefore combines two dangerous elements: a lack of scrutiny and a strong political incentive system. And using these two inputs, it then manufactures a series of highly technical measures that refine the operation of the tax system. This has created the cultural phenomenon of the 'rabbit in the hat', a final flourish of tax policy announced at the end of a Budget to great acclaim in the Commons. It can range from surprise changes in income tax to major reforms of the pensions system. Most Budget days are spent fixating on what this rabbit will be and what it might mean once it is announced. Very few are spent discussing the fact that this is a fundamentally irrational way to develop a country's tax system.

'There have been some gimmicks over the years, including some that have been expensive and wasteful,' Kingman admitted. 'It is also true that the nature of the Budget processes creates pressure for these.'

The political advantages of pulling the rabbit from the hat are questionable. Very often, the rabbit dies upon contact with oxygen. Brown's 2002 announcement of a zero per cent rate of corporation tax was reversed in 2005. His decision to cut the basic rate of income tax from 22p to

20p by abolishing the 10p rate in 2007 caused such outrage he was forced to deliver a £2.7 billion 'emergency Budget' the year afterwards. George Osborne was forced to back down on his changes to VAT, dubbed 'the pasty tax' due to its change to the sale price on hot takeaway food, after the 2012 Budget. In 2016, changes to Personal Independence Payments had to be reversed 48 hours after the Budget statement. Kwarteng's abolition of the top rate of income tax in 2022 had to be abandoned 10 days later in the face of the resultant market chaos.

But the implications for tax policy are far more serious. This approach has helped to create a tax system that is almost completely insane. That is not a purely descriptive use of the word – it is literal. The tax system has no rational structure. It satisfies no possible set of intended aims. It does not look, in the words of former US Treasury secretary William Simon, 'like someone designed it on purpose'.

It is, in parts, regressive – taking money from those with less and giving it to those with more. And it does not even do this purposefully through ideology, but simply as an unforeseen consequence of day-to-day politically motivated policy-making without a strategic assessment to underpin it. It is opaque, in that the variety and jumble of taxes faced by an ordinary taxpayer are so complex that they become incomprehensible. And it is self-defeating, because the convoluted nature of the system provides opportunities for tax avoidance.

'There is no scrutiny on changes to tax,' Portes says. 'You only have to look at the result. Nobody, including in the Treasury, thinks our system is anything but a complete mess. No one thinks we have a decent tax system. We have all these reports that tell us we could do something about it, and they're totally ignored.'

Take VAT. This tax on sales stands at 20 per cent at the time of writing, but some products are subject to VAT at a reduced rate of 5 or 0 per cent. The list of goods that are subject to the tax and those that are not is nonsensical. VAT applies to cereal, for instance, but not to flapjacks. It applies to potato crisps but not tortilla chips. It applies to 'sweet-tasting dried fruit' if it's eaten for snacking but not if it's used in home baking. It applies to gingerbread men if they are decorated with chocolate but not if 'the chocolate amounts to no more than two dots for the eyes'.

Council tax, a tax on domestic property, is based on the value of those properties in April 1991, over a quarter of a century ago. Since that time, house prices have diverged significantly in different parts of the country. Nothing has been done to change the tax.

But arguably the most pernicious effect relates to income tax.

The marginal rate of tax is the tax you pay on the next £1 that you earn. If you were to draw a graph of this system, it would not look like a series of steps, growing larger the more money someone gets. It would look like a series of waves, going up and down, seemingly at random, as it escalates the income scale. This is the result of various bits of tinkering that made perfect political sense when they were introduced and were usually met with great cheers from the government benches in the Commons. But in the long term, they mutilated any moral or intellectual sense from the tax system.

For a married person with children whose partner stays home, the marginal rate goes up once they start paying the basic rate of income tax at £12,571. It then jumps up at £50,001, when Child Benefit starts to be withdrawn at a rate of 1 per cent for each £100 earned. This was a policy from Osborne's 2012 Budget. It spikes into infinity at £50,270, when they hit the higher rate of income tax, because the Married Couple's Allowance is withdrawn. This was a policy from Osborne's 2014 Budget. Once they reach £60,000, the marginal rate falls because the Child Benefit payment is fully withdrawn. It then rises again at £100,000, when the government withdraws the personal allowance. This was a policy from Darling's 2009 Budget. It then falls again at £125,140.

It means that someone earning £61,000 can have a lower marginal rate than someone earning £51,000, and that someone earning £130,000 has a lower rate than someone earning £100,000. Someone earning £1 million would have a lower marginal rate than someone earning £51,000 or £100,000. 'There is no plausible rationale', the IFS director Paul Johnson concluded, 'for a rate structure that looks like this.'

But income tax isn't the end of it. It is conjoined with National Insurance. After the Second World War, this was a distinct payment, which gave out according to what people paid in. But successive governments eroded the relationship between input and output. There is almost no relationship at all between what someone pays in and what they get out. There is no fund being built up or devoted revenue stream being constructed. It is simply a tax on earnings.

And yet it has two qualities that make it different to income tax proper.

The first is semantic. The phrase 'National Insurance', for a time at least, had a different resonance with the public than 'income tax'. This was why New Labour chose to pay for increased NHS spending through National Insurance. 'The preference of Number Ten and Treasury officials was to raise VAT,' Ed Balls later recounted, 'but the idea appalled

Ed Miliband, Gordon and me, and based on our polling the public felt the same. An increase in income tax was slightly less unpopular, but an increase in National Insurance contributions to fund the NHS actually commanded a substantial majority in favour.'

For years, politicians presumed that the phrase 'a cut in income tax' would be politically popular, but that 'a cut in National Insurance' actually sounded frightening – as if something was being taken away from people. It was the tyranny of good branding. The two therefore began to diverge quite significantly. The income tax personal allowance threshold would be raised, while the point where National Insurance applied remained the same.

The second quality is that National Insurance only applies to earnings, rather than income. It hits employers and employees, but it does not apply, for instance, to pensioners. It therefore created a bizarre spectacle where governments would repeatedly stress their commitment to helping 'hard-working families' while in fact penalising them harder than those who earned their income through other means.

The inadequacy of the tax system has been recognised for decades. 'For too long,' Dick Taverne wrote in the foreword to the IFS's 1978 Meade Review, 'tax reforms have been approached ad hoc, without regard to their effects on the evolution of the tax structure as a whole. As a result many parts of our system seem to lack a rational base. Conflicting objectives are pursued at random; and even particular objectives are pursued in contradictory ways.'

In 2009, the Nuffield Foundation and the ESRC funded a two-year inquiry into tax policy chaired by the Nobel prize-winning economist James Mirrlees. It was the most comprehensive and widely respected analysis of the British tax system in a generation. Its findings were damning. There was no coherence between income tax and National Insurance or between personal and corporate taxes. There was no clear approach to environmental taxes. The taxation of land and property was inefficient and unfair, heavily transaction-based, and grounded in 30-year-old property valuations.

'There is a better way to make tax policy,' it concluded. 'There are taxes that are fairer, less damaging, and simpler than those we have now. To implement them will take a government willing to be honest with the electorate and willing to put long-term strategy ahead of short-term tactics.'

Three years later, IFS director Paul Johnson would return to the same theme in a paper called 'Tax Without Design'. 'It is hard to discern a set of principles underlying tax policy over the past decade,' he said later. 'If there is an agenda there, it has certainly not been set out, and it is a good example of making it very difficult for people to manage their finances.'

In April 2016, a joint report by the Chartered Institute of Taxation, the IFS and the Institute for Government came to a conclusion that could have been lifted wholesale from work decades earlier. 'The exceptional processes around tax policymaking – in particular, secrecy, more limited scrutiny and challenge, and the power of the Treasury – have led to an ever-lengthening tax code, beset by a series of problems: confusion for taxpayers, poor implementation, political reversals and constrained options.'

The Treasury's argument against the possibility of reform is the same that it deploys over departmental spending: it is the politicians' fault. Until they are prepared to have a realistic conversation about taxation, nothing is possible. This is because system-wide rationalisation of the tax system would involve a whole host of winners and losers. And the losers, even if they were in a minority, would scream loudest.

If it were to be achieved, it would probably involve temporarily reducing the overall tax yield, which government does not want to do, or introducing a series of overlapping reforms that involve gains and losses for different classes of taxpayer, a project so complex that mistakes would surely be made and the potential for political devastation would be high. No prime minister or chancellor seems to have the bravery to take on that kind of project.

The Treasury is right that politicians live under a constant fear of taxpayer revolt, but the extent to which that fear is valid is highly questionable. In Wales, in 2003, there was a re-evaluation of property values for calculating council tax without mass public outrage. The state pension age was increased in 2007 without riots in Trafalgar Square.

'Raising the state pension age is one of those things that you kind of think "Oh my God, if you say this, everybody is going to go crazy",' said James Purnell, pensions minister under New Labour. 'But you said it lots and lots of times in a series of controlled explosions and it went from page one of the paper, to page three to page five. And by the end it was: "Oh yeah, everybody knows they're raising the retirement age."'

The attempt to lay all the blame on politicians also lets the Treasury off the hook too easily. The department has not merely failed to convince its political masters to reform the tax system. It has conspired with them to make it such a mess in the first place.

It did nothing to respond to the 2009 Mirrlees review mentioned above, or the criticisms from the IFS. It has participated in precisely the type of myth-making that makes the tax system so convoluted. It has no decent scrutiny function for its proposals, which means that they emerge in a dysfunctional state that often falls apart upon contact with reality. And the annual ritual of the Budget sees it pile ever-increasing layers of short-termist politicised technical detail onto a tax arrangement that already makes no coherent sense.

For all its unique attributes and unchallengeable might, the Treasury's policy area has fallen into disarray for the same reason everyone else's has: an overemphasis on party political advantage at the cost of scrutiny and good government.

We've now found a lack of scrutiny and expertise at each level of government – from MPs to the prime minister, the Cabinet and the Treasury. But there is at least one protection that exists independently of the political system: the civil service. And it's this institution that we'll turn to next.

CHAPTER 6

The Civil Service

There's a peculiarly British daydream about the civil service.

It is the dream that someone, somewhere, is keeping things under control. Away from the cameras, in a room with a closed door, a man in a double-breasted suit with a refined accent is putting his hand on a minister's shoulder. And all the silliest plans that minister has are neutralised with a quick-witted bit of procedural obstacle-creation, perhaps without them even realising it's happening. Then, at the end of the day, when the minister has gone home, the man in the suit tucks the latest silly idea away in a little drawer somewhere, never to be seen again.

But the daydream is just that: a dream. In reality, the civil service is subject to precisely the same dysfunctions as every other part of the system: misaligned incentives, generalism, failure of expertise, broken scrutiny functions and fundamental lack of seriousness.

The traditional view of the civil service is called the Northcote–Trevelyan settlement, after the 1854 report that constituted the founding document of the service. It imagined a dual role for civil servants – they were there to advise and to serve ministers.

It's an interesting role, with plenty of potential for contradiction, and it consequently created a highly mercurial culture. Officials were expected to raise objections, warn of incoming dangers, highlight legal problems and notify of practical difficulties. But once the decision was taken by their political masters, they would keep their private misgivings to themselves and help them deliver their agenda. Ministers, for their part, were expected to respect and pay serious attention to civil service opinion, even if the final decision was ultimately theirs alone.

Civil servants were non-partisan and impartial. But that did not mean they were apolitical. They were not independent of government, or even neutral towards it. They served it, whoever it was, on the basis of its democratic mandate. In the US, bureaucrats are legally and constitutionally answerable to Congress, which is their version of Parliament. In the UK, they are servants of the Crown, which means they are the servants of the government. 'The civil service has no constitutional personality or responsibility,' Cabinet secretary Robert Armstrong said, 'separate from the duly elected government of the day.'

For decades, there was a widespread sense that the British civil service was the best in the world. Even Harold Laski, the Marxist political theorist and Labour party chair, thought it 'continuously attracted to its ranks some of the ablest minds in the country'.

But then, in the late 1970s, something changed. And that something was called Thatcherism.

The problem wasn't personal exactly. It was ideological. Thatcher herself rather liked civil servants who answered back. But she was engaged in a revolutionary project to change the face of Britain. She was not interested in moderated power, cautious policy-making or discreet advice about why she might be wrong. The era of a mixed economy, with a large public sector and extensive public services, would be replaced by the era of the full-fledged, no-holds-barred free market. And the era of confidential expressions of caution would pass with it too.

'This was one of the most dismal occasions of my entire time in government,' the prime minister said after meeting a group of permanent secretaries in No. 10 a year after she took office. 'I enjoy frank and open discussion, even a clash of temperaments and ideas, but such a menu of complaints and negative attitudes as was served up that evening was enough to dull any appetite I may have had for this kind of occasion in the future.'

As Thatcher reshaped Cabinet government, so she reshaped the civil service. And this was largely accomplished through the Cabinet, via the political pressures on ministers. The secretaries of state she admired were men of action. That was the way to survive in her Cabinet: doing, not listening, whatever the civil service might have to say about it. Anything else was wet, in manner if not in politics.

As Norman Tebbit said of his predecessor as transport secretary: 'He'd tackled it from an intellectual standpoint and I think he always thought he had to convince people intellectually of the need for a change, whereas I tended to short-cut the people sometimes and tell them what was going to happen. And if they were unconvinced by the arguments, it was tough.'

Civil servants were returned to their semantic roots: servants of the minister. They were not to drive ministers, raise too many problems with what they were doing or even really question very much. As one contemporary official observed: 'I think what happened during the 1980s is that the civil service moved to recognising their job as delivering what ministers wanted. Can-do man was in and wait-a-minute man was out. Ministers not only knew what they wanted, but often how to get there. The civil service role as ballast was sidelined. There was no room for it.'

It's one of the ironies of the civil service that this process was taking place as the comedy TV show *Yes Minister* was being broadcast. Its success convinced audiences that it was an accurate portrayal of the civil service. They were wry, clever, unflappable procedural and linguistic geniuses, who could easily turn ministers to their whim. But while this stereotype held some limited truth in the 1960s and early 70s, it was no longer the case in the 1980s. Just as the public internalised this view, it was out of date.

There was, lurking in the background and occasionally flashing into the foreground, an ideological element to all this. Civil servants were a different type to the public sector worker the Thatcher government was targeting, but they were not altogether different. They were outside of the free market. And the administration's criticism of their work bore an uncanny resemblance to the broader political message. They, like public sector workers, were self-satisfied and anaemic. They were part of the computer-says-no world of the public sector, not the would-you-like-fries-with-that world of the private sector.

Many civil servants thought things would improve when Labour returned to power, but they did not. If anything, the Blairite assault was more vicious than the Thatcherite one. 'The key disempowering moment for the civil service was the Blair government,' Jill Rutter says. 'Until Blair, permanent secretaries saw their role as, first of all, principal policy adviser to the minister, and secondarily managing their departments. Under Blair, they really lost that principal policy adviser role and were told to go back and make their departments deliver for the minister.' This was combined with the introduction of the spad culture at full strength.

Nor did things improve much after that. Conservative ministers would routinely take out their frustrations on the civil service, who were often portrayed as the enemy, and even members of the 'deep state'. By the time the Johnson administration was in power in 2019, the attack had reached unprecedented new heights. 'I found Cummings terrifying as an experience,' a senior civil servant in the Treasury says. 'They were total animals. Saying it's illegal was not an argument against doing something. And that, as an official, was the most frightening experience I've had.'

In the Conservative leadership election after Johnson's departure from Downing Street, the contenders took it in turns to publicly attack the civil service with ever-increasing vitriol. Rishi Sunak accused it of 'groupthink', Penny Mordaunt said, 'Whitehall is broken', Suella Braverman said it had a 'Remain bias' and Liz Truss baselessly claimed it was 'straying into anti-Semitism'. It was an indication of how the civil service was now seen by the Conservative ministerial class.

Ironically, these sorts of attacks came as civil servants went out of their way to fulfil ministers' wishes even when many of them passionately disagreed in private. 'You're given a policy you fundamentally disagree with,' says one civil servant who was involved in Brexit legislation, 'but every morning you have to get out of bed, go in and push it further forward. I was surprised at myself about how cross I would get about obstacles. Without my civil service hat on, I think this Brexit stuff is ridiculous and hideous. But with my civil service hat on, it's my job to make it happen. And given I spend most of my waking hours doing that job, you do actually almost become that person.'

As the Conservative attacks became more colourful and a paranoid conspiracy-theory mindset took root among many ministers, civil servants started presenting practical or legal obstacles to ministers in the softest way possible, in case they were branded political opponents. 'There's definitely a "true believer" test that ministers run against the civil servants they work with,' one says, 'and it's very easy to fail. Providing difficult advice on the merits of doing something, which is our job, has to be presented in a very, very careful way, because if not they'll brand you a Remoaner. Director generals and permanent secretaries are going out of their way to identify very closely with their minister publicly.'

The attack on the civil service from three generations of government – Thatcher, Blair and Johnson – has fundamentally reduced its confidence in itself and its determination to provide ministers with objective advice. Many older civil servants – even those who entered during Thatcher's period – barely recognise the institution they worked in. 'Civil servants are nowadays expected to show a kind of subservience and deference that was neither shown by, nor expected of, the best civil servants when I joined the civil service in 1988,' parliamentary counsel Daniel Greenberg said. 'There is a whole generation of civil servants who have been schooled to think that saying yes to ministers and their close advisers is the only safe method of career progression.'

The near eradication of the civil service's ability to speak truth to power is a blow to scrutiny within government departments. But we shouldn't be too sentimental about the quality of the advice that was offered in the first place. The idea of the civil service as a uniquely effective and clear-sighted bureaucratic entity, such as that put forward by Laski, is largely a myth, and probably always has been.

The key problem with the civil service has been recognised and widely accepted since at least the 1960s. Throughout that decade, disquiet about the Victorian-era Northcote–Trevelyan settlement grew. It was conceived in a simpler time, the argument went, before the dominance of complex systems, massive public sector expenditure, modern technology, increasingly technical public services, and wide-ranging muscular government. It had therefore proposed the kind of system you'd expect for that time: gentlemen generalists – good-old-boy administrators – who could keep things ticking along without too much fuss.

Thomas Balogh, the Oxford academic and Wilson ally who made the case for expert special advisers, wrote an essay in 1959 raging against senior officials. It was titled 'Apotheosis of a Dilettante'. 'It may well happen that both the permanent secretary and the minister arrive simultaneously at a new department,' he wrote. 'Neither of them has made an intensive study of the problems with which they have to deal, or know the personalities and social background.'

By 1968, an inquiry had been established into the subject, chaired by Lord Fulton. Its findings were damning. The problem, Fulton found, was twofold: generalism and churn. There were too few experts. And anyone who might aspire to expertise was prevented from doing so, because they were encouraged to move positions every few years. In other words, they suffered from precisely the same defects as ministers.

Civil servants were highly literate – the kind of people who were adept at papering over difficult issues through the ingenious selection of words – but they were not highly numerate. There was precious little specialist knowledge, or technical skill, or people with qualifications in the hard sciences.

This was not a design flaw. It was the whole culture of the place. The civil service was the cult of the amateur.

'The ideal administrator,' the report said, 'is still too often seen as the gifted layman who, moving frequently from job to job within the service, can take a practical view of any problem, irrespective of its subject matter, in the light of his knowledge and experience of the government machine. Scientists, engineers and members of other specialist classes get neither the full responsibilities and corresponding authority, nor the opportunities they ought to have.' Reform was urgently needed. 'The service,' it concluded, 'is in need of fundamental change.'

But that day never came. Almost all the problems raised in the Fulton report remain today.

Of the various attempts to address them, the most substantial was the Next Steps model in the 1990s, which attempted to create delivery structures in which operational skills would predominate. It started well, then atrophied.

In 2002, Gus O'Donnell, then permanent secretary to the Treasury, commissioned a review that recommended the creation of a variety of career paths for experts and an incentive structure for staff to stay in post for longer. 'I tried to break down the one-dimensional model a bit,' John Kingman, its author, said. 'I suggested there might be certain topics – corporate tax, say, or pensions, or the energy market – that were core Treasury business but that were also ferociously complex and technical, and perhaps not ideally suited to being left entirely to even brilliant twenty-four-year-old generalists. Gus accepted this recommendation. But it hit bemusement more generally – and proved just too weird and counter-cultural. It died a quiet death.'

In 2004, the Professional Skills for Government programme aimed to professionalise the service and move it away from the generalist model. Between 2008 and 2011, the Government Skills Strategy went into operation, again to professionalise the service and share learning and development services. In 2011, the Civil Service Learning programme aimed to improve the quality of generic training. In 2013, the Cabinet Office introduced the Functions initiative to develop and manage specialist skills.

There were, during those various efforts at minor reform, some marginal improvements. There are now more specialist accountants, digital and data experts and project managers. But none of it budged the service's fundamentally generalist disposition. 'They all come in with ideas to reform and reshape the civil service,' a former senior civil servant says. 'They all fucking fail. It's guaranteed. They always lose.'

In July 2020, Cabinet Office minister Michael Gove made a speech that sounded as if it could have been torn straight from the pages of the Fulton report half a century earlier. 'There are a limited number, even in the senior civil service, who have qualifications or expertise in mathematical, statistical and probability questions,' he said. 'The current structure of the civil service career ladder means that promotion comes from switching roles, and departments, with determined regularity.'

A year later, Kate Bingham, chair of the government's Vaccine Taskforce, echoed the point at a speech at Oxford University, as she spoke about her experience trying to secure the jabs during the pandemic. 'The first challenge,' she said, 'is what seemed to me to be a notable lack of scientific, industrial, commercial and manufacturing skills both among civil servants and politicians. The problem was that the department lacked knowledge of the commercial biosciences landscape, and lacked the science and technical understanding needed to be operationally effective.'

The constant merry-go-round of ministerial appointments desperately needs a civil service with deep subject expertise so that it can ground the minister in the objective reality of their policy area. But far from providing it, the rate of job transfer in the civil service is, if anything, faster than in government.

Lord Freud was welfare minister between 2010 and 2016, during which time he helped build Universal Credit. That project was itself in desperate need of long-standing experts to challenge it, during both conception and implementation. Confused project management and missed targets meant it wasted millions in taxpayers' money. But far from being advised by experienced staff, Freud found that he himself quickly became the institutional memory. Between May 2012 and May 2013 alone, the project went through five senior responsible owners in the civil service. 'I sat there for six and a half years,' he said, 'looking at the third, fourth, fifth generation of a person doing a particular area. There is no corporate knowledge retained. That's just a massive vulnerability.'

During that time, Universal Credit's roll-out proved disastrous. It was designed around a stereotypical candidate who was paid monthly, had stable personal circumstances and access to technology and could budget intuitively, but found itself delivering services to people who, in many cases, enjoyed none of those things. It insisted on a five-week wait for the first payment, which drove many people into rent arrears or debt. The rate at which it was withdrawn if someone found work acted as a disincentive to people working or earning more. It made benefit payments conditional on work-related tasks that were poorly suited to jobseekers' personal circumstances.

'The way that Universal Credit has been designed and implemented appears to be based around an idealised claimant and it has features that are harming many, particularly the most vulnerable,' the House of Lords Economic Affairs Committee concluded. 'It is also linked to soaring food bank usage. Housing providers have reported dramatic increases in rent arrears. Many claimants report finding the system incomprehensible. Universal Credit's reputation has nosedived.'

Civil servants are unable to effectively scrutinise ministers, because to all intents and purposes they *are* ministers. They suffer from many of the same defects that afflict their political masters: they were not selected on the basis of their knowledge, they are not incentivised to attain it, and even if they did, they move so quickly that they would lose it.

'You've got these really bright amateurs around,' Nick Clegg says. 'But if you're any good, you move off after two or three years. Expertise and longevity are seen as a sign of failure. That bloke in his mid forties who's been doing rail franchise contract negotiations for the last 15 years? People just snigger. But a Treasury official who did six months with that minister's Private Office and then negotiated with the Europeans and then moved into fiscal policy? Oh, they're a real high-flyer.'

The mechanism by which the civil service punishes expertise is the promotional system. It operates according to grades.

At the bottom, below the grade system, you have administrative assistants and administrative officers, which includes workers like receptionists. Then executive officers, higher executive officers and senior executive officers – ever greater ranks of responsibility and seniority – until finally you reach Grade 7. This is the point at which it gets serious. Grade 7 operates as a feeder grade for the senior civil service. People can then secure promotion to Grade 6 if they prove themselves to be particularly impressive, or are adept at management and suit a team leader role. Grade 5 is the start of the senior civil service. In the old days, this would be the point at which they were included in *Who's Who*. They will now be put in charge of a large policy area, or perhaps be a finance director in a small department.

The system continues like a pyramid, with fewer and fewer people in each rank, all the way up to Grade 1, the absolute peak, for permanent secretaries. People's place in the grade structure defines their pay, but perhaps just as importantly, their social standing. 'The civil service is anti-discrimination of any kind, except one, which is gradism,' a former senior civil servant says. 'If they want to quickly work out how seriously they need to take someone, they work out their grade. The second they know they're talking to a higher executive officer, they think: they're a fucking idiot. Not the smartest. Going to be process-orientated. If they're causing problems I need to work through that person and go up a level to try and get someone who can help me out.'

Not so long ago, most careers in the civil service were defined by the ambition to reach Grade 7 which was considered a senior level. Many civil servants would work their way through the previous grades for 20 years before being promoted to that level. The rare figures who secured it more quickly were typically fast-streamers. These are people who were considered especially bright, arriving from university or another career. They'd be given a series of aptitude exams such as verbal reasoning, non-verbal reasoning, numerical reasoning – basically a glorified IQ test.

Then they'd have certain exercises thrown at them, like being sent emails at a rapid pace and having to manage them, or going into a mock meeting with a card telling them which department they're from and the argument they're required to make. It's telling that, outside of the IQ tests, the exam structure is extremely similar to the approval process for MP selection lists. The test is specifically designed to find bright generalists. It has no focus on, or even any interest in, specialists. Indeed it places no value on expertise, and fails even to look for the people with skills in the areas the civil service knows it lacks – hard science, IT, contract drafting, mathematics, financial services.

Fast-streamers would then be expected to do around four postings before going for a Grade 7 position. Certain very impressive individuals might secure it for their second post, or their third, but most got it on their fourth. They'd be starting on around £28,000 for their first posting and would then get around £50,000 at Grade 7.

Everything happens much quicker now. That is a result of two events: austerity and Brexit. They worked in tandem to speed up the degree of civil service churn, so that people started switching jobs faster than ever before.

Austerity led to a recruitment freeze, a lock on the head count and the freezing of pay. Brexit demanded a huge influx of people to senior positions, either staffing new departments, like the Department for Exiting the European Union (DExEU), or expanding old ones, like the Department for Environment, Food and Rural Affairs, which went from having 6,450 officials in 2016 to 12,600 in 2022. This led to rapid grade inflation, with people being hoovered up into Grade 7 out of sheer desperation. 'The Brexit department was the promotion department,' a civil servant at the time says. 'Hold your nose and do Brexit. Get a Grade 7. Everyone did it. By the time I left, the department was taking fast-streamers after six months and giving them a Grade 7.'

A senior official at the Treasury had the same experience. 'You'd go to a meeting with someone at DExEU,' they say. 'They'd be a very high grade. And I'd be like: fuck me, you're joking. That kid is in nursery school. There was hyperinflation of grades at that point because they had to staff these departments up.'

This dynamic reduced the quality of the people going into the upper echelons of the civil service. And more importantly, it put an even greater emphasis on promotion as the only way to secure more pay in an era of frozen salaries. That meant that the incentive to change roles at speed became even more pronounced.

These calculations do not take place in economic isolation. They take place against the background reality of life in London, which, because of the centralisation of British politics, is where the vast majority of civil servants work. In 1970, the average London house price was 1.2 times the median pay for Grades 6 and 7. That ratio is now 8.4 times. For many talented people, this will have been enough to discourage them going into the civil service in the first place. A potential fast-streamer coming out of university would be looking at £28,000. But if they were to go into management consultancy, they would earn £45,000–£50,000. In investment banking, they would secure around £85,000.

For others, it might encourage them out of the civil service later in their career. In their mid thirties, when they might be thinking of starting a family and buying a house, a very successful fast-track civil servant in the senior levels might be earning as much as £75,000. But a reasonably successful 30-year-old in investment banking would be on around £450,000.

For some people, especially those from wealthy backgrounds who don't have to worry about money, the non-financial advantages of the civil service will be enough to compensate for the low pay. That's particularly the case if they get to work in the relative excitement of the Private

Office and enjoy day-to-day contact with the minister. But it is less the case in the key areas of expertise upon which good governance relies – for instance, developing IT systems for HMRC or drafting contracts in the transport sector. As Kingman said: 'There will always be some who have made their money, or who happen to have no interest in it, or who have private means and want to do public service, or just find government incredibly interesting. There just aren't enough of them to run the British state, especially in the less glamorous mid-level engine-room jobs which really matter.'

The pay issue is a particular deterrent to hard science graduates – exactly the type of expertise the civil service has lacked since the time of the Fulton report. Talented science, technology, engineering and mathematics graduates are highly employable in well-remunerated private sector positions – humanities students less so. The ranks are therefore filled once again with those whose professional qualities are about the skilful management of words rather than the skilful deployment of expertise.

But the crux of the promotional issue is not really intellectual or financial. It is cultural. The civil service has created a workforce that reflects its world view. Its vision of a high-flyer is someone who moves seamlessly from project to project, department to department, amassing two-year cycles of experience as another bullet point on their CV, and managing increasingly large numbers of people. Deep domain knowledge and experience is not considered important. 'I am not sure where this disdain for knowledge and expertise comes from,' Kingman said after his Treasury review, 'but it is deep-rooted.'

The promotional structure has therefore shackled together several distinct elements that should be independent of each other – salary, seniority, management and contact with ministers. In the service's mindset, all four must proceed together. They cannot be separated. More pay is associated with higher grades, which is associated with managing larger teams, which is associated with contact with ministers.

The generalists who enter the civil service sometimes find themselves amassing expertise almost by accident. They go into a department, start working on a project – be it rail franchising, or pensions payment processes, or hospital IT systems – and find that they like it. They then begin to become experts in their field. At this stage, there is absolutely nothing that can be done to reward them while keeping them in position. There is no control over pay. There is no meaningful bonus system. The only way they can secure more money is by going up through the grade system. But to do that, they have to apply to a different position within their department or outside it, taking them away from the area where they have developed the expertise.

'There is no one else who's worked on this for five years like I have,' says one civil servant who is highly regarded and operates in a sensitive area of policy. 'I'm very unusual in basically loving my job so much that I'm willing to forgo career progression.'

This type of figure is rare, but not unheard of. Tory MP Johnny Mercer would do walks around the Ministry of Defence every Thursday morning when he was veterans minister, and talk to staff. It was a highly unusual thing for a minister to do, but it proved revelatory. 'Generally speaking, you would find your most gifted people quietly beavering away,' he says. 'You go to their desk to see what they're doing and you realise all the good stuff from that part of the department came from their desk, not the senior person who signed it off.'

When these people eventually opt for extra money through promotion, they often find themselves delivering considerably worse outcomes than they were before, because the promotional system demands not only that they leave their subject area, but that they become managers. 'The civil service is full of really intelligent eggheads who are shit at management,' a former official says. 'But the way the civil service structure works, you have to become more and more managerial. As you go up from Grade 7 to Grade 6, the main difference is that Grade 6 leads a team of Grade 7s. You have no structure to reward people if they are awesome at their jobs – really sharp, really add value – but are just not cut out for managerial stuff.'

Civil service churn has now reached unprecedented levels. Permanent secretaries, who are supposed to be responsible for the long-term health of a department, average just two years and nine months. That's just one year longer than football managers, who are notorious for the speed with which they cycle through jobs.

There are a smattering of permanent secretaries with long experience of their subject area – people like Philip Barton at the Foreign Office, Jim Harra at HMRC, and Tom Scholar at the Treasury, before the Truss administration sacked him. The rest move regularly.

When a secretary of state does manage to stay in their position for over two years, they will often have more knowledge and experience of their area than their permanent secretary. They will therefore have little need to listen to their advice, which is even more amateur than their own. By the time Mark Sedwill was appointed permanent secretary at the Home Office in 2014, he noted that he was the fourth to have served home secretary Theresa May since she had assumed office in 2010.

The same applies to the rest of the senior civil service, comprising Grades 2 to 5. They are responsible for overseeing and managing the most critical work in British government, including major projects and public services. But on average, they move even faster than permanent secretaries, staying in post less than two years. An Institute for Government report that looked into six government departments in 2019 found that four out of every ten of their senior officials had been in post less than a year.

The picture is the same further down the civil service hierarchy. Some departments, like the Department for Work and Pensions and the Home Office, are good at retaining staff. Others are not. The Treasury, which is notable for having long-lasting secretaries of state, often has the highest rate of annual staff turnover of any Whitehall department. Usually it operates around the 25 per cent mark. This is the kind of turnover you would expect to find in a branch of McDonald's.

Postings in the Treasury are supposed to last between 18 and 30 months, but staff often apply for new positions during an existing posting period. This is encouraged by senior officials, who tell them they need breadth of experience. Analysis by the National Audit Office found that some officials were able to start seeking a new position after they'd been in post just nine months. When the National Audit Office assessed the Treasury's spending team in 2018, they found that staff had been in their current post for a median time of 11 months.

During the financial crash of 2007–8, the Treasury consequently found that it lacked many people with the expertise or experience to handle it. In the seven years beforehand, there had been at least seven different directors general responsible for financial services. There was a grand total of three people on the team dealing with financial stability issues when the crisis struck. By summer 2008, they'd built the team up to 20 and then 45 by October.

There were pockets of in-house expertise. The debt reserves management team understood capital markets and central bank balance sheets and played a crucial role in the run-up to the recapitalisation of the banks. The debt management office had strong working knowledge of markets. The Treasury legal advisers were experts in financial services legislation, public law and state aid. But overall, the picture was grim. 'Going into the crisis, few mainstream Treasury officials had technical banking and financial markets experience or expertise,' the Sharon White review into the Treasury's response to the crisis concluded. 'Officials with relevant background were thin on the ground and most of those deployed to work on the crisis were generalists, who faced a steep learning curve.'

This was the situation as Britain tottered on the edge of financial oblivion. People's lives, homes and material well-being were at existential risk. But the departmental staff in place to handle the crisis lacked the expertise to manage it. Nor were any lessons learned after it passed. Most of the people brought in to handle it left as part of the department's ceaseless churn of personnel. It did not keep a record of the skills it had in-house.

The same dynamic can be found in departments that were once praised for their expertise, such as the Foreign Office. 'I was attending a conference in Eastern Europe,' Margaret Beckett says of her time as foreign secretary, 'and the Dutch ambassador said to me: "I've been here for some time, but I have a weakness. I don't speak the local language.

And of course, your ambassador does. Your ambassadors always do."'

But in the ensuing years, the requirement to know the local language was removed in favour of generic managerial competence. Out of every British ambassador in the Middle East, only three can now speak Arabic. An official who applied for a job in Afghanistan before the Taliban takeover was told that he could not include the fact that he had served in Iran and Iraq and spoke Pashto, because the test was blind to expertise.

Rory Stewart brought with him considerable experience when he entered the Foreign Office as a minister of state. He had worked in Afghanistan, advised Hillary Clinton, written two books on the subject and sat on the foreign affairs select committee. He was shocked by what he found there. 'I was briefed on Afghanistan by a team of five people, four of whom had never been,' he says. 'The one that had was in a junior role, hadn't been there long and didn't speak the language. They were trying to convince me to continue funding the Afghan police. I had written on it a lot – why it didn't work and had no impact. What they were arguing was a mainstream view from five or six years earlier.'

This problem was not just about expertise, but the political willingness to even hear objective information about the world. Stewart started reading the internally classified reports sent in from British ambassadors and was baffled by what they contained. 'Each one was more and more ludicrous,' he says. 'Every one suggested Britain was the most important player in each region.'

Eventually he learned from an African ambassador that this was under instruction from the then foreign secretary, Boris Johnson. He had told them that the reports were to be optimistic and upbeat. 'Johnson called me in and said I needed to stop asking about this,' Stewart recalls. 'He said: "Government is like a rugby match. I used to captain the team. You can't have people saying objectively the other team is better than us. You have to say we're great and we're going to win." It was a sign that Britain simply isn't serious any more.'

The rate of churn doesn't just debilitate departments. It undermines individual projects.

Those tasked with assessing government performance believe the constant changeover of personnel and the absence of any expert knowledge are the key reasons why projects fail so persistently. 'This is something we regularly see evidence of,' the Public Accounts Committee said in 2020. 'Many of the projects and programmes across Whitehall which we scrutinise are afflicted by delays, inefficiencies and budgetary overruns – the root issue of which is often a lack of specialist skills amongst officials.'

The Rough Sleeper Unit was established by New Labour during the 1990s and 2000s, under the auspices of the Social Exclusion Unit in the Cabinet Office. It was composed of around 20 experts and tasked with reducing rough sleeping across England by two thirds within a three-year time frame. It succeeded.

When the coalition government came to power, almost the entire team left or were moved to different departments over the course of two or three years. The number of homeless people then started to rise, due primarily to a shortfall in the delivery of new affordable housing and cuts to housing benefit. Between 2010 and 2018, the estimated number of people sleeping on the streets of England on a single night rose from 1,768 to 4,677. In 2018, the Office for National Statistics estimated there were 726 deaths of homeless people, an increase of 51 per cent in the six years it had collected the statistics. But the government was at a loss as to what to do about it, having discarded the entirety of its institutional knowledge about the problem. It had even lost its knowledge of what it had itself previously implemented. 'There is very little sign,' said Geoff Mulgan, chief executive of the innovation charity Nesta, who was involved in the 2000s policy, 'that either government or opposition is even dimly aware of what was done before.'

Even where officials have picked up experience, the civil service has no idea it happened so is unable to later direct them to a similar project. On a very basic level, government departments have no idea what skills, knowledge or experience their staff have, because no one bothered to track it. Many departments do not collect basic workforce data, such as turnover rates by team. There is no information on how many different departments staff have worked in, or, in many cases, any skills register.

The lack of specialism is particularly painful when it comes to commercial skills. Again, the problem has been recognised for a long time. In 1999, a review into civil procurement in central government by Sir Peter Gershon concluded that commercial skills needed to be raised significantly. Again, various initiatives were launched, such as the creation of the Office of Government Commerce. Again, none of them really worked.

'The problem is not that no one knows what to do,' Colm Reilly, head of government practice at PA Consulting, said. 'It is well known. It is just not done systematically or, sometimes, not done at all. The answer to improving commercial skills is to create the framework of conditions that allow a rigorous and consistent focus on the basics of project management and their implementation.'

But this has never taken place. Wide gaps remain in contract management, the use and management of advisers, risk management, business acumen, information technology, project management and commercial awareness. Reviews by the Office of Government Commerce have found that commercial skills are generally weak across all 16 central government departments.

The lack of commercial skills has a severe financial and organisational consequence. It pushes the civil service towards the use of private sector consultants.

The use of consultants actually went into decline in 2010, after the introduction of an internal review process and a requirement of Cabinet Office approval instituted by minister Francis Maude. But it started creeping up again in 2012, and then skyrocketed during Brexit, which required exactly the types of commercial and project delivery skills the civil service had failed to nurture.

Consultants were brought in across the Brexit policy landscape, tasked with a variety of projects, including providing businesses with information on import and export rules and designing new statutory bodies to carry out functions previously delivered by the EU. Even basic commercial research, such as an assessment of healthcare systems in Europe, was conducted by consultants. The majority of the work went to the big consultancy firms that dominate the industry, like Deloitte, PricewaterhouseCoopers, Ernst & Young and Boston Consulting Group.

Consultants are eye-wateringly expensive compared to civil service staff. A project manager has a daily rate of around £478. They are equivalent to a senior executive officer in the civil service, whose salary has a daily cost of £185–£239. A programme manager has a daily rate of around £600. They are equivalent to a Grade 7, who costs £242–£323 a day.

The problem becomes more severe the higher up the food chain you go. Research from 2016 showed there were 47 consultants working for the civil service with a day rate of over £1,000. That is a higher equivalent salary than that paid to a permanent secretary.

Some consultants come in for a short project and leave quickly afterwards, but others hang around for years. Of the 147 'temporary' external staff employed by the Home Office in August 2015, 121 had been engaged for over a year. Eight of them had been employed for between five and nine years. One temporary staff member at the department was found to have cost £1.4 million in over seven years of continuous employment. A consultant at the Department for Children, Schools and Families cost £1.35 million over three years.

The irony of this system is that consultancy firms are drawing their staff from precisely the same talent pool as the civil service. They are recruiting the bright young things from university that the fast stream looks for. But instead of encouraging them to become generalists, they are turning them into specialists in a key set of commercial activities and then leasing them out to the civil service at exorbitant rates.

As they do so, the civil service goes into sustained decline. It amounts to a degradation of its institutional capacity: a form of conscious deprofessionalisation. Each time skills are sought from the outside, the civil service loses that knowledge on a corporate basis and ceases to be able to properly brief ministers or even really act as an intelligent customer.

'My experience,' Bingham said in her Oxford speech, 'was that officials seemed to use strategic and operational consultants quite freely, and doubtless at great expense. But this has a doubly bad effect: not only does bringing in hired guns from the outside not build real capability within Whitehall itself, it actually reduces the incentive to confront and deal with this problem.' The cycle then continues. Civil service commercial skills are degraded all over again. More consultants are hired to patch over them. And the skills are degraded even further.

The civil service is itself responsible for what has happened to it. Over decades, it has failed to address a lack of expertise and indeed has acted in many ways to worsen the situation. But the blame must ultimately lie with government. The similarity between the job patterns of civil servants and ministers is not a coincidence. It is a demand-side problem. Ministers do not want expertise. They don't want specialism. The more knowledge the civil servant has, the more effectively they can challenge them.

If ministers were yearning for deep subject proficiency, we would see it reflected in the spads they pick. After all, barring interference from Downing Street, they can hire anyone they like for this position, to do whatever they like. If they wanted to, they could use this resource to balance out the generalism of the civil service. But they do not. They hire people to put a further party political spin on the information the civil service gives them.

That gives us a strong indication of what ministers want from civil servants. And that, ultimately, is what they have got: the kind of generalist who has neither the skills, the inclination, the knowledge nor the incentive to object to what they are doing.

Civil servants are professional amateurs because they live in a system dictated by professional amateurs. And that is what the system values.

Next we'll look at political journalists, who stand outside of the formal Westminster system, and are supposed to shine a light on what goes on there.

CHAPTER 7

The Press

Inside the Palace of Westminster, there's a collection of rooms. Physically they're very similar to all the other rooms in the building: rodent-infested, decaying, crumbling at the edges, populated by inflated egos. But constitutionally they are very unusual. They do not relate to the government, or to Parliament, or to the civil service. They are an alien entity.

The collection of rooms is called the lobby and it is full of journalists. Of all the institutions in Westminster, it is perhaps the least understood, which is fitting, because it is also the only one populated entirely by people whose professional role involves revealing things to the public.

Journalism is supposed to act as the last line of defence against bad policymaking. When all else fails, it is meant to shine a harsh light on power and expose it to public judgement. But in fact it is far more complicated than that. Journalism is part of the British power structure. Its editors and proprietors are semi-independent players in the political game. The coverage they provide, whether friendly or hostile, comes from a political perspective and aims to accomplish a political aim.

It is very good at highlighting political misbehaviour – corporate lobbying, affairs, parties during lockdown. It is much less effective at assessing what the government is doing and the impact it has on people's lives. The origin of policy and the effect it has on the public are largely ignored.

And that is the fatal flaw in the way it approaches the business of scrutiny.

At the heart of journalism's problems is financial weakness. News cannot pay for itself. It never has.

Until the early nineteenth century, news was funded by politics. There was no claim of objectivity or impartiality. There was no straight reporting. Political parties provided the funding for a newspaper along with a ready source of ideologically committed readers. It wasn't considered particularly shocking. Even in the late nineteenth century, Robert Lowe would write *Times* leader columns while serving as home secretary in William Gladstone's first administration. As late as 1918, the Liberal prime minister David Lloyd George and his supporters bought the popular *Daily Chronicle* newspaper for £1,659,000, bringing it under the direct control of Downing Street.

But over the first two decades of the twentieth century, press ownership suddenly shifted away from political parties and towards a small group of powerful businessmen – the press barons.

In 1896, Alfred Harmsworth, who later became Lord Northcliffe, started the *Daily Mail* with his brother Harold, who later became Lord Rothermere. Those two names are still synonymous with British journalism. The *Daily Mail*, the *Mail on Sunday*, the *Independent*, the *i*, the *Evening Standard* and the *Metro* are all based in Northcliffe House in Kensington. Rothermere's great-grandson is the chairman and a controlling shareholder of the Daily Mail and General Trust, which owns the *Daily Mail*, the *i* and the *New Scientist*, among other publications.

In an age without mass-market newspapers, Northcliffe and Rothermere managed to create an affordable, energetic paper for the lower middle classes in the form of the *Daily*

Mail. Northcliffe started the *Daily Mirror* in 1903, which eventually became the first mass-circulation paper for the working class. Later, he picked up the *Observer* and *The Times*. By 1914, he controlled 40 per cent of the morning, 45 per cent of the evening and 15 per cent of the Sunday press.

The great heyday of the mass-market British press was between the 1930s and 1950s. By the 1950s, there were 17 million national dailies sold every day. The Hulton Readership Survey of 1956 showed that 88 per cent of the adult population regularly read a daily paper.

The key to this new-found independence from political parties lay in advertising. The 1890s saw a vigorous growth in consumer goods and purchasing power, and the papers had an open space to advertise them. By the 1920s, this advertising accounted on average for 75 per cent of their income. 'For the past three hundred years,' Paul Starr, a newspaper historian, said of the newspaper market in the US, using words that are equally applicable in the UK, 'newspapers have been able to develop and flourish partly because their readers have almost never paid the full cost of production. From the eighteenth century to the middle of the nineteenth century, many newspapers were politically subsidised, directly by governments or through political parties. Then, as consumer markets expanded, newspapers increasingly sold not just news to readers, but also readers to advertisers.' This, throughout its history, has been the key vulnerability in journalism and it remains so today. In general, it costs more to produce than people are willing to pay for it. It has a constitutional function that exceeds its financial capacity.

The advertising revenue came from two sources. The first was display advertising – typically from businesses with ads placed next to editorial content. The second was classified advertising. For many twentieth-century papers, this was the real financial lifeblood. Every day it came in: second-hand cars, houses, children's toys, music lessons, job vacancies, official notifications from the local council, announcements of births, deaths and marriages – all typically printed between the news and the sport.

Classified ads were particularly vital to the local press. 'The massive property section kept the *Ham and High* alive,' veteran political reporter Paul Waugh says of his first job on a local paper. 'I didn't have to chase anything in terms of the money. We just got on with it.' This model provided an extraordinary cash cow for local newspaper owners and shareholders, with profits ranging from 20 per cent to 40 per cent even into the early twenty-first century. Between 2003 and 2007, for instance, Media Wales had profit margins of 34 per cent, making it one of the most profitable companies in Wales of any kind.

Late-twentieth-century journalism was a kind of Eden. And like Eden, it flourished on the basis of innocence. It was an age in which no one had access to information, outside of the basic data on audience numbers provided by the Audit Bureau of Circulation. Businesses had almost no understanding of how many readers saw their adverts, let alone whether they went on to buy anything from the company. For all they knew, they glanced right over them onto the next news story. But it was one of the few avenues they had to attract the public's attention, so the money kept flowing in.

The same went for editors. They didn't have any real understanding what people were reading. 'You had no idea why people were buying the paper,' says Alan Rusbridger, editor of the *Guardian* between 1995 and 2015. 'There were things called reading and marking surveys. You would literally get 12 readers into a room with a copy of the *Guardian* and a felt-tip pen, then you would ask them to go through it and highlight the things they read. At the end, the digest told you that something like 9 per cent of readers read editorials, 11 per cent of readers read Hugo Young and 33 per cent of readers read the royal story on page three. What am I supposed to do with that? Am I going to sack Hugo Young tomorrow and have royal stories? No, of course not.'

It was a veil of ignorance, stretched luxuriously over a whole industry. And as long as it stayed there, the money kept flowing in.

This model gave reporters the one quality that above all else allowed them to scrutinise the activity of the government. It gave them time. They would be expected to write one story a day, perhaps two at a maximum. They would only have one deadline. If they were on a morning paper, it was between 6 p.m. and 8 p.m. – a few hours before the paper went to print. That gave them the entire day to dig into the story they were going to tell: reading reports, calling sources, chatting with experts, meeting politicians, attending press conferences and mulling the whole thing over.

When a new policy emerged, journalists would often call the government department's press office. These had started with Lloyd George, who appointed William Sutherland as his press secretary in the period after the First World War. The No. 10 press office itself was established after the Second World War, then slowly spread out from there until there was one in each department.

There was a fairly solid wall between the press office on the one hand and the minister on the other. The former was staffed by civil servants. They would provide information about a policy and try to explain it. They would also clarify any issues journalists had, after checking the details with officials. They were not in charge of advertising the policy. It was more like a public information campaign. 'People in press offices read all the documents,' veteran *Guardian* home affairs correspondent Alan Travis says. 'You could have a proper conversation with them.'

The minister, on the other hand, would do the persuasion. There was a sense that this was part of their job. They wanted to make their case, even to hostile journalists. And that applied to political enemies too. Hard-line Conservatives would typically still be open to speaking to left-wing journalists. 'When I started in 1992,' Travis says, 'I was taken out by the director of communication and head of news at the Home Office and they ran through with me in great detail every active issue in the department, in a completely open and discursive way. When Michael Howard became home secretary, he was happy to sit down for an hour and answer questions from home affairs correspondents in detail. For four years, practically every week, I met him and his ministers. We had the same with Jack Straw and David Blunkett.'

Since the very beginning, journalists have always attempted to influence politicians and politicians have always attempted to influence journalists. The press is not just a fearless speak-truth-to-power watchdog for the public interest. It is a part of the events it is reporting. Sometimes a tiny part, sometimes a major one. But always involved.

'I am but a comparatively young journalist,' the Victorian editor W. T. Stead wrote in 1886, 'but I have seen Cabinets upset, ministers driven into retirement, laws repealed, great social reforms initiated, bills transformed, estimates remodelled, programmes modified, Acts passed, generals nominated, governors appointed, armies sent hither and thither, war proclaimed and war averted, by the agency of newspapers. There were of course other agencies at work; but the dominant impulse, the original initiative, and the directing spirit in all these cases must be sought in the editorial sanctum rather than in Downing Street.'

Speaking to a Royal Commission on newspaper ownership in 1947–9, press baron Lord Beaverbrook was perfectly clear about his intentions. He owned his newspapers, he said, 'purely for propaganda and with no other purpose'. Decades later, Australian newspaper magnate Rupert Murdoch echoed him when asked if he interfered with his newspapers' editorial policy. 'I did not come all this way,' he said, 'not to interfere.'

In 1979, his *Sun* newspaper swung hard behind Thatcher in the general election. A year after that, editor Larry Lamb was rewarded with a knighthood. Its enthusiastic support for the government allowed Murdoch to purchase *The Times* and *Sunday Times* without reference to the Monopolies and Mergers Commission. During a brutal dispute with print unions, Murdoch used recent government anti-strike legislation to establish a new subsidiary company so that his workforce's action became secondary picketing and therefore illegal. A massive police presence was approved to support him. Murdoch was simply following the footsteps of proprietors through the centuries: as political players in their own right – altering policy, taking down opponents, influencing government. And doing so as much for personal commercial reasons as ideological ones.

These political relationships are not simple. They do not mean that newspaper owners and editors are always entirely aligned with a favoured party. They can and often do fall out. Sometimes editors decide that a party is going to fail and start to distance themselves from it. Other times they conclude that its actions are so egregious that they must strike out against it. Sometimes they just happen to disagree on something.

John Major discovered this during Black Wednesday in September 1991, when Britain fell out of the European Exchange Rate Mechanism. He called *Sun* editor Kelvin MacKenzie to ask how the paper was going to report the story. 'Let me put it this way,' MacKenzie said. 'I have two buckets of shit on my desk and tomorrow morning I am going to empty both of them over your head.'

Tony Blair and his press secretary Alastair Campbell worked hard to convert that fractured relationship into Labour support. The Labour leader flew to Australia to get Murdoch on board in July 1995. 'If the British press is to be believed,' the media tycoon said, 'today is all part of a Blair–Murdoch flirtation. If that flirtation is ever consummated, Tony, I suspect we will end up making love like two porcupines – very carefully.' But make careful love they did, and *The Sun* and *The Times* swung behind the Labour leader in the 1997 election.

Under the administrations of Theresa May and Boris Johnson, the relationship between Downing Street and the right-wing press became more incestuous than at any other point in the modern era. James Slack, the home affairs editor of the *Daily Mail*, was appointed the prime minister's spokesperson under May. He became No. 10's director of communications under Johnson, and then announced that he was leaving to go back into journalism as deputy editor of *The Sun* in March 2021.

Slack's Downing Street leaving do the next month, held during a COVID lockdown, constituted one of several celebrations that became known as the Partygate scandal. It was a story of almost biblical proportions – a classic tale of politicians breaking the laws they themselves had written. It dominated the political conversation for months on end and ultimately led to Johnson's departure from office. But despite all the press coverage, *The Sun*, where Slack was now working, repeatedly held back from featuring the story on its front page. And that made perfect sense, because it was itself deeply involved in the unfolding scandal. To have covered it would have conceded that it was a player in the events it reported on. Slack was then succeeded at Downing Street by Jack Doyle, another *Mail* home affairs editor. And so the cycle continued.

In November of that year, *Mail* editor Geordie Greig, who had featured extremely critical coverage of the Johnson administration, was suddenly and unceremoniously sacked. No one could work out why. The *Mail* had only recently become the UK's highest-selling newspaper, overtaking *The Sun*. But then it became clearer. Paul Dacre, former *Mail* editor and a close Johnson ally, was made editor-in-chief of the publishing company that owns the newspaper. Immediately afterwards, the *Mail*'s editorial position changed to become vociferously pro-Johnson. Over the course of 2022, Johnson repeatedly tried to secure Dacre a peerage for the House of Lords.

The relationships that cement these sudden changes in coverage are typically conducted in Downing Street or the prime minister's country residence, Chequers. Editors are invited in for a friendly chat, they're called up by the prime minister for a conversation after a major event, or they spend the weekend together. It is extremely difficult to secure information about these relationships, even though they can have a decisive impact on political outcomes. After all, who would report them? 'There's that sense of walking up Downing Street to go and have a cup of coffee with the prime minister,' Rusbridger says. 'It's a very bad thing for the ego, it really is. You think: "Oh, I'm a real person of consequence." It's a compromising relationship, a blurring of the social and the professional in ways designed to make you feel that you're friends. And then they can call you up and ask a favour.'

The impact of those conversations can be felt throughout the newspaper. Murdoch continued to talk to the editor of *The Sun* several times a week throughout his career. He was more hands-off with *The Times*, although editors would always have a sense of his view without necessarily needing to ask. That unspoken approach exists all the way down the publication hierarchy. Often journalists pick up on a change in political direction without being told anything, simply by looking at story placement. They will check the news list – a live document showing which stories will be on which page of the paper the next day – and notice the items that reliably move towards the front.

Sometimes it's more direct. Editors give clear instructions in morning news conferences about what they want and what they don't. 'That's spread down the chain to reporters who aren't in news conference,' a former senior reporter at the *Mail* says. 'You might get the odd comment like "they're not bothered about that", "they're definitely keen on this", "we need to keep going on this", "we need new lines on that". There's times where the line's more heavily dictated than others.'

The effect of this political element is that journalistic scrutiny is selective. Sometimes it is selective between the parties, offering one an easy ride and another a hard one. Other times, it is selective between figures within a party, targeting the rivals of a favoured individual. But either way, it does not provide a universal scrutiny function. It provides a partial one.

The key daily event in political journalism is the lobby briefing, in which the prime minister's spokesperson updates journalists on what has been happening and takes their questions. There's one in the morning and one in the afternoon, although the afternoon session is largely irrelevant and will only be well attended on a big news day. Lobby meetings typically become less interesting over the course of the week.

The primary feature of the lobby briefing is stonewalling. The spokesperson comes in with a set of lines they will give in response to questions and they will proceed to give those lines no matter what they are asked or how many times they are asked it. Generally speaking, those lines have been carefully formulated to reveal nothing at all. 'These people are basically just reading from a script,' says Jim Pickard, chief political correspondent at the *Financial Times*. 'That doesn't tell you anything. They're not lying. They're just not confirming anything and they're not providing detail. The more adept ones will deviate a little and give the impression of candour but in reality cling pretty close to their pre-written script.'

Sometimes journalists find a weakness in the account they're being given and are able to exploit it. 'It's 90 per cent not very useful and 10 per cent useful,' says Adam Bienkov, who has been in the lobby for over a decade, 'but that 10 per cent can be very, very useful. Occasionally you ask something that hasn't been written down and you get a chink of light.' At this point, the assembled journalists will often start hunting as a pack – picking up on an inconsistency in a previous answer or pressing further on a line of questioning established by another reporter. It can become a feeding frenzy. 'There's no escape,' Waugh says. 'You have to stand there. You have to answer the questions.' At these moments, the lobby can be very impressive. It can tear apart a government position, which then translates into bruising morning newspaper headlines, which typically translates into a much more aggressive approach from the broadcasters.

But there is a flip side to the pack hunt. It is groupthink. Working together in the same building, day after day, means lobby reporters are prone to gathering together after an event and chatting about what just happened. Very often, they arrive at a shared view, which is then transmitted out across the newspapers. 'When you get together after an event,' says Jason Beattie, assistant editor at the *Daily Mirror*, 'you share with each other what's the line. It's partly to cover your own back and partly because it's easier. But it means there's less independent thinking.'

The same process applies to which stories are covered, as well as how they're covered. Lobby journalists often fall into subject matter homogeneity. 'There's no big central decision on what the subject of the day is,' a *Mail* political reporter says, 'but if you go to lobby and all the questions are on one thing, you think: "Oh shit, that's the important story of the day." You obviously get sucked in.' Important stories are therefore left uncovered. This is particularly the case if they are complex, unusual, policy-heavy or do not fit easily into an ongoing Westminster narrative.

Homogeneity is particularly dangerous for the lobby because it is already engaged in a very specific form of political journalism. It does not focus on the development of policy, or its long-term consequences, or the real-world impact it has on people's lives. It focuses on the daily party political frenzy of Westminster – rising and falling stars, disputes within and between the parties, scandals and resignations. Court intrigue.

In some ways, that is a function of the job. Most lobby journalists are not working in the world on which policy impacts. They are working – like MPs, civil servants and ministers – in Westminster. And they soon internalise the dynamics and the assumptions of that place, alongside those they are meant to scrutinise. 'To call it fast food is knocking it too much,' one newspaper editor says, 'but it's immediate. It's here and now. Their ability to think laterally is close to zero.'

The primary basis on which policy is measured by the lobby is its effect on the standing of political parties or their leaders, not the impact it might have. 'Often the most notable story was the battle in Westminster over who's in and who's out, who's up and who's down,' Rusbridger says. 'There's a disconnection between the specialist journalists who really know their stuff, often more than the ministers, and the way the lobby operates, which tends to skim the surface.'

Once a policy has been passed, it effectively ceases to exist for the lobby. There is very little political coverage about the impact of Universal Credit, say, or the privatisation of probation, or the decline of the homelessness unit. That is old news, something happening out there somewhere, whereas the lobby is dedicated to what is happening now. 'It covers the battles over an issue while it goes through government and Parliament,' says Peter Riddell, a former columnist at *The Times*, 'but very seldom its implementation. Take Michael Gove's education policy. How has it actually worked out? No one talks about it. Those are the types of things there ought to be much more focus on.'

Lobby journalists are themselves aware of this process and the way their coverage starts becoming more myopic by virtue of the workplace. 'I started in political journalism writing commentary for the *Birmingham Post*,' Beattie says, 'and I think I had a better view of Westminster in Birmingham than in the Houses of Parliament. I had perspective.'

The structure of lobby briefings changes depending on who the prime minister's spokesperson is, but typically speaking, it will often be followed by a secondary briefing. Unlike the first, this will be off the record. It is given to a smaller group, who tend to stick around while others drift off. It is known, in a somewhat tongue-in-cheek way, as dark lobby. 'The wire services like Reuters are in a rush and they don't do off-the-record, so they go,' says Dan Sabbagh, who covered for colleagues in the lobby during their maternity leave as associate editor of the *Guardian*. 'There was a kind of an understanding that if you were junior, you would disappear after a bit. This is Britain, so no one would say anything, but you knew. The heavyweights stay. I wasn't always strictly welcome, but the first thing I learned as a journalist was to follow your opponents and hang around them like a grisly smell.'

At this point the briefing becomes more indiscreet and confidential. The information at this stage might be about an upcoming prime ministerial trip that could not be revealed publicly for security reasons. But it can also be used to impart more detailed information to senior journalists, especially if the spokesperson trusts the outlet to deliver it in a favourable manner. During the Brexit negotiations, for instance, this was typically when the more accurate briefings would be given. 'As it became a smaller group,' Sabbagh says, 'it became progressively more off the record and a bit better in terms of information.'

Unlike the normal briefing, in which comments are ascribed to 'the prime minister's spokesperson', the designation can sometimes change at this point so that it refers to 'a Whitehall source', or even 'a party source'. This was the case for Guto Harri, who was director of communications towards the end of Johnson's time in government. 'Having seen how the sausage is made, you can see how the attributions are dishonest,' one lobby journalist says. 'Guto Harri is not a party source. He's the prime minister's comms chief. He's giving a briefing on the basis that he's referred to as something he isn't.'

Almost all governments have tried to bring the lobby under their control, but some have been more effective at it than others. New Labour attempted to contain it by threatening a removal of access if journalists didn't give them the coverage they wanted. 'The lobby used to be totally captured under New Labour,' Pickard says. 'And the reason was that Labour was politically omniscient. It looked like there was no chance of anyone else being in government from 1997 to probably 2007. And therefore no journalist was really thinking "let's cultivate loads of Tories". All the focus was on Blair and Campbell. So they bullied the fuck out of journalists and made clear that if they wrote negative stuff, they would be cut out of the circle of trust.'

Journalists who wrote critical coverage, or who failed to give the stories handed to them the appropriate spin, were out in the cold. But this period of control eventually faded. Soon enough, the war between Blair and Brown became so intense that they started fighting it through briefings to the press, and the control the leadership was able to exercise deteriorated significantly. 'The dominance didn't last,' Riddell says. 'After the 2001 election, the real dynamic was the rivalry between the two, and in place of a united government line, journalists were offered alternative official lines on domestic policy.'

During the Johnson administration, Cummings and Slack tried to formalise the dark lobby system by restricting lobby briefings to sympathetic journalists. The plan fell apart when the lobby as a whole refused to attend unless their colleagues were included.

But the biggest threat faced by political journalism did not come from politicians. It came from the collapse of the financial model.

The internet was the single biggest change to hit journalism since the development of consumer advertising. It was a Year Zero event: an existential crisis that completely reorientated the incentive structures for organisations and individuals, with far-reaching implications for their capacity to scrutinise power.

The first impact was obvious and devastating. People stopped buying newspapers. In 2007, *The Sun*, at the top of the market, was selling 3,031,724 copies a day. By 2017 it was selling 1,602,320. The *Guardian*, at the bottom of the market, was selling 366,233. By 2017, it was selling 154,431. Essentially, newspapers lost half their print audience in a decade.

They tried various gimmicks – distributing bulk copies for free to hotels and airlines, offering two-for-one holidays or cinema tickets or city-break deals. None of it worked. The decline was relentless.

The fear in the industry, starting from around the turn of the twenty-first century and becoming more intense every year, was of a death spiral. Circulation decline would lead to advertising decline, which would lead to revenue decline, which would prompt management to issue redundancies, slash marketing, dump investment plans and freeze wages. And then, with the few remaining journalists being asked to work twice as hard, the product would go into editorial decline, meaning readers would lose interest and the circulation would plummet even further, only for the cycle to begin again.

In reality, newspapers were not actually losing readers. They were gaining them. They lived in a world of painful commercial irony, in which they were read by more people than ever before while securing less revenue than they'd ever known.

In June 2006, the *Guardian* had four million unique online users in the US alone – a marketplace where it was previously a complete unknown. The trouble was, they couldn't monetise them. The total revenue generated by those four million readers in 2005–6 was just £73,000. And the reason for that was that readers weren't interested in adverts.

The luxurious opacity of the old system, where neither the newspaper nor businesses really knew if the ads were being read, was replaced by one in which they had a very good idea indeed. The internet offered data right down to the granular level: how many people had seen the ad, how many had clicked on it and how many had gone on to make a purchase. The new key metrics were revenue per thousand eyeballs, known as RPM, and click-through rates, known as CTR. Neither of them looked very promising.

'We have a problem,' the *Guardian*'s commercial director wrote around 2001. 'People come to our sites to read stories – not click on ads. Our response rates are very, very low – particularly on our news site, where we have the most inventory. This means we often find ourselves falling off schedules after advertisers evaluate their performance on our sites.'

Classified advertising was hit even harder than display. The Craigslist website, established by a web enthusiast in San Francisco, went online in 1996. It offered everything the classified sections did, and mostly for free. People could find work, or cars, or even dates through its pages. By 2016, it was hitting 20 billion page views a month. It almost singlehandedly broke the financial model of many newspapers.

The *Guardian* lost £36.8 million – 15 per cent of its income – in two years. The *Sunday Times*, which at one point made £1 million in profit a week, was rumoured to be losing £15 million a year. The impact on the local press was even deeper. ABC figures – industry-standard circulation data – from 2016 showed that every single paid-for local daily was losing readers. The *Wigan Evening Post* lost 36 per cent in a single year. Even the best-performing, the *Yorkshire Post*, fell 3.6 per cent. There was an average decline of 12.5 per cent. The decline hit prestigious local papers as hard as it hit the others. In the 20 years leading to 2016, the *Express & Star* went from selling 217,000 copies to 54,890, the *Manchester Evening News* from 214,000 to 46,738, and the *Liverpool Echo* from 173,000 to 43,836. Over two decades, they lost three quarters of their customers.

Local journalists are the policy front line. They do not focus on the origin of policy, or the way it passes through Parliament. They look at its impact on the streets of their patch. Their local area is their expertise, and the good ones know it like the back of their hand – the police, social services, councillors, planning meetings, hospitals, youth centres. 'Regional media are a canary down the mineshaft,' a national newspaper editor says. The decline of the traditional financial model meant that many of these areas turned into news deserts. Magistrates' courts and local council meetings went unreported. Increases in crime, or A&E waiting times, or school failure simply had no one to cover them.

The large companies that hoovered up local titles, like Newsquest and Local World, started piping bland uniform central content, defined by search engine optimisation parameters, onto their websites, then cramming them full of pop-up ads and videos that played without warning, making the reading experience corrosive and unwelcoming.

A new corporate culture emerged, with no local roots or concern for journalistic standards. David Montgomery, the CEO of Local World, told the Culture, Media and Sport Select Committee that local newspapers would have to be 'truly digital', with content 'harvested and published without human interface'. This would mean further job cuts. 'Much of our human interface,' he said, using a euphemism that revealed much more than he intended, 'will have disappeared.'

The internet changed the entire pace of journalism, at both national and local level. With fewer staff and less money, editors were forced to ask those who remained to cover more and more stories. This cut away their chief investigative attribute – time.

The effects were already noticeable in 2006, when the journalist Nick Davies undertook a study with researchers from Cardiff University looking at news stories from *The Times*, the *Guardian*, the *Telegraph*, the *Independent* and the *Daily Mail* between 1985 and 2005. They found that the average journalist was filling up three times as much space in 2005 than they had in 1985. They had, typically speaking, a third of the time to do their job. It escalated from there. The old practice of being able to focus on one story over the course of the day – with the various meetings, phone calls, investigations and press conferences that would entail – faded away. It was replaced by the frenzied demands for content online.

'I contrast my first days in the lobby with how it is now and it's a massive change,' Waugh says. 'Hacks that are new to the lobby, they're podcasting, tweeting, live blogging, writing for the web within fifteen minutes of a story breaking, coming up with long reads, TV appearances, plus checking and accuracy – you name it. There's massive demand on individual reporters. You are so time poor.'

The same applies on broadcast news, which has changed pace to keep up with people's changing consumption habits. 'If you're at the Beeb,' a senior BBC journalist says, 'it's multiple track with multiple different deadlines. We're many years from when print filed once a day and we filed three times – morning, teatime and evening. There's now one continual cycle.'

The internet provided detailed information about advertising performance, which proved financially catastrophic for newspapers. But it also did the same for editorial, with similarly catastrophic potential consequences for their decision-making if the data was not used wisely. 'Now we know exactly what's read,' Rusbridger says, 'how long it is read for, when people stopped reading, whether they stopped reading at the fourth paragraph.'

In a desperate bid to stay afloat, some editors made the basic metric of page views the sole criterion of editorial success. 'One of the broadsheets used to have a screen in the middle of the room, literally showing you the most read stories,' Pickard says. 'There was a period where something like "Woman With Five Nipples" would be beating some Brexit story. And so, inevitably, some editors end up wanting more of the nipple stories and less and less of the stories about the Northern Ireland Protocol. As soon as you start doing that kind of thing, you end up with clickbait.'

The tyranny of metrics pushed journalism towards what interested the public and away from the public interest.

The newspaper editor Harry Evans, who helped cement the reputation of the Insight team of investigative reporters at the *Sunday Times* in the late 1960s, was fond of telling colleagues that newspapers were only on the verge of securing real change when they had begun to bore readers. He'd picked this up during a long crusade at his first newspaper, the *Darlington Northern Echo*, fighting to clear the reputation of Timothy Evans, who was wrongly convicted and hanged for murder. The coverage helped spur the movement against capital punishment.

Rusbridger learned the lesson well. 'If your whole news organisation is terrified of boring readers, then you'll never get Watergate,' he says. 'Watergate took two years to report. And if you go back and read it, a lot of it was a single column on page five, which just added a tiny little bit of incremental information. Flush out the context. Get it on the record.'

Instead of patience, the dominance of metrics pushed in precisely the opposite direction. One of the core triggers that reliably provides page views is outrage. In political journalism, there is arguably no stronger motivating factor in reader behaviour. And the same applies to social media, where vitriol, condemnation and vociferous expressions of emotional disapproval typically result in a strong response from fellow users. News desks soon found that these expressions of online outrage could be fed into the editorial machine, being cheaply repackaged as stories that attracted huge numbers of page views with barely any editorial time needed to write them.

'It speeded up the cycle for everybody,' a senior figure at the BBC says. 'Nadine Dorries says something relatively punchy in a tweet. The Guido Fawkes website writes it up. The *Guardian* writes that. It goes into Mail Online. Someone replies to that and then, before you know it, you have a story. It took five minutes to write, gets the clicks and takes up half a page in the paper. Everyone knows it's a load of old bollocks, but it's almost free and people click on it.'

As the internet was detonating its financial model, political journalism was facing another seismic change in how it operated – the development of the spad system.

Under Blair and Campbell, the Government Information Service, which oversaw departmental press offices, was subject to a sustained attack. 'I had the first formal heads of information meeting,' Campbell wrote in his diary within days of the 1997 victory. 'There was definitely a culture gap. I said things I thought were blindingly obvious e.g. about planning of events coming up and they didn't seem to get it. What was clear was that the department press heads had very little clout within departments. They were a pretty dull and uninspiring lot.'

Existing communication officials were told to step up their performance or go. Many chose the latter option, especially in the upper management tiers which were almost completely defenestrated. Departmental press offices went into terminal decline. The days when a reporter could call up a press officer and have an informed conversation about a policy were gone. Instead, reporters were asked to send in their questions by email so that answers could be approved by a media spad. It functioned less as an exchange and more as an early-warning system for stories.

The idea of a civil servant who is informed about a policy and able to have an independent conversation on it is now almost laughable. Journalists barely bother to call up departmental press offices at all, except sometimes to tell them what they are about to put in a story so they can send a response. 'It's frustrating,' Beattie says. 'A really good press officer who knew their subject backwards was in a really good position to limit the damage. They can steer you away from problematic areas, they can soften it. But more and more now, they refuse to engage at all.'

The role of formal civil service communication was supplanted by media spads. Of the two spads secretaries of state were expected to have, one focused on policy and the other on media relations. Gradually a more informal system developed of background briefings of journalists by these political advisers. To most journalists, it was considered perfectly acceptable. The spads were a rich source of stories. 'The thing is with spads,' Sabbagh says, 'even though they're in their twenties or early thirties, they can bypass the whole Whitehall system.'

The media spads did to journalism what the policy spads had done to the civil service, in both positive and negative ways.

Sometimes they were useful. They provided an information conduit. The ministers would be too busy to talk to journalists all day, just as they were too busy to talk to civil servants all day. So as long as the spad knew their boss's mind, they would be able to facilitate communication, messaging reporters on their views on a topic, or when an announcement might be forthcoming.

But as with policy spads, many media spads started to form a cocoon around the ministers, preventing journalists from securing access. Veteran correspondents such as Travis, who'd grown used to weekly in-depth conversations with home secretaries like Michael Howard, now found the door closing in their face, even when reporting on a government that was ostensibly more politically sympathetic. 'John Reid had a complete hooligan of a spad who just put the phone down and refused to deal with me,' he says. 'Alan Johnson had a spad who hated the *Guardian* – said he hated Trots and liberals. Very hard to deal with. Chris Grayling actually banned *Guardian* journalists from visiting prisons.'

As the years wore on, the power of the spads grew. Instead of communication taking place on the phone with an official, it took place on WhatsApp with a political adviser. 'Literally your whole job was to get the WhatsApp numbers of spads,' Rusbridger says of lobby journalists. 'You're entirely dependent on 27-year-olds – if you could get their numbers, if you can get them to reply. If you're lucky, they respond with a one-line answer. The whole thing is unattributable, unaccountable and deniable. And it's done on a favour-for-favour basis to the ones they trust. The lobby journalists will tell you that they're really tough, they're holding these guys to account. But the danger is that it can become a form of client journalism.'

That then raised the question of what happened if a journalist did something the spad did not like. What would happen if they wrote or tweeted unfavourably, or covered a story in a hostile manner? The answer, in many cases, was that they would be frozen out.

'Go back to Dom Cummings and the Barnard Castle affair,' Pickard says, referring to a story in which Boris Johnson's chief adviser was caught breaking COVID regulations. 'If you look at the Twitter feeds of certain prominent political journalists, they were silent for five days during that period. There are definitely political journalists who aren't going to rock the boat too much, because they rely on their sources for their stories, and those sources are deep in the heart of government. Does that mean that they're writing propaganda? No. But are they going to gun for someone who's handing out stories regularly to them? Also no.'

Unlike press officers, spads were not responsible for explaining policy. They were tasked with improving the standing of the political party in general and their minister in particular. Their dominance exacerbated the pre-existing lobby tendency towards personality and court intrigue over the detailed assessment of government proposals. That took place against a declining financial backdrop in which journalists were under enormous strain to churn out multiple stories a day. It created a pincer movement, where they were more reliant on the information being given to them by party political operatives, without the time or resources to verify it.

'You have to bring your own scepticism to things or that's your journalistic integrity gone,' Sabbagh says. 'But at the end of the day, you need to give the news desk something. There's a bias to writing things. Let's say No. 10 gave you nothing and a spad gave you a tiny bit. I would be thinking "I'm fucked" but you have to thread something together based on what little you have.'

The combination of technological and constitutional change had served to amplify journalism's weaknesses and quieten its strengths. And as the financial pressures continue and the spad system grows, there is little sign of it resisting.

In the next chapter, we'll return to the Commons, to see how things operate now that MPs have got settled in. But first, we'll take a short interlude and look at a case study of British incompetence that brings together the various failings we've encountered so far.

Interlude: Evacuation

On 15 August 2021, Kabul fell to the Taliban. What came next was a disaster for the people of Afghanistan. It was a return to fascistic theological government, which would systematically abuse human rights, oppress women and drive the country into starvation. But it also demonstrated something else. It was an object lesson in the deterioration of British governance. For 11 days, in the heat of the summer, the full dysfunction of the state was laid bare.

It provides a grim case study of the numerous dysfunctions we have seen so far in this book: from prime ministers, secretaries of state, civil servants and journalists. It was about a failure of expertise, particularly in country-specific intelligence and project management. It was about the state's responsibility to the people who sustain it and the things that happen when it no longer takes that task with the seriousness it deserves. And ultimately it was about blood, spilled on starched earth, and the final redundant pleas of those who still believed that Britain was better than it was.

The preparation to evacuate people from Afghanistan should have begun in February 2020. That was when US President Donald Trump announced his decision to withdraw troops from the country. Failing that, it should have started in April 2021, when the US's intention was confirmed by Trump's successor, President Joe Biden. No meaningful preparation took place on either occasion.

At this stage, there were two central facts that should have been guiding the behaviour of the British government. The first was that countless Afghans had helped the UK over the two decades it had operated in the country. And the second was that they were vulnerable to reprisal killings by the Taliban when they took over. Neither of these facts was given serious attention.

British intelligence failed to predict the speed of the Taliban advance. It simply did not have the resources or the know-how to assess the situation on the ground. This was due to failed promotional arrangements, failed assessment systems and failed cultural priorities.

Other countries were not taken by surprise. The French government began evacuating its local Afghan staff, including cooks, drivers and cleaners, on 10 May 2021. It repeatedly told its citizens to leave. It aimed to have only French staff remaining by July, a project it accomplished successfully. Some 623 people were flown to France in the weeks before the takeover. The final evacuation for non-essential staff took place on 17 July, four weeks before the fall of Kabul.

On 8 July, nearly a month after France started evacuations, Boris Johnson told the House of Commons that there was 'no military path to victory for the Taliban'. By 14 July, the Taliban had seized all the major border crossings into Tajikistan, Iran and Pakistan. By 21 July, they had control of half the country. The British intelligence assessment finally changed on 22 July. 'Peace talks have stalled,' the Foreign Office's principal risk report read, 'and US NATO withdrawal is resulting in rapid Taliban advances. This could lead to fall of cities, collapse of security forces, Taliban return to power, mass displacement and significant humanitarian need. The embassy may need to close if security deteriorates.' But the

British travel advice for those going to Afghanistan did not change until 6 August.

The foreign secretary at the time was Dominic Raab. He was a former solicitor with no expertise in foreign affairs or any meaningful accomplishments either in his constituency or his ministerial career. His time as Brexit secretary was principally remembered for his admission that he 'hadn't quite understood the full extent' of how much UK trade relied on the Dover–Calais crossing. But he had endorsed Johnson in the Conservative leadership election in 2019 and was duly rewarded with one of the great offices of state.

His only direct engagement about Afghanistan with one of the country's neighbours in the eight months before the takeover was a single phone call with Pakistan's foreign minister in April. In the six weeks before the takeover, he engaged in only one international meeting, with the head of the United States Agency for International Development (USAID). As the situation deteriorated in the first half of August, he held just two one-to-one conversations with the British ambassador in Kabul. When Kabul eventually fell, he was on holiday. So was the prime minister, the minister with responsibility for Afghanistan, and the permanent secretaries at the Ministry of Defence, the Home Office and the Foreign Office.

There were three sets of people the government needed to evacuate from Afghanistan: UK nationals, Afghans who worked directly for the UK government, and Afghans who had supported UK objectives – such as journalists, judges and women's rights activists.

The second group was dealt with by a Ministry of Defence programme called Afghan Relocations and Assistance Policy (ARAP). It was deeply flawed, failed in its central mission and ultimately buckled under the demand. But it was at least set up in advance of the fall of Kabul. The policy was approved in December 2020 and the programme was opened in April 2021.

There were no plans whatsoever for how to evacuate those in the third category. It was only after intense lobbying from MPs that the Foreign Office even undertook to establish the scheme, initially by trying to widen the criteria for ARAP and then by creating a separate category of so-called 'special cases'. The design of the category was eventually submitted to the foreign secretary on 19 and 21 August, four days after the fall of Kabul and five days before the end of the evacuation programme.

We would have no clear idea of what happened next were it not for two whistle-blowers in the civil service who worked in the Foreign Office's Special Cases team. One was Raphael Marshall, a higher executive officer. The other was Josie Stewart, a Grade 6. 'My actions are likely to result in my dismissal from the Foreign Office,' Stewart said. 'I loved my job. I loved working with my regular team and department. I cannot, however, accept the lack of accountability that I have seen for failures in the civil service system.'

What they described was one of the most comprehensive moral and operational failures in the history of the civil service.

British allies in Afghanistan were encouraged to send an email to a Special Cases inbox so that their claim could be processed and they could secure a place in the evacuation. The emails had titles like: 'Save my children'. Many were never even read. At any given moment between 21 and 25 August, there were over 5,000 unread emails in the inbox.

On the afternoon of the 21st, Marshall was tasked with monitoring the inbox. At this stage, he was the only person being asked to do so. When he looked at the screen, he realised that no emails had been opened for the last 24 hours. There were at this point two other people on the Special Cases team, but both were primarily dealing with other tasks. One of them was not even on shift, but had decided to stay. Marshall himself was not rostered, but opted to work out of moral obligation. Had he not done so, there would have been no one monitoring the emails at all. The thousands of people sending last-minute desperate pleas for help would have been doing so to an empty office cubicle.

On 22 and 23 August, no night shifts were allocated. The inbox sat with no one monitoring it. Because Afghanistan is 3.5 hours ahead of the UK, the period in which no one was reading the emails would have stretched until after noon local time. On the 22nd, three days before the end of evacuation, things marginally improved when six Foreign Office staff working in the Department of International Development were drafted in to help. But they could not offer much assistance, because a lack of integration in the two departments' IT systems meant they were unable to share documents or access the inbox.

Stewart arrived the next day. She had been trying to join for a week, but had been ignored. 'I first volunteered to work on the crisis on 16 August,' she said. 'I repeated my offer at least once daily, both proactively and in direct response to daily requests for more volunteers, until 23 August when I decided to just turn up, at which point I was warmly welcomed by an under-resourced team.'

There was no induction process for new staff, nor any introduction to what they were doing. There was no clear tasking, or system for recording decisions, or arrangements for handover between shifts. Every single member of this team was new to the Afghan crisis. 'I believe no member of the Afghan Special Cases team had studied Afghanistan, worked on Afghanistan previously, or had a detailed knowledge of Afghanistan,' Marshall said. 'My own knowledge of Afghanistan is largely limited to reading Rory Stewart's book.' Nevertheless, despite having only worked on the team for one day, he was considered an expert in the process and was asked to integrate the Department of International Development team and instruct them in the criteria for eligibility.

'On the night of Saturday 21st,' Marshall said, 'I individually briefed the two people who came on shift to prioritise the emails. One was clearly scared by being asked to make hundreds of life-and-death decisions about which they knew nothing. They initially essentially declined to do the task. I persuaded them that unless they accepted the task, the emails would not be read at all, which would be worse.' He assessed that one was either an administrative officer or an executive officer – both well below a Grade 7. The other was a second-year fast-streamer.

Those with outside expertise who offered to help the Foreign Office were ignored. A volunteer group that had been assisting with Afghan evacuations told MPs: 'Of all of the Western governments we and others worked with, the sheer lack of communication with friendly volunteers and organisations was seen as a startling contrast to the approach of other Western governments. The Danish government, the German government, the French government and the Canadian government showed more responsiveness to external support, more coordination of the process of extracting vulnerable Afghans, and more practical responses to fast-changing conditions.'

The civil service team were being asked to prioritise requests with no background understanding of the politics of Afghanistan or the complex web of identities that constitutes its society.

The principal ethnic groups in Afghanistan are the Tajiks, the Pashtuns, the Hazara and the Uzbeks. The Taliban core is composed of Pashtuns. The risk of genocide under their rule was particularly pronounced for the Hazara population, who had experienced targeted attacks and the destruction of their religious and cultural property. But far from being able to make detailed assessments about ethnic identity, the team leader on the Special Cases team did not even know what the correct term was for people from Afghanistan. They referred to them repeatedly as 'Afghanis'. 'Although I am sure they meant well,' Marshall said, 'in my opinion this indicates they did not have sufficient expertise.'

There was no access to additional information about the individuals or organisations being discussed except for that available on Google. There was no ability to process applications in any language other than English. There were no Foreign Office research analysts available to provide expert advice.

The Special Cases model required the team to judge who was eligible for evacuation using three criteria: their vulnerability, their support for UK objectives in Afghanistan, and 'significance/sensitivity'. The first two criteria matched almost every email received in the inbox, so were of no use in prioritising them. The third was never defined and was considered by those working on the evacuation to be functionally meaningless.

At this point, the MP constituency function kicked in. MPs started getting calls from Afghan families in their community, their supporters and people they had known in the country. So they did what MPs do when it comes to constituency work. They got involved. 'We were all desperately trying to help people we knew,' Stewart said. 'Doubtless I would have done the same, had I been in a position of political influence. But the cost and implications of this should not be overlooked.'

The pressure from MPs meant that the scant resources of the Special Cases team lost any remaining commitment to the idea of prioritisation on the basis of need. Instead, cases were prioritised on the basis of whether an MP was interested or not. 'The very significant pressure and lobbying by MPs on behalf of particular individuals and cohorts,' Stewart reported, 'meant that most of the focus of the Special Cases team was on tracking down correspondence or data on individuals with connections, when it could otherwise have been spent identifying and ensuring we helped the most vulnerable people.'

At one point, the team leader told the staff that the meaning of 'significance/sensitivity' was literally that an MP had lobbied on the individual's behalf. This became, for a time, the only basis upon which emails were processed. As the days wore on, the team was told to focus solely on opening emails from MPs about cases they had taken up, rather than exercise any independent assessment about need.

Raab then made a public commitment. He told MPs that the Foreign Office would reply to all MPs who wrote in about an Afghanistan case. Suddenly the mailbox teams were bolstered with additional staff. However, they were there not to assess the emails that were coming in, but to focus solely on identifying and opening emails from MPs. 'This was purely in order to enable the foreign secretary to say that all emails from MPs had been read, and to issue a generic response,' Stewart said. 'I do not believe that anything was actually done with any of the information in these emails at that time. The only urgent requirement was to manage the political fallout and to appear to MPs as if something was being done.'

Those emails that were read and considered eligible, according to the vacuous criteria given to the officials, were entered into a spreadsheet alongside a short summary of the case. There was no guidance on what was required in this summary, so they varied massively. In some cases, the whole email was copied out. In others, only a short sentence was provided. With no expertise, the officials were unable to make judgements on the contents of the emails, for instance between how likely a group was to face reprisals.

These summaries became the guide for whether applications made it onto ever-diminishing shortlists. They were hastily written, with no contributory expertise, on the basis of no guidance, according to meaningless criteria, by a handful of understaffed and overworked junior officials. And on this basis decisions of life or death were made.

Throughout this process, officials were denied a clear line of command from ministers.

Lord Ahmad was a former vice chair of the Conservative party who'd been given a life peerage in 2011 and then an ever-growing series of ministerial responsibilities at the Foreign Office. By the time of the Afghan evacuation, he was responsible for the United Nations, the Commonwealth, preventing sexual violence in conflict, and South and Central Asia. Afghanistan therefore fell under his remit. His brief was far too broad and vague to have brought any specialist knowledge to the process, but to his credit, officials reported that he was highly engaged with the evacuation process. That alone did not improve matters, however, because he had not been given the authority to make decisions. The one minister who tried to understand the problems with the Special Cases system was denied the ability to do anything about them. Instead, all decisions flowed to Raab, who, for long stretches of the evacuation, seemed to disappear altogether, creating a decision-making bottleneck.

At this point, conditions around Kabul airport had descended into total chaos. The UK-controlled entrance, at the Baron Hotel, was surrounded by a crowd of 25,000 people trying to enter. Several were crushed to death. Those who were authorised for evacuation had to first get past the Taliban, who were beating people with sticks to stop them approaching the airport, and then fight their way through the crowd. Successful evacuations involved sending small teams of soldiers out to grab people and then bring them back safely to the waiting plane.

In total, this process was estimated to take twelve hours or more. As the clock ticked down to the end of the evacuation, time was therefore of the essence. Every second of delay cost lives. Every second meant more people would be left behind, at the Taliban's mercy.

The team working on evacuations adopted a system of last resort. They started to submit exceptional cases to the foreign secretary for approval in a desperate bid to get them out.

Raab then made a choice that would have a profound impact on the people awaiting evacuation. He could have permitted the Crisis Centre to make the authorisations on his behalf, without his involvement. But he did not do that. He reserved the decision for himself. And then he failed to make it. For several hours, as the evacuation window closed, the foreign secretary did not engage with or respond to any of the notes sent to him.

The team sent over the names of people who needed urgent evacuation. There was silence. Then, after a long delay, Raab's Private Office said that they would not look at individual cases and needed them in one 'well-presented' list.

In those last hours, with lives held in the balance, the clock ticking down, and British soldiers being forced to make life-threatening trips into the crowds, the evacuation team was reduced to reformatting an internal document so that it met the presentational specifications of the foreign secretary.

On 25 August, the day before the end of the evacuation, Lord Ahmad himself intervened to secure the evacuation of a senior Afghan soldier, his adult children and his young grandchildren. The soldier had been authorised but his children had not. He refused to leave without them, knowing that if he did, they would be murdered by the Taliban. He told the Foreign Office he would rather stay and die with his family. The Crisis Centre tried desperately to submit his family as an exceptional case to Raab's office. 'The foreign secretary did not respond for several hours,' Marshall said. 'I believe this family did not succeed in entering the airport.'

Finally, at the very end of the process, there was a sudden effort to secure evacuations. But it was not for humans. It was for dogs.

It concerned an Afghan animal charity called Nowzad, which was run by a man called Pen Farthing. On the basis of the Special Cases criteria, there was no justification for evacuating the team or its animals. The Taliban were not a threat to cats and dogs. The charity was not vulnerable. It had not assisted British aims in Afghanistan. And it had no 'significance/sensitivity', under any objective understanding of the term. The Ministry of Defence and the Foreign Office concluded that there was no risk to the staff. An internal Foreign Office investigation determined the group was not eligible.

But Nowzad had one thing other evacuees did not. It had a media campaign.

The press had struggled with Afghanistan for years. It was a military and diplomatic engagement that had gone stale, carrying on month after month, decade after decade and involving a complex interplay of ethnic, economic, religious and political elements. It did not break down easily into good guys and bad guys. The coalition-backed government was far superior to the Taliban and it broadly respected women's rights, but it was also deeply corrupt. For years, the internet traffic to stories about Afghanistan was low to non-existent.

Coverage, on the other hand, was extremely expensive. Sending someone there would involve flights, security and interpreters. They would need to be there for a long time, understanding the social and ethnic dynamics, before they had anything useful to report. It simply didn't add up financially. A quick-turnaround story about the latest outrage on Twitter would get many times the volume of traffic and cost almost nothing to produce.

The withdrawal from Afghanistan did command media coverage throughout the 11 days. But it was akin to the coverage of a natural disaster: a great swell of human misery without a clear sense of focus.

Farthing provided the focus that was missing, offering a tangible narrative that could be understood by anyone. It was almost too perfect. In a sea of brown faces, he was white. Not only that, he was British, a former Royal Marine commando, and he was protecting dogs and cats in a war zone. It was as if a Hollywood scriptwriter had come on board. Farthing became the human face of the disaster, appearing on Sky News and the BBC almost daily and featuring in newspapers at the same rate, under increasingly desperate headlines demanding something be done for him. Celebrities like Ricky Gervais swung in to encourage their fans to back his campaign, drumming up support on social media.

Farthing was adept at utilising this media focus. On 23 August, he called Peter Quentin, the defence secretary's spad, to demand he secure his evacuation. 'Get me out of Afghanistan with my staff and my animals,' he said. 'I served for twenty-two years in the Royal Marine commandos. I am not taking this bollocks from people like you who are blocking me. You've got until tomorrow morning. I'm on Sky News around about 7.45 and your name will be the only name people are talking about.'

Later that day, the Special Cases team received a ministerial request from Wendy Morton, the minister for Europe, to evacuate the group. Marshall initially thought it sounded reasonable and asked a member of staff from Permanent Joint Headquarters, the nerve centre for overseas military operations, about it. The charity said it could supply its own plane, so it wouldn't be taking up any capacity that could have been used for refugees.

The headquarters official was unimpressed. The problem wasn't the planes. The government could charter as many planes as it liked. The problem was the operational capacity. The relevant constraint was the limited number of soldiers they had at the airport to get eligible people past the crowds, and the time they had to focus on each case. Every minute they spent on one would mean that someone else in the endless inbox of unread emails was being left to their fate. There was no reason to think the Taliban would target animal charities, so why spend that time and capacity somewhere it was not needed rather than on all the desperate cases where it was? The Special Cases team passed that message on to Morton's Private Office.

But then, in the early hours of the 25th, it was overruled. The defence secretary sent out a tweet saying that Nowzad had been cleared for evacuation. With a click of a button, he overrode the entire Foreign Office prioritisation process.

A spasm of confusion followed. Officials at the Foreign Office sought rapid confirmation from the national security adviser, Stephen Lovegrove, who agreed to seek 'clear guidance from No. 10'. At this stage, the prime minister almost certainly authorised the Nowzad evacuation. Downing Street has denied this, and several ministers have gone out of their way to pretend otherwise, but there is no other possible explanation for what followed, because shortly afterwards, Lovegrove called the Foreign Office and confirmed that the Nowzad group should be called forward.

'It was widespread knowledge in the Foreign Office Crisis Centre that the decision on Nowzad's Afghan staff came from the prime minister,' Stewart said. 'I saw messages to this effect on Microsoft Teams, I heard it discussed in the Crisis Centre, including by senior civil servants, and I was copied on numerous emails which clearly suggested this and which no one challenged.'

In the months that followed, there would be a purposeful cover-up of that decision-making process. 'We asked the Foreign Office for an explanation of the Nowzad case on many occasions,' the Foreign Affairs Committee said. 'We repeatedly received answers that appeared calculated to mislead or to evade our questions and that were contradicted when new facts came into the public domain.' The committee's conclusion was simple. 'Multiple senior officials believed that the prime minister played a role in this decision. We have yet to be offered a plausible alternative explanation for how it came about.'

On 28 August, Farthing was evacuated from Afghanistan on a private aircraft. Soldiers were sent out to retrieve him from the crowd. US troops helped load animals onto the plane. Permissions for the charter were sought and supported by the Ministry of Defence. UK air staff in NATO's Combined Air Operations Centres facilitated the landing slot.

'Permanent Joint Headquarters was organising the largest European evacuation of Kabul,' said Admiral Ben Key, who was overseeing the general evacuation. 'We were in command of the only carrier strike group at sea in the Western Pacific Ocean on that day. We were also overseeing the battle group that was operating in very difficult conditions in Mali. The majority of my time on that day had been dominated by managing the narrative and outcomes of Nowzad.'

There were 230 empty seats on the plane, but none of them were occupied by refugees. Instead, Farthing brought around 200 cats and dogs with him, which were put in the hold.

'My colleagues and I eliminated thousands of Afghan friends of the UK at risk of murder from the evacuation lists,' Marshall said. 'We were instructed to do this due to lack of capacity to process people at the airport. On Wednesday 25 August, many people referred by secretaries of state were rejected due to limited capacity. This capacity was subsequently used to transport animals.'

Once the evacuation was over, the government promised to get as many people as it could out of Afghanistan through other means. On 15 September, Raab said: 'Since the completion of the evacuation phase, the Foreign Office has been urgently working through the correspondence.'

This was false. 'The claim is not accurate,' Stewart said. 'There was no urgency whatsoever accorded to doing anything actually meaningful with any of the emails at this stage.'

We don't know how many British allies were murdered by the Taliban after the withdrawal. Somewhere between 75,000 and 150,000 people applied for the Special Cases scheme, the vast majority fearing for their lives and those of their families as a result of their connection to the UK. Fewer than 5 per cent received any assistance, comprising a total of 483 people.

Two months later, the Foreign Affairs Committee held an evidence session with Shaharzad Akbar, chair of the Afghanistan Independent Human Rights Commission. 'Targeted killings are happening,' she said. 'Most of my colleagues are in hiding, but, to the extent that they could document it, over a hundred people were killed in targeted killings in forty days of Taliban rule. The number of cases is probably much more than that. They were detained illegally and then killed by people affiliated with the Taliban.'

No lessons were learned from what happened during those few days in 2021. The Foreign Office has not admitted any shortcomings. When the foreign secretary was asked what the department could have done better, he was unable to name a single thing, except for regretting the fact that he had not returned from holiday sooner.

Even if he had had eyes to see it, it would have been too large for him to do so. It is not about the failure of a particular project. It is systematic and existential. It is about a ministerial class that is not selected on the basis of competence or expertise and is therefore unable to do the job asked of it when it really matters. It is about a civil service that has no specialist capacity, either in subject areas or operations. It is about a media that has become infantilised into promoting human interest stories over structural analysis. And it is about a national leadership that responds more diligently to that pressure than it does to genuine social need.

In short, it is about whether this is a serious country or not. And on those late summer days of 2021, as thousands crammed in around the airport in Kabul and Britain's allies were left at the mercy of the Taliban, there was only one possible answer to that question.

CHAPTER 8

The Commons

The first thing you notice about the Commons is the noise.

It's hard to capture on TV – the microphones in the Chamber are pointed directly at the person speaking, so the background shouting sounds far quieter than it is in real life. Even if you attend in person, the bulletproof glass shield in front of the public gallery prevents the full scale of the sound from penetrating.

Inside the Chamber, it is deafening, particularly during set-piece events like PMQs. The Commons is the debating chamber for 650 elected MPs. They sit on all sides, shouting encouragement or abuse. Someone speaking from the front bench will be presented with rows of opponents, stretching from left to right and rising up to the back benches, creating a wall of human disdain. It is a bear pit. And unless you have a firm core of inner resilience, it is hard to maintain your composure and press ahead with your speech in the face of it.

This is what the prime minister is presented with when they try to speak. Even if they can get past the Treasury, the civil servants and the media, they must still reckon with one of the most raucous and chaotic legislatures on the face of the earth.

At its strongest, the bear pit can destroy prime ministers and end governments. On 7 May 1940, in the opening stages of the Second World War, prime minister Neville

Chamberlain's critics turned a Commons debate into a howl of despair against early Allied failures. Conservative MP Leo Amery ended his speech by echoing Oliver Cromwell's words when he dissolved the Long Parliament in 1653: 'You have sat here too long for any good you are doing. Depart, I say, and let us have done with you. In the name of God, go!' Chamberlain submitted his resignation to the king three days later.

There are plenty of other examples in the modern period that, while not as historically decisive, altered the political dynamic, be it Geoffrey Howe's resignation speech against Thatcher, or Robin Cook's resignation speech against Blair. 'The extraordinary thing is that the Commons Chamber can be absurd and very superficial, or it can be an enthralling theatre,' former Labour leader Neil Kinnock says. 'When it's absurd and superficial, it's a bloody nuisance and no help with democracy at all. When it's enthralling theatre, it can ultimately bring down the government, because of authentic, fluent, deadly passion on a major issue. There are occasions where enthralling theatre really does shift the terrain.'

But this theatre conceals an embarrassing secret. Behind all the shouting and the showmanship, the Commons is an empty shell. It doesn't really stand up to government at all. It cannot. It has all the trappings of democracy but none of the mechanisms required to make it real. 'As a legislative assembly,' political scientists Anthony King and Ivor Crewe wrote, 'the Parliament of the United Kingdom is, much of the time, either peripheral or totally irrelevant. It might as well not exist.'

The chief reason for this is the government majority, handed to it by the first-past-the-post electoral system. With that in place, a government can do whatever it likes. Barring backbench rebellions, it can pass any law it wishes. Most of the time, it doesn't even have to think about Parliament's response. It's simply not pertinent. 'It's remarkable, thinking back on it, how little I was encouraged to think about Parliament,' former deputy prime minister Nick Clegg says of his time in Downing Street. 'Of course, there were crucial moments, like the Syria vote, or dare I say it the tuition fees vote. But on the whole, it's actually remarkable how little time I really spent worrying about getting stuff through.'

The noise of the Commons might be deafening, but it has a hollow ring to it. MPs can blast out indignation. They can launch forensic logician assaults on government legislation. They can mock and they can castigate. But none of it matters. Once the noise subsides, there will be a vote. And the government will win that vote, no matter what was said beforehand.

If it stopped at that fact, it would be bad enough. But the problems with the Commons run far deeper than that. Governments through the ages have not sat back and enjoyed their majority. They have gone much further, taking full control of almost every aspect of the House's operations and then finally moving to sideline it altogether.

The chief way the government asserts its dominance is through the control of time.

Over the course of a century, from 1811 to 1911, the executive achieved functional dominion over the legislature through the use of standing orders. These are the rules of the House we looked at in chapter 2, which have been passed by the Commons to govern its affairs. To a certain extent, change was necessary. The pre-Victorian Parliament was a place of chaos. It was politically, procedurally and legislatively incoherent. The various rules of the Commons in operation at the time were decided on the basis of ad hoc motions, meaning you couldn't consult them in advance or get any sort of handle on how things would be done. Eighteen debatable motions were required just to get through the stages of a bill, and that was before you reached amendments or clauses. You just couldn't use the system to make law.

But the changes that were ultimately put in place were far more draconian than whatever was required to fix the problem. They wiped out the Commons as a viable legislative chamber.

In 1811, a distinction was made between 'orders of the day' and 'notices of motions' – the first referred to government business, the rest to everything else. Gradually government business was given more and more time. It grew remorselessly, like a blob, eating up ever-increasing amounts of the Commons schedule. Then, on 11 April 1902, any lingering pretence was removed. The kill shot came in the form of something called Standing Order No. 14.

This is arguably the most important of all the rules in the British Parliament. And it makes that claim on the basis of one devastating implication: it ended the operation of the Commons as an independent body. Under its provision, government business took precedence at every sitting. The government had taken complete control of the Commons Chamber – it decided what could be discussed, when and in what order. It decided when bills were debated and at what point that debate would be terminated. This standing order is still in place today. And it continues to suffocate the life from the legislature.

Standing Order No. 14 contains a few minor exceptions. Thirteen Fridays in a parliamentary session – the phrase used for a parliamentary year – are given over for private members' bills. This allows individual MPs to put forward proposed legislation, but it's of little consequence, because none of them have a chance of turning into law unless the government gets behind them.

There are also 20 days a session given over to opposition parties to hold debates, the last vestigial remnant of the huge amounts of time available in the nineteenth century for debating and authorising public expenditure. During that day, they can debate what they like. But they can't decide when to hold the debates – that's up to the government. And the votes they hold have no legislative impact. Finally, there is a limited allowance for backbench business – a chronically misunderstood provision we'll come to in a moment.

The basic reality is ultimately the same today as it was in 1902. The government has control of time. And this control allows it to restrict the extent and the type of scrutiny legislation is subject to. Many congresses or parliaments have a business committee or bureau that decides what business to propose. It then sets a draft agenda, which is voted on by its members. They are independent bodies, which make their own decisions about what they want to do. But in Britain, the system is entirely different. The Commons is told what it is going to do and for how long it is going to do it, every Thursday at 10.30 a.m. by the leader of the House.

That job title is very revealing in and of itself. They are not, in reality, the House's leader in its relationship with the government. They are the government's leader in its relationship with the House.

The moment at which the government unveils upcoming Commons debates and the introduction of future legislation is called Business Questions. The leader of the House opens the event by outlining the timetable for the next two weeks. The first week is usually described in detail and the second week in a rough outline. MPs cannot amend the timetable and they cannot vote on it. The one thing they can do is comment on it, but even this they rarely do. They typically just raise a series of unrelated matters.

Ministers, on the other hand, can amend the timetable as much as they like. The agenda is not definitive or exhaustive. They can add whatever they want to it, whenever they want, whether or not it featured at Business Questions. The only restraint is that they issue an additional business statement if there's a substantial change to the timetable, and even this is a courtesy.

The sole moment of participation in the business agenda from anyone outside of government is through informal talks with the official opposition in something called 'the usual channels'. This, as its name suggests, is an incredibly opaque and mysterious institution. We'll come to it later and it won't make a pretty picture.

Most of the time, MPs seem barely aware that things could work in any other way. They don't rail against the headlock they've been put in. It's been this way so long, most of them hardly notice it, or if they do, they actually celebrate it as the British tradition of strong government. As the reforming MP Tony Wright said, they 'have been willing accomplices in their own subjugation'.

But during the last half-century, three crucial events have taken place that shifted power back to Parliament in small but important ways. They were the emergence of the select committee system, the Wright reforms, and the changes introduced by Speaker John Bercow. None of them were revolutionary. None of them fundamentally altered the power dynamic in Westminster. But they represented a concerted effort to turn back the tide of government control.

*

Select committees have existed, in some form or other, since the sixteenth century. In 1571, for instance, there was a Committee on Examination of Fees and Rewards taken for Voices. In 1652, there was the magnificently named Grand Committee for Evils. These early committees were ad hoc and intended to solve a given problem, basically like a judicial inquiry today. By the late nineteenth and early twentieth centuries, committees had become highly partisan and almost completely ineffective.

But then in 1979, everything changed. The date was not a coincidence. We repeatedly see the same pattern. Generally speaking, the best shot at constitutional reform comes in the first two or three years of a new government, when the politicians who said all sorts of idealistic things in opposition suddenly find they need to act on them. After that point, the momentum is usually lost.

In 1979, the man the moment fell to was a liberal Catholic and moderate Conservative called Norman St John-Stevas. He didn't survive the Thatcher regime for very long. She saw the world in black and white, he concluded, but 'the universe I inhabit is made up of many shades of grey'. He had the questionable honour of being the very first moderate Conservative, known as 'wets', she dismissed from Cabinet, in January 1981. But in the year and a half he had available to him as leader of the Commons, he did something remarkable. He created the modern select committee system.

Soon enough, Thatcher would realise the mistake she had made, but at the time she had other things on her mind. Stevas, however, knew exactly what he was doing. 'The principal reason why I was so keen, along with many other members of Parliament, to introduce the comprehensive system of select committees,' he said, 'was in order to seek to redress the balance between the House of Commons and the executive.'

Select committees are now a fixed part of the Westminster system. They are standing entities. They stay in place month after month, year after year, only re-forming after an election. Since 2010, the chairs have been elected by the Commons and members are elected through an internal process within the parties, in proportion to membership of the Commons Chamber. The job of the committees is to investigate a subject area, launch inquiries into particular aspects of it and write up their findings in a report. Twenty-one of the committees map onto government departments. Several others cut across departments, like the Public Accounts Committee and the Environmental Audit Committee.

They are exceptionally well staffed. The 30 committees operating in the Commons have a total staff of 280 people. Departmental committees usually have about six full-time staff, led by a clerk of the committee.

Clerks are effectively the civil servants of the House, with a similar grading system and similar pay. They are the robed, wigged, barrister-type figures you see in front of the Speaker during parliamentary proceedings. They are not employed by Parliament in general, but by the Commons and the Lords respectively. They are therefore independent of ministers. Their loyalty is to Parliament, not the government. They typically start as an assistant. If they're promising, they'll make clerk of a select committee after around five years. This would be roughly equivalent to Grade 5 in the civil service. There they act as principal adviser, manage the team, and work alongside the chair in compiling the report.

The committees have a tremendous degree of power over what they do. They are fully autonomous organisations. They decide what to investigate, how to investigate it and who to call in for questioning. They decide what gets put in their report and how it is written. Those reports have no direct impact on the government. The only requirement is that it responds in two months, but it's perfectly at liberty to dismiss it out of hand, and often does. Nevertheless, the committees have proved surprisingly influential. A study by UCL's Constitution Unit found that governments accepted 40 per cent of their recommendations between 1997 and 2010, including a third of recommendations suggesting significant policy changes. These included a complete ban on smoking in public spaces, strict requirements for shotgun licensing, and the creation of a government strategy for 'honour'-based violence and forced marriage.

Ultimately, though, the significance of committees is not really about their power or their influence. It's about their culture.

Stevas managed to create something truly alien in Westminster: an institution that breaks nearly all the traditional rules of how the British political system operates. Instead of generalism, it is based on expertise. Instead of machismo, it is based on compromise. Instead of partisanship, it is based on cooperation. And instead of vitriol, it is based on evidence.

The staff include one or two committee specialists, who are experts in their field, providing in-depth research and briefings. They are bolstered by specialist advisers from outside, typically of high prestige, who assist either part-time or on a day rate, helping MPs understand issues that are often highly technical and complex. There are normally about 120 specialist advisers at any one time. 'We normally have at least two specialists,' a select committee chair says. 'We also have access to the National Audit Office, sometimes on secondment or ad hoc, to sit in briefing meetings with us.'

In the Commons, the Speaker is a kind of neutral referee. They are not there to push debate in any particular direction, but merely to make sure the rules are followed and MPs get time to speak. Select committee chairs are different. They are active participants. They are tasked with creating an evidence-gathering process, keeping the conversation focused on what is being discussed and, most importantly of all, reaching a consensus.

In the Commons Chamber, the whips dominate proceedings. But select committee discussions after an evidence hearing are conducted in private. They are unwhipped, so MPs can express without consequence ideas that are at odds with their party's official policy. This culture repels the classic adversarial archetype of Westminster and instead attracts a different type of person – one who prefers to work with people rather than against them. 'I'm not a confrontational politician,' a former select committee chair says. 'I don't like confrontation. When I have to do it, I have to do it, but I really don't like it. So I enjoy the cross-party stuff. It suits my temperament.'

The research into select committee MPs is instructive. Those members of Parliament who were most restrained in their actions and preferred to avoid conflict with others were 55 per cent more likely to join select committees, on average, than those who scored lowest for those values. The Democratic Audit in 2016 found that select committee chairs rebelled against their party majority more frequently than their backbench colleagues. The data suggests that the causation therefore goes both ways. The select committees attract people who want to step outside of the whip system, and encourages an independent mindset once they've done so.

In fact, committees can arguably be seen as one of the informal parliamentary groups that provide strategic and emotional support to rebel MPs in Westminster. You will often see members of a committee on different sides of the Commons refer to each other as 'honourable friend' – typically used only for members of your own party – when in the Chamber. The friendship is often genuine as well as professional. Committee inquiries can last a long time and often involve foreign trips. The members end up getting used to one another. That relationship is a kind of forbidden love affair in Westminster. It is an antidote to the tribal shouting of the Commons Chamber – a reminder that good people can come from a different tradition and good ideas can come from a different direction.

After years on the committee, MPs develop a deep granular expertise about the subject they cover. When they stand up in the Commons Chamber, they tend not to deliver lines-to-take from the whips, boilerplate party political generalities or a ham-fisted rhetorical flourish they've practised in front of the mirror in the hope that it'll be clipped for the nightly news. They deliver actual insight, moderated by a rounded understanding of the subject matter, and grounded in empirical knowledge. The reports they produce are the result of an evidence-gathering process, informed by outside specialists. And that process is not distinct from the consensual cross-party solutions they end up proposing. It is the cause of it. Once debate centres on evidence rather than partisanship, consensus becomes that much easier. 'People often start off with quite hard-and-fast rules on a subject,' a select committee chair says, 'but once they're exposed to the evidence, most people will follow it.'

There are plenty of disagreements between select committee members behind closed doors. Chairs often have to work hard for the committee to establish a joint position. But most people who participate in the system are struck by how natural it feels to behave cooperatively when they're away from the angry shouting of the Chamber. 'I tend to find that there's a consensus on most issues, actually,' says Damian Collins, former chair of the Digital, Culture, Media and Sport Committee. 'The witnesses you call forward, the evidence you get – most people would agree on what seems right and what seems important.'

A generation after Stevas, another opportunity to claw back power from government emerged.

It sprang out of the MPs' expenses scandal, a grubby and painful episode in 2009 in which several MPs were found to have misused the expenses system, tapping into precisely the suspicions the public had about them. In the months that followed, the outrage was so severe, and MPs' sense of vulnerability so acute, that several options opened up that wouldn't have been possible in normal times.

One of them was parliamentary reform. Strictly speaking, it didn't have much to do with expenses. But people were grasping for ways to placate the chorus of public anger, and this was one of the measures they came up with.

On 10 June 2009, Gordon Brown gave way to growing parliamentary pressure by asking Tony Wright, chairman of the public administration select committee, to establish an inquiry on reform of Commons procedures. Almost as soon as he gave the commitment, he had second thoughts. A motion to establish the committee did not appear for five weeks. When it was presented to the Commons, no time was given to debate it. No. 10 ultimately allowed time for debate on 20 July, the last opportunity before MPs departed for the summer recess. It was passed a full seven weeks after Brown announced it. 'This matters,' Wright later said, 'because it illustrates one of the key problems. This is the impotence of the House to find time to debate and decide its own internal affairs, unless the government enables it to. This is not a satisfactory situation for a sovereign legislature.'

When it came, Wright's report was devastating. It was as if all the frustrations and weaknesses of over a century had finally come boiling to the surface, and for a brief moment it seemed as if something might actually be done about it. The Commons, Wright found, was in a coma. And that was due, more than anything, to the stranglehold over the timetable. 'It is wrong in principle that, in addition to controlling its own legislative timetable, the government rather than the House decides what is discussed, when, and for how long,' the report concluded. 'We consider it for example unacceptable that ministers can determine the scheduling of opposition days without reference to others, that they have an untrammelled power to decide the topics for general and topical debates, that they can determine which issues in major bills are debated on the floor of the House and by corollary which issues are not.'

The report recommended a two-stage solution to the timetable problem. First, it demanded the creation of a Backbench Business Committee, composed of elected backbench MPs, to agree what would be debated in time set aside for all non-government business. Second, it demanded the creation of a House Business Committee, which would be composed of frontbenchers nominated by the party leaders and the MPs from the Backbench Business Committee. This second committee would draw up a draft agenda for the week ahead, including government business, and it would put it to the Commons for a vote.

It was a crucial moment. The report was taking direct aim at Standing Order No. 14. MPs would be given back control of the timetable. The Commons would function like a free, independent legislature. It would decide when and for how long it scrutinised legislation.

Brown would probably have ignored the report if he'd had a chance. Prime ministers are rarely in the business of giving up their power over Parliament. He'd therefore been wary of it almost as soon as he promised it. But the opportunity was taken away from him. The election of 2010 threw Labour out of power and brought in the Conservative–Liberal Democrat coalition. That opened a window of opportunity. It was a new government. It had Liberal Democrats in it, who would pressure the Conservatives on reform. And David Cameron had made George Young, who had served on the Wright committee, leader of the House. It was as if the stars were aligned. Everything had come at the right time.

But even then, it wasn't enough.

The government accepted the creation of the Backbench Business Committee and let it decide what to do with 27 days a year on the floor of the House. It then promised to introduce the second part of the jigsaw – the House Business Committee – by 2013. But that never happened. The momentum died and the prospect of radical change died with it. Downing Street couldn't bring itself to give up its control over the timetable. The idea was quietly killed off.

It was one of the greatest wasted opportunities for constitutional reform in the modern era. But there was, even after all that, something striking about what had taken place.

The Backbench Business Committee couldn't control what happened with government business, but it had control over an awful lot of Commons time. And in that time, MPs could do whatever they wanted. They could potentially even vote to temporarily suspend the standing orders and take control of additional time. Finally an avenue had been provided for them to take on the government.

And MPs, with grinding predictability, then proceeded to do absolutely nothing with it.

The only figures who noticed how much freedom they'd suddenly been granted were the Brexiters. 'I was sitting in the tearoom next to David Cameron one day,' Tory Eurosceptic Peter Bone says, 'and I said: "Wonderful about the Backbench Business Committee." He replied: "Yes, it is really good." Then I said: "The fact that we can actually put substantive motions on and have votes." He was just drinking his tea at this time and spluttered it out.'

The 27 days controlled by the committee establishes an important principle. It provides time, free from the government, for MPs to debate whatever they want. The amount of time spent in the Commons on backbench business increased from around 10 per cent to around 25 per cent. But the full scale of its powers has not been realised. It's as if someone left a constitutional grenade launcher lying around and no one thought to pick it up.

'I genuinely struggle to understand why it hasn't worked,' says Meg Russell, one of the country's foremost authorities on parliamentary procedure. 'I originally devised that mechanism and was then a specialist adviser to the Wright committee. I proposed it in order that they could use it to do bold things. But they're not doing what it was for. There have been big, important topics that MPs complain government isn't scheduling for debate, which they've then failed to schedule themselves. They've got the structure, but somehow the politics is not enabling it to be used.'

The third major opening for reform came with the election of John Bercow as Speaker. It was another unintended consequence of the expenses scandal. The existing Speaker, Michael Martin, was considered deaf to the outrage and had to step down. His replacement proved to be one of the most ferocious Speakers in the modern period.

The Speaker's day starts with the Speaker's conference, a few hours ahead of proceedings in the Commons, when they sit with their three deputies to look at the agenda. The Clerk of the House – the most senior clerk in the Commons – will run through the order paper, which contains the day's business. Typically it will involve departmental questions and debate over a piece of legislation as well as a few other bits and pieces.

They will talk through several things that might happen. They will discuss potential points of order, which are supposed to be procedural complaints by MPs but are usually just excuses for grandstanding. They will consider proposed amendments to legislation and whether they're within 'scope', which means pertinent to the bill. And they will work out the Speaker's response to any problems that might arise.

The Speaker's powers are quite extensive. They choose the amendments, they choose who gets to speak in a debate, and they choose how long it runs on for. But their most significant power is interpretation – assessing the jumble of precedents, rulings and standing orders that dictate Commons life and applying them to whatever is going on that day.

Bercow's approach was to interpret them in the most liberal way possible, by constantly adopting whichever interpretation made it easiest for the Commons to have its say. 'This was the problem,' he says. 'It wasn't just expenses. It was that this House needed to get off its knees.'

His first salvo came during the Queen's Speech in 2013. Standing Order No. 33 clearly limited the number of amendments to a motion on the Queen's Speech to two. But

Bercow wanted to accept three: one from the opposition, one from the Welsh nationalist party, Plaid Cymru, and one from the Tory backbencher John Baron about a referendum on EU membership, which was then a twinkle in Eurosceptics' eyes. He was told by the clerks that he could not. But the clerks can only advise. It is up to the Speaker to make the decision. 'The standing order says "a further amendment",' Bercow says. 'The spirit of the thing was probably as the clerks said, but it did not say so precisely.'

Bercow was playing around with the interpretive possibilities of the House's rules in order to give backbenchers more of a say. At this stage he was doing it for Eurosceptics, who were then a minority in the Commons.

Later he did the same for Remainers, who were by then themselves a minority. On 9 January 2019, he allowed a vote on an amendment to a government business motion to give MPs a say over Theresa May's Brexit deal. This time it wasn't just a dusty and arbitrary restriction relating to the Queen's Speech. Bercow was tampering with the government's cherished monopoly over the timetable. Again the rules were pretty clear: he couldn't do it. Again the clerks advised against it. And again he ignored them. Whenever he did it for one side of a political divide, the other would become outraged. But in each case, he followed the same principle: standing up to the government and giving the House a say.

Bercow then dusted off two powers that had been lying around without being used very often.

The first was the emergency debate, which could be activated using Standing Order No. 24. It triggers a three-hour debate on a matter the government is failing to allow time for. Yet another scrap of Commons time was being clawed back for MPs.

In truth, it's a fairly blunt tool. Three hours sounds impressive, but the format inevitably leads to parliamentary grandees making long speeches. It rarely allows for a sustained interrogation of a minister. Yet the government finds it inconvenient. And because it finds it inconvenient, it can be useful. Since Bercow left the role, his successor, Sir Lindsay Hoyle, has kept it in reserve as a form of leverage against the government. 'It's part of my toolbox,' Hoyle says.

The second power Bercow used was the urgent question. This is a request by an MP, made at least an hour before the House sits, to ask a question of the relevant minister in the Commons. It's discussed at the Speaker's conference. If they decide that it satisfies the criteria, a warning is displayed on the annunciators around the parliamentary estate. It is an effective vehicle for scrutiny – taking place at short notice, often before the government has resolved its position on a matter, on a matter of general importance. Unlike emergency debates, it involves the minister having to answer question after question from around the House. It's a much more focused form of interrogation. Before Bercow, there were very few urgent questions. There were just nine in 2006–7. In 2016–17, there were 74.

One of the first urgent questions Bercow granted was from shadow children's secretary Michael Gove to children's secretary Ed Balls in 2009. Balls had ignored the advice of the Commons children's committee in his appointment of the children's commissioner and was facing accusations of trying to railroad through MPs objections. He instantly called up the Speaker's Office. 'What was obvious was that he was accustomed to the idea that he phoned the Speaker and would get what he wanted,' Bercow says. 'He'd done this for Brown when he was a spad. It was almost surreal that Balls was expecting the conversation to finish with me saying "thank you, it won't be granted". I said: "You'll hear when we make a decision." In fairness to him, he came to the Chamber to answer the question and never mentioned the matter again.'

The urgent question has now become a key element of day-to-day parliamentary scrutiny of the government. It has been kept up by Hoyle as it was by Bercow.

Select committees, the Backbench Business Committee and the Bercow reforms have all provided incremental improvements to Westminster. They have loosened the government's vice-like grip on Parliament. But they have also been met by a counter-reaction. Under the May and Johnson administrations in particular, No. 10 has forcefully pushed back.

Between 2016 and 2020, as the debate over Brexit raged and MPs increasingly tried to make their voices heard, the government opted first to silence and then completely close down parliamentary democracy.

May took aim at the opposition days that are available under Standing Order No. 14. These constitute one of the few moments in which the government does not control the timetable. Under the standing order, there must be 20 of them in a parliamentary session. But there are two weaknesses in the provision. The first is that sessions do not always last a year. If a government wants, it can extend them. This is precisely what May did, stretching the session out from 2017 to 2019, with no commensurate increase in the number of opposition days. The second is that the government controls when the opposition days will occur. The timing, as with everything, is entirely at its discretion. So the prime minister simply refused to make the time. For a five-month period, the government did not table a single opposition day. When she did eventually table them, she instructed her MPs not to vote on the motion they put forward. The opposition victories piled up – 299 to 0, 288 to 0, 238 to 0. But they were completely meaningless. She had made the entire concept of opposition days null and void.

Under Johnson, the attacks stepped up a gear. On 28 August 2019, he initiated an unlawful prorogation of Parliament.

Prorogation closes a session. Everything shuts down: the Commons, the Lords and all the committees. Usually it's an uncontroversial administrative function that brings the parliamentary year to a close once all the political business has been wrapped up. Previous prime ministers had played some grubby games with it, like when John Major brought it forward for the 1997 election at the height of the cash-for-questions affair, in which MPs were paid bribes to ask questions in Parliament.

But nothing like this had been seen for centuries. The last time anything even approximating it took place was in 1629, when Charles I dissolved Parliament and initiated the Eleven Years' Tyranny. For the first time in the modern era, Parliament was suspended against its wishes. It was a moment in which the government's true attitude towards the Commons was revealed. The full extent of its subjugation was now plain for anyone to see.

But the chief mechanism that modern governments have used to silence MPs is far less dramatic. It is an administrative function, which few people care about or have even heard of.

It allows government to sidestep Parliament altogether and pass law without it, through ministerial fiat. And it threatens to become the default setting of British law-making.

The mechanism comes under various names. Sometimes it is called secondary legislation – as opposed to primary legislation, which is the term we use for Acts of Parliament. Sometimes it's called subordinate legislation, or delegated legislation, or statutory instruments. Technically speaking, a statutory instrument is a type of delegated legislation, but they're so common that the term works as a substitute. They're all very boring names. But then as a general rule, the most boring names in politics are the ones that are worth looking into, because they're where the most disturbing items are hidden.

The reason it's called delegated legislation is because Parliament is delegating its law-making power to someone else. That can be an institution or professional body, but typically it's the minister proposing the law. They turn themselves into a mini one-person Parliament, able to operate as they wish without reference to anyone else.

Statutory instruments have been around for a long time, but their use was formalised in the Statutory Instruments Act 1946. They were meant to satisfy a couple of issues. First, they'd let ministers get on with innocuous, uncontroversial technical adjustments without bunging up the legislative process in Parliament. And secondly, they'd provide the law with the flexibility to meet changing circumstances with the requisite speed. And that, on its own terms, is perfectly reasonable. Nobody needs Parliament to be consulted every time ministers modify the specifications of speed cameras. Most changes to the social security system by the Department of Work and Pensions are similarly very technical and granular. You'll always want some kind of option for this type of law-making.

But Westminster is based on the centralisation and concentration of power. So, in an entirely predictable way, these instruments have long been misused. And now the extent of that misuse has become so severe that the walls between primary and secondary legislation have started to break down completely.

As the decades wore on, the volume of delegated legislation grew remorselessly. There were 6,644 pages a year of new statutory instruments in the 1980s, 8,705 in the 1990s, and 10,421 in the 2000s.

Increasingly the two principles of statutory instruments fell away. Instead of being reserved for uncontroversial technical issues, they were often used for highly controversial non-technical issues. In 2014, they were used to regulate the depiction of various sex acts showing female domination in online pornography. In 2022, they allowed the home secretary to unilaterally define the meaning of 'serious disruption' during protests. Later that year, the government tried to use them to effectively pass all future education policy. 'In the last few years of my time as parliamentary counsel,' Daniel Greenberg said, 'I had an increasing feeling that there was coming to be a consensus, albeit an unspoken consensus, within the public service that primary legislation is an unrealistically unwieldy way of running the country and that ministerial diktat is so much more effective for everybody.'

This system has its own legal momentum. Each time new ministerial powers are introduced, they set a precedent. From that point on, a minister often claims another power on the basis of what has come before. It only ever works one way: towards expansion. These are 'extremely unhealthy trends', Labour peer Ann Taylor warned in September 2021. 'The more significant problem is not the issues in each individual bill but the underlying trend we are seeing of moving away from Parliament making our laws and ministers increasingly taking powers to change the rules, regulations and guidance.'

The powers conferred on ministers generally do not go away once they are used. They stay there, ready to be used again whenever they decide they want to.

In 2021, the UK experienced a shortage of HGV drivers, as a result of the pandemic and Brexit. The government's response to this problem was to activate a series of statutory instruments that it had lying around. It used at least eight of them, which had been introduced in legislation going back as far as 1971. Far from being uncontroversial, the instruments were used to make changes with a potentially profound impact on public safety. One of them removed the requirement for car drivers pulling certain kinds of trailers to take an additional driving test, so that they could free up capacity at examination centres. Four separate instruments were used to extend the number of hours drivers could legally be at the wheel.

Statutory instruments are unamendable. The only thing Parliament can do is accept or reject them. But in practice this is a false choice, because it almost never rejects them. The Lords, which is far more vigilant against statutory instruments than the Commons, has only defeated the government six times over these powers – once in 1968, twice in 2000, again in 2007 and 2012, and then finally in 2015, when it voted to defer consideration of the Tax Credits (Income Thresholds and Determination of Rates) (Amendment) Regulations.

As ever, the name is tremendously boring. And as ever, that's where they hide the mucky stuff. The regulation radically altered people's entitlement to tax credits, in a bid to save the government £4 billion a year. A highly controversial measure of that sort with a profound impact on people's lives had no business featuring in a statutory instrument and should have been properly debated in Parliament. The

Lords voted against a motion that would have rejected the regulation outright, and instead took the more moderate approach of supporting two motions saying they would 'decline to consider' it unless the government undertook certain actions. Nevertheless, No. 10 reacted in a spasm of incandescent rage, setting up a review that contemplated removing 'the House of Lords from statutory instrument procedure altogether'.

Nothing came of it – the report faded away, and it was all anyway overshadowed by Brexit. But the report hangs like the sword of Damocles over the Lords. They know that if they consider even deferring another statutory instrument, let alone rejecting one, the government is likely to retaliate by reopening the review.

Statutory instruments are made possible by an Act of Parliament. The government will add a clause to a bill which gives a minister the power to do certain things, typically using a statutory instrument. The instrument itself can then be introduced by the minister at a later date, when they want to implement their new power.

There are two main kinds of statutory instrument: negative and affirmative.

Negative statutory instruments become law automatically unless MPs or the Lords object to them. Very occasionally there's a 40-day period for parliamentarians to object before they become law. These are called 'draft negative'. Usually they become law instantly, but parliamentarians are given 40 days to object afterwards. These are called 'made negative'.

Made negative is by far the more common procedure. It's used for all sorts of things. In August 2021, for instance, the government used one to unilaterally give itself planning permission to convert the Napier military barracks in Folkestone into a form of punishment accommodation for asylum seekers. During the 2019–21 session, 904 made-negative statutory instruments were laid before Parliament, forming 65 per cent of the total number of instruments introduced by the government.

Parliament can reject these instruments by 'praying' against them. It's an archaic bit of terminology that refers to its method of communicating with the Crown. In this case, the Crown is the minister. So of all the archaic terminology in Westminster, 'praying' against a statutory instrument is actually quite revelatory, because it demonstrates the truth of the power relationship. Ministers are acting like absolutist monarchs. MPs are acting like serfs.

The prayers of Parliament will not be answered. According to the 1946 Act, the government must revoke the instrument if either the Commons or the Lords approves the prayer motion. But there's a catch. It is the same old catch that applies across the parliamentary system: the government controls the timetable. It can decide whether or not to allow a debate on a negative statutory instrument. Predictably, it doesn't like doing so. The only scenario in which it is likely to allow a prayer motion is when it's from the leader of the opposition.

In the two-year parliamentary session of 2019–21, only 13 made-negative instruments were prayed against. Five of those prayers were simply ignored. Eight were debated. Of those eight, seven were from the leader of the opposition and the other was from the SNP's Westminster leader, Ian Blackford. Out of the tens of thousands of negative instruments laid since the 1950s, only seven have ever been rejected. The last time the Commons rejected a negative instrument was in 1979.

Affirmative instruments are ostensibly used for more controversial powers, and are supposed to consequently enjoy higher levels of scrutiny. In truth, neither of these elements really holds up. Plenty of contentious powers are included in negative instruments, and the scrutiny available to affirmative ones anyway remains almost non-existent. They have the same structure as negative instruments – they can be 'draft' or 'made'. Draft affirmative needs the approval of Parliament before it becomes law. Made affirmative come into force as law instantly but needs the authorisation of Parliament if it is to remain law beyond a certain period, which is usually set at 40 days. Like negative statutory instruments, the affirmative procedure is used for all sorts of things. In 2019, it was used to change the UK's carbon reduction commitment.

Affirmative instruments are supposed to be scrutinised in something called delegated legislation committee, during sessions that last no longer than 90 minutes. But the committee cannot reject them. It can only debate them. They are then sent back to the Commons, where they can be voted on but cannot be debated. There is, needless to say, no sensible reason why you would separate out the debate from the vote. But in truth, it is of little consequence, because the committee itself is constructed specifically to make sure that there is no meaningful assessment of the instruments. The delegated legislation committee is where scrutiny goes to die.

The MPs attending the committee are selected by the whips. They typically have no idea what is being discussed and no experience at all in the technical area the instrument covers. They sit there, bored and confused, waiting for it to end. 'I was sent off on a three-line whip to one on double taxation,' former Tory MP Sarah Wollaston wrote in the

Guardian. 'I struggle with the law on any kind of taxation, let alone double taxation, and sent a worried note to the whip in charge, wondering whether there had been a horrible mistake. I received a note to inform me that my only duties were to turn up on time, say nothing and vote with the government.'

The end comes quickly. The Institute for Government found that in 2017–18, the average duration of a delegated legislation committee hearing was just 26 minutes. Two meetings during the session lasted less than a minute.

Typically speaking, the minister in charge will make a speech. That will be followed by a speech from the official opposition. MPs will often be dealing with constituency correspondence or taking care of office work. It is considered bad form to speak in any way, let alone stand up and express an opinion. Doing so merely delays the process. Soon enough, the formalities end. The instrument is sent back to the Commons and is passed without debate.

The only bodies in Parliament that really bother to scrutinise what is happening with delegated legislation are in the House of Lords. They're called the Delegated Powers and Regulatory Reform Committee and the Secondary Legislation Scrutiny Committee. The former looks at the powers ministers are asking for and the latter looks at the statutory instruments that have been laid using those powers. The Delegated Powers and Regulatory Reform Committee in particular is of pivotal importance. No one has heard of it. Most people in Westminster have no idea it exists. But since 1992, it has almost single-handedly provided a defensive shield against the growth of ministerial power.

It looks at all government bills and reports on whether the powers ministers have handed themselves are appropriate. As the Hansard Society said: 'The work of the committee provides the nearest thing to a form of jurisprudence in the area of delegated powers.'

It is a lonely job and an unsung one. It is also a largely ineffective one, because although the government will sometimes reverse course in the face of the committee's criticisms, it has never shown the slightest indication of improving its approach to statutory instruments. Quite the opposite. It has expanded their use beyond any possible conception of parliamentary democracy.

The expansion of executive power through delegated legislation often takes the form of a linguistic sleight of hand.

Ministers often create the power for a limited situation, then say it can be exercised to make 'other provision generally'. They say the power 'may, in particular, include' something, thereby creating a formulation that tacitly admits that it can be used in all sorts of other, unspecified ways. They authorise ministers to 'simplify or improve' legislation, which is so broad a construction that it allows them to basically do whatever they want. They let ministers mitigate 'any failure of law to operate effectively' or 'any other deficiency', thereby providing extremely wide powers with no set definition. These are all real examples taken from real legislation.

There are three chief reasons why they're written in this way: either the government cannot properly articulate what it wants to do, or it is in a rush, or it actively and consciously wants to give itself excessive powers. 'I've definitely been in that situation,' Carl Gardner, a former government lawyer, says. 'You sort of want the power to be as wide as possible. Everybody in the system knows that you're going to want those powers to be wide to make your own life easier.'

Eventually ministers stopped bothering to write legislation with any degree of specificity whatsoever. The temptation of statutory instruments was so great, and the scrutiny of them so feeble, that they simply dashed out some powers in the broadest manner imaginable.

The 2018 Healthcare (International Arrangements) Bill, for instance, was meant to allow the government to continue reciprocal healthcare agreements between the UK and EU member states after Brexit. But rather than write out in detail the powers it would give ministers, it simply allowed them to do whatever they wanted. It created an open power for the funding of healthcare all over the world. The powers in the bill provided no limit to the level of payment a minister could authorise, or who could be funded, or the type of healthcare that could be supported, or the powers that could be conferred on anyone, or the functions anyone could be given, or the number of Acts of Parliament that could be amended. 'If the secretary of state wished to fund wholly or entirely the cost of all mental health provision in the state of Arizona, or the cost of all hip replacements in Australia, the regulations would only be subject to the negative procedure,' the Lords delegated powers committee concluded. The bill passed anyway.

Far from being relegated to technical, uncontroversial matters, statutory instruments are now routinely used in areas of acute political sensitivity. This extends to basic individual rights and free expression. The right to protest in Britain, for instance, is currently maintained at the whim of a minister.

Home secretary Priti Patel's Police, Crime, Sentencing and Courts Act 2022 outlined a series of new conditions that could be imposed on demonstrations. If a senior police officer believed that the noise produced by a protest 'may result in serious disruption to the activities of an organisation', for instance, they could change its route, its destination or the number of people who could attend. Basically, they could close the demonstration down. Anyone on the protest who failed to abide by the conditions could be imprisoned for a year.

That was already an extremely broad piece of legislation. It is hard to think of a single demonstration that does not disrupt an organisation in some way, even if it's simply the noise disturbing a shop nearby. But Patel went a step further.

The definition of the phrase 'serious disruption to the activities of an organisation' did not feature in the bill. Instead, it gave the home secretary the power to define the expression through a statutory instrument – whenever she liked, for whatever reason she liked, on whatever basis she liked. In case that wasn't enough, Patel also gave herself the power to define the phrase 'serious disruption to the life of the community' via statutory instrument, which would again authorise police intervention against demonstrators.

The next home secretary, Suella Braverman, picked up the baton with the Public Order Bill 2022. It created something called a 'serious disruption prevention order'. They could be imposed on anyone who the police believed had previously caused 'serious disruption' during a protest and was planning to do so again in future.

The orders were very severe. They allowed the courts to impose 'anything' in the form of restrictions or prohibition, including barring the protester from particular places, or meeting particular people, or participating in particular activities. It even allowed the authorities control over their social media accounts. These restrictions could apply even if the person had never been convicted of a criminal offence.

On the face of it, the bill handed extraordinary powers to the police. But in fact those powers rested with the home secretary. It contained powers that allowed her to issue 'guidance' to police, including on how they should exercise the orders and who they should target. That guidance wasn't optional. The police 'must have regard to' it. The home secretary had effectively used statutory instruments to hand herself the power to deprive protesters of their freedom without them having committed a criminal offence.

Statutory instruments sometimes take the form of so-called Henry VIII powers. These allow ministers to amend or repeal an existing Act of Parliament. It is in effect a power grab. It takes primary legislation, which has been subjected to the more rigorous requirements of parliamentary debate, and allows the government to change it using the barely-existent requirements of delegated legislation. The name comes from Henry VIII's loose approach to law-making. But in fact it is too understated, because the king never enjoyed this degree of control.

Henry VIII powers were deployed to spectacular effect during Brexit, when whole areas of British law were suddenly subject to them as a way of quickly copying-and-pasting European law into a post-EU legislative landscape. The European Union (Withdrawal) Bill, the Lords committee said, included 'wider Henry VIII powers than we have ever seen'.

In some areas, the process of delegated legislation has gone so far that the government has effectively given up on writing legislation altogether. Instead, it has started to write bills with so little content, and so many powers for ministers to legislate later using statutory instruments, that they are in the end effectively just an index of ministerial powers. These are called skeleton bills, because they contain the bone structure of legislation, but all the meat is added later by the government without any meaningful consultation of Parliament. 'Skeleton legislation signifies an exceptional shift in power from Parliament to the executive,' the Lords committee said, 'and entails the government, in effect, asking Parliament to pass primary legislation which is so insubstantial that it leaves the real operation of the legislation to be decided by ministers.'

The danger of skeleton bills was clear as far back as 1932, when an inquiry into delegated legislation led by the Earl of Donoughmore raised concerns from critics that it had 'so far passed all reasonable limits, as to have assumed the character of a serious invasion of the sphere of Parliament by the executive'. Those now seem like halcyon days of innocence compared to what is happening now. Even in the first five years of its operation in the late 1990s, the Lords committee only found it necessary to denounce four bills as skeletons.

Today, skeleton bills are passed that allow ministers to rewrite the entirety of a regulatory framework at the stroke of a pen. The Haulage Permits and Trailer Registration Bill did it for haulage, and the Healthcare (International Arrangements) Bill did it for healthcare. The Medicines and Medical Devices Bill, the Lords committee found, conferred 'very wide powers to almost completely rewrite the existing regulatory regimes for human and veterinary medicines'.

The 2018 Agriculture Bill was intended to replace the European Common Agricultural Policy, which provided subsidies for farmers and funded rural development programmes. According to the government, it would 'provide the legal framework required to transition out of the EU' and 'move away from the rigid bureaucratic constraints' of the European policy. The 'legal framework' they ended up producing was a skeleton bill that conferred 26 powers on ministers, to make law through two dozen classes of statutory instrument, in just 36 clauses. The powers included giving ministers the ability to create criminal offences punishable by up to two years in prison and unlimited financial penalties. They were given these powers indefinitely. It was as if Parliament was watching powers flying far overhead. They had soared across the sky, from the EU to the government, without ever touching down in the House of Commons.

In recent years, the government has gone beyond even the powers of secondary legislation and started to create a whole new legal ecosystem of so-called tertiary powers. This is where the power to make law is handed from a minister to a third body, like an institute, a professional standards organisation or HMRC, where there are almost no scrutiny functions whatsoever. They can just start pumping out law without it even coming into contact with Parliament. Even the poverty-stricken standards of statutory instruments look robust in comparison.

This type of power is never called legislation. It is hidden away under numerous euphemisms: guidance, determinations, protocols, public notices, directions, arrangements, rules and codes of conduct. But that is all a mask. It is legislation in disguise. If you contravene it, you are subject to the loss of your liberty, just like with any other law. 'How are you meant to know what the rules are?' asks Dheemanth Vangimalla, a researcher in statutory instruments at the Hansard Society. 'How are you meant to know what the law is if it's not necessarily published where you think it will be published and not by means that you think it would be normally legislated for?'

This tactic involves the abuse of language to the point of logical impossibility. Take 'guidance'. It features in two bills from the 2017–19 parliamentary session – the Ivory Bill and the Mental Health Units (Use of Force) Bill. They are on very different subjects and yet both contained the same striking provision: the power to issue guidance that, like Braverman's Public Order Bill, people must 'have regard to'. In other words, it was a requirement. It was, the Lords committee concluded, a form of mandatory guidance. 'The very concept,' they said, 'is a contradiction in terms.'

Although a recent innovation, tertiary legislation is already expanding so quickly that it is threatening to engulf the UK's entire regulatory framework. This is partly a result of Brexit. The act of taking decades of EU law and switching it to the UK statute book in a short timetable meant that ministers could insert all sorts of powers into the bills with a minimum of fuss.

The European Union (Withdrawal) Bill introduced various tertiary powers with no requirements for any of them to be subject to parliamentary procedure or even the stick-thin scrutiny requirements of statutory instruments. And yet the extent of those powers was extraordinary. The bill allowed ministers to create bodies that could legislate, without any oversight at all, in any of the areas that had previously been covered by EU law, including aviation, banking, investment services, chemicals and medicines.

Clause 7 of the bill allowed ministers to do whatever they think is 'appropriate' to address 'any failure of retained EU law to operate effectively'. There was no definition of what 'effectively' meant or what might be considered an 'appropriate' response. There was no assessment of what it might mean in practice, or the extent of the ineffectiveness that might trigger the power. There was no detail as to whether it related to multiple sectors or could apply to just one.

The British government had handed ministers the power to make these changes, for whatever reason they liked, with almost non-existent parliamentary involvement, across the entire landscape of European legislation.

Then COVID-19 hit. And the statutory instrument system reeled completely out of control.

On the face of it, the pandemic offered a good example of when you might legitimately want to use delegated legislation. Rapid technical changes in law were required, time was of the essence, and it was often impossible for parliamentarians to meet because of lockdown rules. Indeed, that is the kind of scenario envisioned by the 1984 Public Health (Control of Disease) Act, which the government heavily leaned on for its COVID-era statutory instruments.

But what was understandable in March 2020, when the first lockdown was imposed, was less understandable by Christmas time, when another was imposed. And yet as time wore on, and the excuses for haste fell away, the government continued using statutory instruments regardless. On 15 February 2021, nearly a year after the first lockdown, they were still using a negative statutory instrument to create a new system of quarantine and testing rules for travel to other countries. It came into force three days after it was published. The government continued legislating this way throughout the entirety of the pandemic.

Ministers grew accustomed to being able to legislate as they wished, without the inconvenience of parliamentary involvement. 'There are reasons why a COVID government might want to legislate very quickly,' Jonathan Jones, former head of government legal services, says, 'but that should not become the norm. It's not normal that ministers are signing off really complicated controversial legislation at 11 o'clock at night to come into force at midnight. That is not a good way of legislating.'

The most draconian rules imposed on the British public in modern history, including the command that they only leave their homes for certain purposes, were introduced by statutory instrument. Hundreds upon hundreds of them were passed, using powers granted to government in 134 separate Acts of Parliament. Most received no scrutiny at all. Of the 504 statutory instruments deployed by September 2021, only around 30 were debated in Parliament before they came into force. Fifty-six of them came into force before they were even laid in Parliament.

On 13 May 2020, the government laid a statutory instrument that permitted people to leave their homes for reasons other than exercise. MPs were allowed to look at it a month later, on 10 June. But by then, the rules had already been superseded by another statutory instrument, which came into effect on 1 June. This one allowed people to leave home for any reason, as long as they stayed in overnight. By the time the Lords were able to assess that one, on 12 June, it had itself been superseded by another, which allowed the re-opening of shops and the introduction of support bubbles.

The statutory instruments were introduced so late that the very concept of law started to dissolve. The 13 May regulations on permissions to leave the home came into effect at midnight, but were only laid before Parliament at 9.30 the following morning, when they were published on the government website. So for nine and a half hours, the public was subject to laws they were unable to read.

Even if they could have read them, they would have made little sense. Instead of being published in intelligible English, the statutory instruments took their classic form: 'Paragraph 13(1) does not prevent P carrying on a restricted business, or providing a restricted service, of a kind specified in paragraph 19(2)(a) to (e) between the hours of 22.00 and 05.00,' read one. Others bore the classic scars of amendment-stitching, asking to omit words from one sentence to another in, for instance, regulation 4, paragraph 2, subsection b of another instrument. Instead of being replaced, statutory instruments were simply amended over and over again, going from 11 pages at the first lockdown to 130 pages by the end of the last one. Soon enough, no one really knew what the rules were – not the politicians, or the police, or even the ministers themselves. In November 2020, Michael Gove enthusiastically told voters that golf courses and tennis clubs were about to open before quickly having to correct himself.

'We have seen legislation imposing the most profound, intrusive restrictions and requirements on our national life,' Jones concluded, 'on us all as individuals, on businesses, schools, universities, cultural organisations – being made at high speed, on the basis of policy created and announced by ministerial statement, drafted often overnight with no or limited parliamentary consideration, coming into force within days or even hours, and then quite often needing to be corrected or changed again at short notice.'

Once it became possible to behave this way, the government continued to do so, even when any real justification had faded away. A year and a half into the pandemic, on 5 August 2021, it was making changes to the testing and self-isolation requirements on people arriving into the UK a day before they were laid in Parliament and three days before they came into force. Regulations on the import of animal products were made at 10.17 a.m. on 28 September and then laid before Parliament at 2.30 p.m., before coming into force at midnight.

'I worry about the eradication of the rule of law,' Hoyle says. 'Because that's what we built ourselves on. That's my job, to make sure the voice of this House is heard and that the executive must be accountable to the people who've been elected who serve this country. We can't bypass that. Unfortunately, COVID allowed us to do things differently. We've lost a lot of what the House is about.'

What began as an understandable technical provision has increasingly become the de facto model for government legislation. As its use has become mainstream, the two Lords committees have found themselves issuing more and more strenuous warnings, in a desperate bid to get parliamentarians to see the danger staring them in the face. Their last reports were called 'Government by Diktat' and 'Democracy Denied'.

But still no one listens. Most MPs will have no idea those reports were published. And in a way, why should they? They know a horrible secret: even when the government resists the temptations of statutory instruments, publishes primary legislation and experiences the full weight of the Commons process, it will still receive hardly any scrutiny at all.

The gap between a full Act of Parliament and delegated legislation has narrowed to the point where you can look at one and then the other and find yourself barely able to tell them apart. And that grim process is what we'll turn to next.

CHAPTER 9

The Law

The legislative process is a maze with no centre. You're told that at some stage detailed scrutiny takes place. But when you walk through the corridors and peer around the corners, you never find it.

The reason it cannot be found is because it does not exist. Even when governments avoid statutory instruments and pass full Acts of Parliament, there's so little actual examination of the bill in the Commons that it often might as well not happen at all.

When we think of legislative scrutiny, we imagine the Commons Chamber rammed with MPs making passionate speeches for or against a piece of legislation. But this isn't where scrutiny takes place. It's not even where it's meant to take place. This chapter will tell the true story of legislation, throughout its life in the Commons, to demonstrate how it really works.

Legislation starts as a twinkle in the eye of the Parliamentary Business and Legislation Committee, or PBL. Very few people have heard of it and newspapers almost never cover it. That's not an accident. As a general rule, the stages of a bill's life that are talked about most frequently are completely inconsequential and the stages that are never mentioned are absolutely pivotal.

The PBL committee sits in the Economic and Domestic Affairs Secretariat in the Cabinet Office. Its membership is like a who's who of all the most quietly influential positions in government outside of the prime minister: the leader of the Commons, the leader of the Lords, the chief whip, the chief secretary to the Treasury and the attorney general. The task of this committee is to collate all the laws the government wants to pass into a full legislative programme, which is then presented during the King's Speech – the event that launches the new parliamentary session. It's also meant to scrutinise each individual bill to make sure it's fit for purpose. It does the first job poorly and the second not at all.

The process starts when PBL writes to departments asking them to put in bids for the next parliamentary session. There are around two dozen slots for legislation, give or take. These are highly prized. The Treasury has its slots by default. Other big departments, like the Home Office, will expect one or two. Some, like the Ministry of Defence, rarely need one. The PBL committee is supposed to assess the need and urgency of the legislation, but in truth the legislative scramble has very little to do with genuine demand and a lot to do with power. 'The bigger and more important the department,' Margaret Beckett says, 'the more legislative items you have to have for your own prestige. And the bigger and more important the secretary of state, the more determined they are to have their legislation in the programme. So you've got this ridiculous process where, if you're a very macho man with a strong sense of your own importance, you're going to demand your legislation comes top of the queue, which may or may not have anything very much to do with what should be the political priority of the day.'

The bids are also dependent on prime ministerial interest. PBL will have communicated the kinds of things that are required to fit with No. 10's political narrative. For Johnson, for instance, it was levelling-up and post-Brexit benefits. Departments are then meant to tailor their bid to that agenda or emphasise any aspects that fit with it. They're trying to build a storyline, connecting the poetry of the prime minister's speeches with the prose of the legislative agenda.

The bids come in. There are usually about twice as many as there are slots. PBL goes through them, often with assistance from the Policy Unit, and sends suggestions to the prime minister. 'Both Boris and May would say: "Where's my bill on X?"' former director of legislative affairs Nikki da Costa says. 'So you give them the narrative top line. "Prime Minister, this is what we think, based on your speech on the steps of Downing Street, we should prioritise." That sort of thing.'

PBL will then start chopping and changing bill proposals to make everything fit the limited number of legislative slots – a Home Office bill, for instance, might have some measures from the Department of Culture, Media and Sport thrown into it if they can't find them their own slot. 'They will go for the most politically virile bills at the top,' says a civil servant who was involved in the process. 'Then they'll work their way down.'

At the end of the process, the leader of the House gives the departments drafting authority. This means that they have a guaranteed slot and can begin the process of writing the bill. At this point, one of the strangest and most eccentric operations in Westminster takes over. It is the Office of the Parliamentary Counsel (OPC). These are the people who write the laws.

The point of writing a bill marks the first stage at which a political idea receives some form of genuine scrutiny. It is a very narrow form of scrutiny. It's not about the wisdom of the policy or its evidential basis. It is about what the law is trying to achieve and how to turn the proposals into something with legal clarity.

It starts with lawyers in the government department writing instructions to counsel about what they want the law to do. Under no circumstances are they to try and offer a draft. That's considered unimaginably rude in the rarefied environs of the OPC. Instead, they have to describe what they want in prose. 'It's a really long letter,' says Gardner. 'You would set out what the law is now, what ministers want to change it to, the different outcomes they want to achieve, and then perhaps some thoughts on how it might be done.'

The OPC is structured into four teams, each covering a cluster of departments, with one of them specialising in Treasury legislation because of its technical nature. Each one has a team leader, the equivalent of a director general in the civil service. At the top is the first parliamentary counsel, equivalent to the permanent secretary.

Bills are written according to a 'four eyes' process. They're drafted by one staff member and checked by another. Those pairs involve one senior figure and a more junior figure, who has historically been called a 'devil' – a term borrowed from the Bar. When counsel receives the instructions, they typically approach it in one of two ways. Some of them start writing instantly as they read the letter, refining as they go. Some sit and think about it, collect their thoughts and then write it out in one go. Either way, they will have a long back-and-forth with the department, interrogating the policy so it can be expressed in legislation.

This can be a challenging intellectual process. 'It's only when you start trying to put the words on the page that you realise there's a little gap here, a little gap there,' a former parliamentary counsel says. 'I was doing a bill where a clause turned on the definition of the word "near". But this is very imprecise. What if you're five metres away? What if you're using a drone from 100 miles away? So it often involves you putting lots of hypotheticals to departments to try to establish what they are trying to achieve. And often it turns out they don't really know what they mean.'

Counsel choose every word in the legislation. There is therefore a curious subculture of legislative literary appreciation, where those in the know – a couple of dozen people at most – will be able to spot a particular drafter's legislation from its manner. One counsel, who was called by a former assistant to ask about a piece of legislation, was told that they hadn't bothered asking who wrote it because they instantly recognised the 'peculiarly staccato style'.

Counsel do their work diligently, but there are several things that can go wrong in this process.

The first is that the instructions are of poor quality. Most departmental lawyers are very good, but occasionally you get a bad one. When that's the case, the system falls down. 'Despite the creativity at the heart of what parliamentary counsel do,' former counsel Daniel Greenberg wrote in his book on the subject, 'ultimately they are to some extent machines that require to be driven by departmental lawyers. If the driver does not fully understand the capabilities of the engine and how it requires to be handled, it is not possible to produce a creditable result.'

Sometimes the departmental lawyer is strong but will be sidelined by the ministers and their spads. Outside of being presented with a draft of the law, there's nothing counsel hates more than a minister getting involved. 'It's a nightmare to deal with because they don't understand what a bill is trying to do,' one says. 'I remember doing a bit of work with Oliver Letwin. He was very interested in drafting and that led to long meetings that didn't go anywhere. I had a colleague who worked with David Davis. He was awful. You'd get the text of the bill back covered in red pen.'

You can spot ministerial interference in legislation fairly easily. It'll usually emerge with what amounts to a press release stuffed into the face of the bill, like someone inserting a laminated menu into a restaurant's food. Dominic Raab's Bill of Rights Bill, for instance, opened with an 'introduction' about free speech and rebalancing law away from Europe. Liz Truss's Northern Ireland Protocol Bill started with an 'overview of main provisions', which insisted the deal the UK made with the EU did not have effect. Neither of them had any legal meaning and would never have been written by counsel of their own volition.

Sometimes ministers demand changes that counsel cannot bring themselves to make. Greenberg, for instance, was told by a minister to change a heading in a bill so that it would conceal the fact that the legislation allowed for properties to be searched without a warrant. 'I refused on principle,' he said, 'to adopt a heading that deliberately concealed the effect of the section.' In the end he threatened to consult the attorney general, and the minister backed down.

The ability to sound a warning with the attorney general was once a valued last-chance emergency provision for counsel. This no longer applies, however. The avenue was eradicated by the politicisation of the attorney general role, particularly under Suella Braverman in 2020. At this stage, it ceased to have any pretence of objective legal advice or a role in the protection of legal standards and instead became a mouthpiece for the government's position. 'That function does not exist any more,' a former parliamentary counsel says. 'And it has led to a diminution in counsel authority.'

But the biggest problem is time. Everyone is always in a rush. Ministers draw up an idea quickly so that they can get a legislative slot, because this is how they secure a promotion in the next reshuffle. The government stacks together lots of legislation to show that it's getting on with things. This creates a strong sense of forward momentum for ideas that have often not been formulated properly. 'If it's something that a minister wants to do and it's got a lot of political capital behind it, it can move quite quickly,' Gardner says. 'It can move ahead of thinking.'

The pace means ministers often have very little patience with the intellectual process counsel is pursuing. Corners are cut, pressure is applied and deadlines bear down. And in legislation, that usually translates into broad powers. Instead of trying hard to define words like 'near', counsel are forced to go with what they're given.

It's this kind of pressure that results in legislation like the Public Order Act 1986, section 5 of which outlawed 'threatening, abusive or insulting words' which might cause 'harassment, alarm or distress' – big, broad terms without any concrete meaning. Between 2001 and 2003 alone, 51,285 people were convicted under this section, 8,488 of whom were between 10 and 17 years old.

'The less time I have to prepare a draft, the more likely I am to have to legislate in broad terms,' Greenberg wrote, 'and to take wide powers, which may go further than is required by the essential policy aims, but which can be guaranteed to achieve those aims and more. The result is legislation that is more intrusive upon the citizen than is necessary.'

That sense of frenzied legislative urgency means bills are now sent off to Parliament well before they're finished. Once upon a time, this was considered an embarrassment. Now it is the norm. Counsel know they're not finished, but time has run out. So instead, they finish the legislation on the run, as it is passing through Parliament, by having the government add amendments to it. As we'll see in the next chapter, these amendments are typically made in the Lords. In the 2016–17 session, 2,270 amendments were made to government bills in the Lords, only 36 of which were forced on the government by a vote.

When counsel is done with it, the bill returns to the PBL for a final meeting. This takes place in the Large Committee Room. 'It's a very claustrophobic windowless room, where the leader of the House sits on a grand wooden chair,' a bill team civil servant says. At this point, the legislation is supposed to be subject to scrutiny once more. It's not objective scrutiny and it's not on the policy itself. It's self-interested party political scrutiny, in which the committee tries to make sure that the bill won't fall apart in public and embarrass everyone. 'Often they just turn around and say "no way",' one official who has been on the receiving end of the process says. 'When that happens we just have to go back to the drawing board and start again.'

Governments often insist that this is a bruising process in which every aspect of the bill is challenged. Speaking to the Delegated Powers and Regulatory Reform committee on 20 July 2022, chief whip Mark Spencer insisted it was as ferocious as ever. 'I think it is very robust and very tough,' he said. 'There are some ministers that have literally been munched up and spat out in PBL. You really do get under the skin of the legislation. You test ministers' knowledge of the policy. You properly take them to task in private before it meets the sunlight of public scrutiny.'

This is false. We can't see for ourselves what goes on in the committee hearing, but we can see what comes out of it. And the product of its deliberations is near-total legislative chaos.

In January 2022, for instance, the government added a host of controversial police powers, including the right to stop-and-search someone 'without suspicion', to a bill right at the end of its legislative progress, after it had passed through its main scrutiny stages in both the Commons and the Lords. That was either the result of gross scheduling incompetence or, more likely, a conscious attempt to introduce wide-ranging legal changes that fundamentally altered the relationship between the citizen and the state with minimal parliamentary involvement. The Lords voted them down at the last minute, one by one, in 14 consecutive votes – the worst series of government defeats in the Lords' modern history.

Just 10 days before Spencer had assured peers of the robustness of the PBL process, the government had scrapped the entire first half of its schools bill, containing 18 separate clauses, and pledged to rewrite them as the legislation continued to go through the Commons.

The clauses had proposed that all maintained schools be turned into academies and that ministers be given the power to dictate the entirety of their decision-making, from the curriculum to the length of the school day, exclusively through statutory instruments. In other words, they all but eradicated parliamentary involvement in education policy.

In both cases, the bills involved massive executive power grabs, which fell apart almost as soon as they were exposed. Neither indicates that the PBL process is working effectively.

When PBL is done with the bill, it is finally cleared to be introduced to Parliament. Counsel now send it to the House authorities, and from that point on, it goes from being a government document to a parliamentary one. Further changes can no longer be made at the flick of a draftsperson's pen. They must be done by amendment.

And yet the scrutiny process, if anything, becomes more seriously flawed.

Bills can start their progress through Parliament in either the Commons or the Lords. We'll assume here they start in the Commons, but the process is roughly the same whichever way it begins. The bill enters the Chamber through first reading, which is a purely formal process, and then is given second reading. When you see MPs debate legislation on TV, this is usually the stage you'll witness. But it is not meant to be a particularly meaningful moment. It is supposed to be a general debate on the ideas in the bill, rather than a detailed assessment of it.

Throughout that debate, you will often hear ministers refer to the forensic scrutiny the bill will receive later. Backbenchers will often say that it can be improved further on in the legislative process. All those assurances are empty.

Second reading usually lasts a day, which in practice means about six hours of debate, typically between 1 p.m. and 7 p.m. If it's a major bill, it'll be given more. At the end there is a vote, which the government will almost always win on the basis of its majority.

With that out the way, the real business of passing legislation begins. Even most of the people who consider themselves seasoned Parliament watchers never see what comes next. Very few, if any, pay attention to the core stages of a bill, where the line-by-line scrutiny is supposed to take place. And they will therefore never know that this line-by-line scrutiny never happens and is in fact largely a myth.

It starts with committee stage. This involves an assessment of the bill by something called a public bill committee.

Most democracies have a version of this process. In Germany, the committees resemble, in composition and function, Britain's select committees. They are thought of as specialised parliaments within a parliament, composed of members who know a lot about the bill and the subject matter. The chairs aren't neutral. They are actively trying to facilitate agreement and find consensus, even if they're from the opposition. Ministers and whips are absent. In their place there is a strong committee staffing contingent and lots of civil servants. The committee is there to improve legislation, not to rubber-stamp it or oppose it outright. It is conversational, rather than confrontational. It collects evidence and holds hearings.

There are similar systems around the world. The Netherlands and the Nordic countries behave in a similar way, as do Scotland and Wales. In Scotland, the select committees and public bill committees are the same body, so the politicians looking at the bill are well staffed, are already familiar with each other and have a deep knowledge of the subject matter. They consult widely, collect evidence and hold hearings if necessary. Tellingly, they also behave largely in a collegiate way, despite the fact that party political tensions outside of the committee are just as ferocious as they are in Westminster.

Back in London, the opposite situation holds. If you wanted to design public bill committees to be as useless as possible, you would create a system very much like the one we have now. On every point and in every aspect, they motivate MPs away from detailed consideration and cross-party improvement of legislation and towards the vacuous machismo of the Commons Chamber.

Indeed, the Commons Chamber, with all its flaws, is replicated at a small scale in the committee room. This is actually a literal process – the room is laid out as if it were a mini version of the House of Commons, with benches of opposing MPs facing each other, rather than the collegiate horseshoe shape of the select committees.

The whips select the MPs who sit on the committee. They even attend themselves. Those on the committee are encouraged to blindly support or oppose the bill and not think deeply about it. The chair functions as the Speaker does in the Commons rather than like their counterpart on a select committee, acting as an impartial referee as opposed to someone tasked with finding consensus. The government comprehensively outguns the opposition, with access to massive civil service resources. The committee has no specialist staff and is ad hoc – it does not have the kind of permanent existence that allows it to amass expertise.

The committee system is therefore one of the great abiding lunacies of the Westminster system. It has developed a world-class select committee structure for assessing policy but a disastrously ineffective public bill committee structure for passing legislation. 'When I joined my first select committee as a little clerk in 1983,' Paul Evans says, 'there were just two of us and only forty-two staff supporting these activities. When I retired, I was in charge of all the staffing in select committees. There were about 300 of them, probably. So that side of scrutiny has massively grown. Whereas with legislative scrutiny, we're still just leaving MPs swinging in the wind.'

Committee stage can technically go to a select committee instead of a public bill committee, but that's vanishingly rare. It can also go to a so-called committee of the whole House if it is particularly uncontroversial or particularly constitutional. This is what happened with the European Union (Withdrawal) Bill in 2017–19, for instance. But generally speaking, governments will try to avoid this, because a committee of a few dozen MPs is far easier to control than 650 of them.

Public bill committees typically have a membership of between 16 and 30 MPs. Occasionally the whips will bring in a sceptic from their own benches to placate backbenchers, but it's rare, and anyway makes no difference to the outcome. The MPs are selected as lobby fodder: a human rubber-stamping machine.

The membership reflects the composition of the House, so the government's majority has as much force in committee stage as it does on the Commons floor. For committees with an odd number of members, the government must have a majority. It is given a majority even when it does not have one in the Commons, as Theresa May's administration demonstrated when it secured a committee majority despite being a minority government.

These two key qualities – the selection of MPs by the whips and the replication of the Commons majority – means that the government will always get its way in committee. The bill will always go through and every opposition amendment will be defeated. 'It's worse, actually, than the Commons itself,' former Liberal Democrat leader Tim Farron says, 'because you're not going to get any rebels. There's no question that it will do anything other than what it is whipped to do.'

The committee goes through the bill clause by clause. The chair, with the assistance of the clerks, will group the amendments according to theme, and one amendment is picked as the lead amendment for each group. This grouping of amendments is a key dynamic in the life of a bill, with dangerous consequences that we'll come to later. There's a debate on the motion 'that the amendment be made', which includes all the others in that group. Then the committee votes. If any amendment succeeds – which, unless it's by the government, it won't – it is added to the bill. Finally the bill, as amended or otherwise, is reprinted for the next stage and off it goes.

These committees and their predecessors, which were once called standing committees, have always been useless. For as long as anyone can remember, they've been a redundant procedural formality in the legislative system.

'The procedure of standing committees is insane,' Richard Crossman, a Labour leader of the House in the 1960s, said. 'Under the present system there is no genuine committee work, just formal speech making, mostly from written briefs.'

Ferdinand Mount, head of the Policy Unit under Thatcher, took the same view. 'The ministers wearily reading out their briefs,' he said, 'the opposition spokesmen trotting out the same old amendments purely for the purposes of party rhetoric and without any serious hope of improving the bill, the government backbenchers – pressed men present to make up the government's majority – reading the newspapers or answering their letters.'

Nothing had changed by the Blair era. 'During the standing committee stage of line-by-line scrutiny,' *Times* journalist Peter Riddell said, 'government backbenchers are actively discouraged from participating lest their speeches delay progress on a bill, so they can be seen doing their constituency correspondence and, depending on the season, their Christmas cards.'

The situation today is largely unchanged. The names change, and a few procedural alterations have been made. MPs now sit absorbed in their phones and iPads rather than the newspapers. But the committees remain as redundant as they were half a century ago.

Opposition MPs and shadow ministers will make all sorts of speeches about how disgraceful the bill is. Sometimes they will even put down amendments to try to improve it. But regardless of what they do, those amendments will not succeed. 'The system is set up to encourage the opposition just to grandstand,' Farron says. 'It doesn't encourage you to actually forensically engage in the legislation, which is why very often it's bad.'

Even if they did want to properly scrutinise the legislation, the opposition would struggle to do so because of the inequality of arms between them and the government. There are no committee staff to do policy analysis, number-crunching or fact-checking. There are no outside experts, as there are on select committees. There's just the clerks, whose job is to ensure the correct conduct of proceedings, not do research or assist in evidence-gathering.

The government has the massed ranks of the civil service behind it. The minister has the support of an entire bill team of officials. But the opposition has almost nothing, except for whichever pressure group has been briefing them – and these groups will have their own agenda, which may or may not accord with the need for the bill to be scrutinised properly.

There are a few bits of assistance available to the opposition. The Public Bill Office in Parliament will help MPs draft amendments. The Commons Library will produce short neutral factual papers on significant bills. And there is something called 'Short money', which is intended to fund policy research by the opposition front bench. But it is nothing next to the government's access to resources.

There are occasional flashes of decency. It's quite striking that such a thing happens at all, given the range of forces against it and the pressure of the whips, but it does. 'I think they can't help it,' a former clerk says. 'If a politician sees a bad bill, they want to defeat it or change it for the better. They get no credit for it. But they're not just there for credit. They're there for their own self-respect.'

Many frontbench politicians have stories of the times they fought to improve a piece of legislation despite it doing them no good whatsoever. 'We do it despite the system,' Labour frontbencher Lisa Nandy says, 'not because of the system. That's the problem with British politics. Everything from our electoral system to our way of governing and debating and voting – it's all set up to be a fight. One side wins, the other side loses. But most of the challenges we face are in shades of grey, not black and white. When it works it's because you've thwarted the system that you're stuck in.'

After committee stage, the bill moves to something called report stage. This is without doubt the most important stage of a bill's progress through the Commons.

It is the only opportunity for the House as a whole to engage in the detail of the legislation. It's the only chance for all MPs to propose amendments and vote on the specific proposals contained within it. It's the only moment for backbenchers with knowledge of the subject to have a chance to participate. It therefore goes without saying that this is the stage where the dead hand of control comes down hardest. 'The single greatest cause of dissatisfaction which we have detected with current scheduling of legislative business in the House,' the Wright committee said, 'arises from the handling of the report stage of government bills.'

There are two aspects to what happens next that serve to eradicate meaningful debate. The first is an artificial constraint on time and the second is an artificial constraint on subject matter.

The control of time is achieved by something called a programme motion, which contains the timetable for debate over the bill. It is introduced at the end of second reading and is put 'forthwith', which means that it is not debated and is unamendable. Sometimes a supplementary programme motion is added before report stage which is amendable, although the opportunity is rarely taken to do so.

But it is not decided by the government on its own. It is done through 'the usual channels' – the communication forum between government and opposition. On the face of it, that sounds healthy – a rare example of cross-party cooperation in the otherwise hyper-partisan environment of the House of Commons. But this cooperation is done in a very specific way: according to no rules, in private and without transparency.

The usual channels reveals something fundamental about the dynamic of the Commons. It is not just about the government versus Parliament. In many ways, it is about the government and the official opposition versus the backbenchers. 'It's organised to suit the two front benches,' a former clerk says. 'The government pretty much has its foot on the neck of the House. But the other foot, I sometimes think, belongs to the official opposition.'

The phrase 'usual channels' is shorthand for all sorts of different conversations between business managers in the two main parties. It covers relatively uncontroversial chats about the timing of recess, general agreement on the timetable, the timing of bills, the length of debates on them, which select committee gets chairs from which parties, and when it's time to get their respective backbenchers to start wrapping up speeches at the end of the debate. They also arrange 'pairing', where an MP from one side can be away from the Commons Chamber during a vote if the other side agrees that they will reduce their vote to balance things out. It's a civilised agreement that makes life bearable for MPs, meaning they can go to a hospital appointment or attend their child's play at school.

These conversations involve the government and opposition chief whips, as well as the private secretary to the chief whip. Some conversations are arranged ahead of time, but many of them happen minute by minute and hour by hour, often 'behind the chair', which means literally a whispered conversation around the back of where the Speaker sits. It is all completely opaque. 'The system for scheduling business is not transparent to many inside the House, let alone those outside,' the Wright committee concluded. 'Even the term "usual channels" has a distinct air of mystery which demonstrates the difficulty of establishing who has made or can make a particular decision. There is no consultation with minority parties or backbenchers. Most decisions are taken in private, do not have to be justified in public and can sometimes only be gleaned after the event.'

The conversations in the usual channels typically involve horse trading between the two main parties. Others struggle to get a look-in and are only consulted on certain occasions. To even be part of the usual channels you need at least three MPs in the Commons. This means that someone like Caroline Lucas, the sole Green MP, is completely excluded. The only reason she gets any information over and above a normal member of the public is because the Plaid Cymru party takes pity on her and passes it on.

And yet the usual channels works to exclude MPs in a much more structural and pernicious manner than simple party snobbishness. Its primary effect is to shut out any knowledgeable or independent-minded MPs from the debate.

The key to understanding this dynamic lies in the incentives of the respective party leaderships. The government's motivation is not complicated – it wants to get its legislation through. The opposition's motivation is more nebulous. If the Westminster system was rational, it would be trying to improve the government's legislation and only voting against it where it was still not satisfied. But that is not how Westminster works. The first-past-the-post electoral system has handed the governing party a Commons majority. This means that any opposition amendment, no matter how reasonable or constructive, will be defeated. There are therefore no rewards to this approach.

And yet other opportunities are in play. Debates in the Commons are sometimes watched by journalists and covered in newspapers. Clips of political leaders fiercely denouncing government legislation can be published on social media. If they're really lucky, they might appear on the evening news. So while the opposition is unable to improve legislation, it can use amendments to galvanise its base and appeal to voters. There is therefore a strong pull away from forensic assessments and a strong push towards tub-thumping fire-and-brimstone party political grandstanding.

It might look as if parties are ferociously opposed to one another, representing inimical world views. But in fact they are united by strong underlying assumptions about how things should proceed. They like it this way. They actively choose, day after day, to set up big elemental moments of political conflict instead of engaging in detailed work towards a compromise position. 'When you know in the back of your mind that the government's going to win this,' SNP MP Alyn Smith says, 'your political brain kicks in and you make a different speech to the one you'd make if you wanted to reach the middle ground. If I thought there was a realistic chance of winning the government over to an amendment, I'd say: "Well, look – we agree on this general objective, I think it would be better met by doing that." But even if I turn into a modern-day Cicero, whatever speech I make doesn't matter, so I just call them a shower of bastards.'

If you watch closely in the Commons, you will often see the opposition chief whip looking vaguely uncomfortable, or sitting with a stone-grey poker face, when their own side is complaining about the small amount of time granted to a particular stage of a bill. The reason for that is that they agreed to it. 'I don't think the opposition whips mind as much as they make out,' a former No. 10 civil servant says. 'They can live with a lot more than they imply. And often they quite like it, because it means that they don't have to put as much pressure on their side to stay in the Chamber and vote. That's the reality of what it's like to manage a political party and schedule business.'

This is the core dynamic of the usual channels: the government's desire to pass legislation versus the opposition's desire to grandstand. The government will stress how quickly it wants to get on with the legislation and the opposition will say which issues it wants to hold votes on. This conversation will then dictate how long is allocated for report stage and the way it is structured.

Typically speaking, the programme motion will allow one day for report stage. Very occasionally, if it's a major piece of legislation, it's given two. On a few vanishingly rare occasions – three times in the decade 2000–10 – it's given three. But the overwhelming majority of bills get one.

The use of the word 'day' is a euphemism. It begins after the end of ministerial questions, ministerial statements, urgent questions and whatever else happens that morning. In the evening, it must end an hour before the 'moment of interruption' – the fixed endpoint of the parliamentary day – so that the bill can go through third reading, which we'll discuss in a moment. What this means is that report stage typically lasts about five hours, sometimes less. It usually starts around 1 p.m. and ends around 6 p.m. In 2016–17, report stage took up just 6 per cent of time on the floor of the House.

This problem is actually worsened by the otherwise beneficial reforms Bercow introduced when he was Speaker. With lots of urgent questions allowed during the day, the time for report stage is pushed further and further back, until the actual business of scrutinising a bill becomes an afterthought. 'Bercow would allow four UQs,' says Evans, 'So if you have four UQs, we'd have four hours of that, and then we'd have an hour and a half to deal with the whole of a big bill. That would happen.'

Report stage is therefore a race against the clock. There is no reason for this clock to exist. It is a completely unnecessary imposition. It makes no difference whether a bill is passed today, tomorrow or the next day. The clock is there simply to prevent any meaningful analysis of the legislation. This restriction in the time available is then used to justify a reduction in the number of votes on amendments.

Superficially, it seems as if any MP can put down an amendment to the bill. And indeed they can. Amendments are grouped together, subject by subject, just like they were at committee stage. And just like committee stage, they are headlined by a lead amendment. When the debate over each group is finished, MPs move on to vote. But in practice, only amendments put down by the leadership of the official opposition party, and perhaps one from the leadership of another smaller opposition party, will be voted on. There might be one other amendment in its group or a hundred – it doesn't matter. All other amendments will typically be ignored.

Very occasionally, the Speaker will select an amendment by a backbench MP that has support from high profile figures across the House. At other times, the official opposition will get behind one of its backbencher's amendments rather than try to formulate its own. But these moments are the exception. The vast majority of amendments selected for a vote are written by the leadership of the official opposition or the second largest opposition party. Of course, none of these amendments will succeed. They will lose all of them. But they are not there to succeed. They are there to grandstand.

During the course of report stage, two things happen that reduce the opportunity for debate.

The first is that the government itself uses up all the time. A minister leads the debate on each of the groups. They stand and give a long statement running through the amendment and why they disagree with it. And every second they speak is another second that the backbenchers are unable to discuss their own amendments. 'Because you have a minister leading it, they will be taking up most of the debate,' Commons Speaker Sir Lindsay Hoyle says. 'That's the problem with knives.'

The second is voting. Each vote takes about fifteen minutes. The Speaker shouts 'division', which announces the vote. The MPs flood out of the Chamber into the division lobbies. The numbers are counted by the tellers. The whole theatrics of the voting process must play out. 'The Speaker can't just call amendment after amendment, and if he did, he'd quickly become extremely unpopular,' a former clerk says. 'The House doesn't want to have lots of votes. The whips will tell you this. The members want to go home.' The Speaker has the same view. It's a common refrain in Westminster. MPs claim to want lots of votes, but when the immediate practical consequences become apparent, they are less eager. 'All the MPs want divisions,' Hoyle says, 'But if there are ten of them, they'd soon not do.'

Of course, there is no reason for votes to be conducted according to this antiquated system. They could be done electronically. And in fact they were – during the COVID-19 pandemic, electronic voting worked extremely well. This would allow the Commons to vote on as many amendments as it wanted.

But even before the pandemic was over, the leader of the Commons, Jacob Rees-Mogg, scrapped the system. At the time, people were startled at the sudden retreat into the old way of doing things, but it made perfect sense. Electronic voting opened up new avenues of participation for MPs. It allowed for votes on multiple amendments without any practical consequence in terms of time or organisation. So naturally it had to be dismantled. 'Electronic voting is perfectly feasible,' a former clerk says. 'We know because we did it. But the rules have been drawn up through the whips. They know what effect they have. They are not intended to lead to having lots of votes.'

Those few backbenchers with a specialist knowledge of the subject area who might put forward useful amendments to improve the bill are frozen out of this process. The government does not want to hear from them, and the opposition does not want to hear from them either. So their amendments are not selected.

Stephen Timms, for instance, is one of the most highly regarded politicians in the Commons. He does not make grandiose speeches. He does not share gossip with journalists over lunch. He has very little name recognition outside of Westminster. But he was a former chief secretary to the Treasury in government and shadow work and pensions secretary in opposition before he became a backbencher in 2015. He arguably knows more about social security than anyone else in the building. But if he wanted to propose an amendment to a piece of legislation, he would simply be blocked by the usual channels. He could draft it, table it and get it on the order paper. If he was lucky, the Speaker might allow him to talk about it in the Commons for four minutes. But he is very unlikely to get it to a vote, because all the time has been eaten up by the amendments from the official opposition. 'Someone like Stephen Timms will never get an amendment voted on, because the usual channels will sort it out between them,' Evans says. 'His amendment and all the others would be thrown into this big miscellaneous bucket of everything. He may not even get called to speak. He almost certainly won't be able to push it to a vote.'

Report stage is gradually changing. The number of groups of amendments is being slowly whittled down. Instead of four or five groups, there are now often two, or even one so-called 'supergroup'.

This sounds like a healthy response. It reduces the amount of time a minister can use up, means votes take place in one go rather than throughout the afternoon and allows as many MPs as possible to speak about their amendment. 'The purists may not like that,' Hoyle says, 'because you have a very disorganised debate. But I think it suits the modern member. Lumping together where we can.' But this approach does not actually solve the core problem, which is that the front benches have a stranglehold over amendments.

The reason the government doesn't mind the change is because debate is only meaningful if it leads to votes. Reducing the number of groups has no impact on votes. 'The government, unless it's playing tough, doesn't really give a shit what's debated,' a former clerk says. 'I mean, why should it care as long as it gets its bill through?'

The lumping together of amendments in massive groups also has a dangerous consequence. It turns the only moment of pinpoint House of Commons debate on the detail of a bill into just another general chat with no specificity, like second reading. 'Nobody listens,' Evans says. 'Nobody hears. The minister is not challenged on any detail. They can just respond with another set of sweeping generalisations. The opposition picks a few things to have a symbolic vote on. And that's it.'

This is a pattern that is played out across the Commons landscape: from estimates debates in which MPs are supposed to track spending by government departments to delegated legislation committees. Whenever MPs are tasked with forensic analysis, they retreat back to generalism. And that is a product ultimately of the selection process. They were not chosen for their ability to scrutinise. They were chosen for their ability to campaign. So when the system demands that they fulfil their democratic function, they find themselves intellectually incapable of doing so.

'It lets everybody off,' Evans says. 'It lets ministers off the hook, because they can easily get away with not replying to a point made two hours previously by some obscure backbencher. But it also lets the backbenchers off the hook, because they don't have to keep to the point. They don't have to try to craft their speech to a specific issue. They don't have to think about it very hard. They can get away with just the usual empty rhetoric.'

At the end of the allotted time, the debate suddenly comes to an end, regardless of how much progress has been made.

Any parts of the bill which have not been covered will simply go through undebated. Government amendments or new clauses are passed with no scrutiny and no discussion whatsoever. They are simply agreed to in a kind of humiliation ritual. Even highly charged and controversial areas of politics, like changes to judicial decision-making on extradition cases, have been passed in this way. But even if a section was debated, it will have made little difference. Report stage's bland generalities and broad-strokes rhetoric will have left most of the detail of the bill unaddressed.

The Commons will then spend an hour on third reading. This is usually a valedictory affair, in which MPs, and particularly those who served on the public bill committee, will speak wistfully and sentimentally about its progress. It is then passed by the Commons. The bill is wrapped in a green ribbon. The doorkeeper shouts: 'Message to the Lords.' The doors are thrown open and it is walked by one of the clerks through the Members' Lobby, past Central Lobby, to the Bar of the House of Lords.

As it leaves, the more thoughtful MPs in the Commons Chamber might recognise something. That despite all the soothing after-dinner speeches and the grand send-off they just witnessed, no real scrutiny of that bill took place.

It did not take place at the PBL committee. It did not take place through the needlessly rushed writing process at the Office of the Parliamentary Counsel. It did not take place at first reading, which was a formality. It did not take place at second reading, which was a general debate. It did not take place at committee, which was purposefully structured to prevent meaningful assessment or improvement. It did not take place at report stage, which was stitched up between opposition and government to prioritise theatrics over substance. And it most certainly did not take place at third reading, which acted as if the preceding stages had been more meaningful than they really were.

But they will know something else too, which may or may not be a source of comfort to them: that the bill is now in the Lords. The adults are in charge. And the bill will finally receive the kind of scrutiny it should have been subject to in the Commons.

CHAPTER 10

The Lords

There is a place with a proud record of standing up to government. It works diligently and thanklessly to improve legislation. It applies expertise to policy. It seeks consensus. It is independent-minded and rejects partisan points-scoring. It acts with a seriousness that is absent almost anywhere else in the political system.

It is the House of Lords.

That obviously seems an insane thing to say. This is a place that looks like it's been ripped from the medieval ages. It's occupied by people with names like 'lords spiritual' and 'lords temporal'. The latter category includes hereditary peers, a vestigial link to the era of power through bloodline. It has no democratic legitimacy whatsoever. Even traditionalists concede that it is anachronistic. Most progressives think it is a national embarrassment. It is the one institution in Westminster that apparently everyone agrees must be reformed.

But through a strange combination of circumstances, the Lords has developed into something unusual in the British political landscape: a functioning chamber. It is, simply put, one of the only aspects of our constitutional arrangements that actually works.

The Lords operates in a shadow world of legitimacy. On paper, its powers are considerable and it is fully autonomous.

In practice, it lives under the constant knowledge that the Commons can challenge its existence pretty much any time it likes. If it were ever to start really acting up, it would almost certainly be completely overhauled. 'There has to be a recognition that the Commons is the elected body and therefore has to win,' crossbench peer Lord Judge says. 'It has to win. We can improve, we can propose amendments, but we cannot win. That principle cannot be ignored.'

The starting point for this constitutional settlement between the chambers came in 1911. Back then, the Lords had powers that were almost equal to those of the Commons. But after several decades of deferring to the Commons on budgetary matters, it proceeded to make a terrible mistake.

A bill was going through Parliament that introduced the idea of progressive taxation and included new taxes on inherited wealth. It was a threat to the aristocratic interests of the hereditary peers who occupied the Lords Chamber, so they vetoed it. That was a decision they came to regret. In a sudden defensive spasm of constitutional reform, the Commons hit back. The Lords' veto was scrapped and replaced with a power of delay. It could hold back legislation for two sessions, but no longer.

The Parliament Act of 1949 involved another significant reduction in its power. Now it could only delay legislation for one session. The Lords can still kill a bill sent to it by the Commons, but it is only a temporary measure. If the bill has passed the Commons in two successive sessions, it can be given royal assent without the agreement of the Lords. The sum effect is to limit the Lords' power of delay to 13 months.

The Parliament Act is a gun. It is hardly ever used because it hardly ever has to be used. It has been deployed just four times since 1949. Its chief function is as a deterrent and a reminder of what the Lords is supposed to be: not an equal Chamber, but a revision Chamber. Somewhere that improves legislation where it can and warns about it where it cannot.

Far more important than the Parliament Act is the Salisbury Convention. It states that the Lords will not impede the passage of legislation if it was included in the manifesto of the winning party at a general election. It is a self-denying ordinance that severely restricts the actions of the Chamber.

The Lords are also unable to amend bills of 'aids and supplies', which includes the annual finance bill implementing tax proposals made by the chancellor in the Budget. Only the Commons can authorise taxation and spending. On financial matters, the Lords is almost completely silent. This is a big part of the reason that the legislative record of the Treasury is such a terrible mess.

The Lords agreed to these restrictions because they were afraid of what would happen to them if they didn't. It was clear that if they blocked the government's legislation, it would eradicate them. Indeed, the introductory text of the 1911 Parliament Act warned that the government 'intended to substitute for the House of Lords as it at present exists a Second Chamber constituted on a popular instead of hereditary basis'. It never happened.

There was another major shake-up in 1958, when Harold Macmillan passed the Life Peerages Act. At this point, the Chamber was composed of law lords, bishops and hereditary peers. The Act retained the hereditary peers, but it also created a new type of lord: life peers. They were granted peerages but were unable to pass them down to their children.

The Labour government under Tony Blair then undertook another reform at the turn of the century. It summarily dismissed hereditary peers. Out of over 600 of them, just 92 were allowed to remain – a sop to the House to contain its disgruntlement.

It also created the House of Lords Appointments Commission. This had two roles. First, it would vet the nominations put forward by the political parties for their people to become peers 'to ensure the highest standards of propriety'. And secondly, it would itself put forward non-party-political crossbench peers for a position in the Lords Chamber. Those it put forward would be people of significant achievement, with a commitment to the highest standards of public life and independence from any political party.

As in 1911, it was meant to be a first step towards further reform. A royal commission was set up under the chairmanship of Lord Wakeham to explore avenues for change. It decided that things ought to stay largely as they were, but that the power to appoint life peers should be taken from the prime minister and handed to an independent appointments commission.

At that point, progress halted. Executive powers have a habit of staying precisely where they are, zealously guarded in the various nooks and crannies of Downing Street, and that's exactly what happened here. The prime minister remains the gatekeeper. They decide when a list of new members is announced and the number of names it contains. Other party leaders are then invited to make their own nominations.

It's this element of the system that has fallen into a state of advanced moral decay. A succession of prime ministers have exploited the nomination system as a clearing house to reward loyalists from their time in government. Boris Johnson used it to nominate Evgeny Lebedev, the Russian-born billionaire owner of the *Evening Standard* newspaper, despite reported warnings about him from the security services. He also gave a peerage to Peter Cruddas, a billionaire party donor, despite contrary advice from the Appointments Commission.

There was another effort at reform in 2003, with a joint committee of the two Houses putting down seven options – from a fully elected Lords Chamber to a fully appointed one and everything in between. The Commons rejected the lot. 'We should go home and sleep on this interesting position,' leader of the Commons Robin Cook said, after months of his intensive work had turned to ash. 'That is the most sensible thing that anyone can say in the circumstances.' There was a final attempt at reform under the coalition, but that failed even faster than Cook's had done.

And that brings us to where we are now. The Lords currently has 25 bishops, 666 life peers and 91 hereditary peers, adding up to 782 members.

For many people, that storyline will sum the whole thing up. The Lords is a remnant of aristocratic power. It is stuffed with people who have no business sitting in a modern legislature, like the bishops or billionaire party donors. It has no democratic mandate and therefore does not deserve influence over political life. The fact that it is still there, a Frankenstein's monster of various failed efforts at reform, is a testament to Britain's constitutional anaemia.

But when you look a little closer, it becomes more complicated.

Blair's reform had two explosive political effects. Firstly, it created the modern crossbench system, which would slowly drip-feed non-party-political figures with deep background expertise into the Lords through the Appointments Commission. Secondly, it created a chamber with no majority.

Until the twenty-first century, the Lords had a massive Tory majority – nearly twice as many peers as Labour and the Liberal Democrats combined. Afterwards, Labour and the Conservatives had roughly the same number of lords. By the end of Blair's premiership, the number of Labour peers pulled slightly ahead, but no party had overall control. And they never have since.

There are currently more Conservative peers than there are for any other single party, but they do not have a majority. They are outnumbered by those from other parties and the 183 crossbench peers.

In a political system defined by the ability of the governing party to bludgeon its way through opposition, the Lords stands apart. Its behaviour is therefore strikingly different to what we see in the Commons.

First of all, it simply will not do what it is told. This was the lesson New Labour discovered, much to its horror, after basically creating its modern incarnation through the expulsion of the hereditary peers. Between the 1999 reform and the 2005 general election, the Lords defeated the government 283 times. On over a third of those occasions, the government gave way. On two occasions, it dropped a bill completely. Among other things, the Lords killed off a planned offence of inciting religious hatred, made sure that control orders in the Prevention of Terrorism Bill were subject to judicial rather than political decision-making, halted an increase in the pre-charge detention of terrorist suspects from 28 days to 42, denied the government the power to use delegated legislation to make ID cards compulsory, and prevented the restriction of trial by jury on four separate occasions.

This process has continued since the Labour years and remains the case today. The Lords is one of the few parts of the political system that is prepared to stand up to executive power. It is the only place on the parliamentary estate where the government is regularly defeated.

But it is something even more seminal than that. It is the place where bills are improved. In the 2016–17 session alone, there were 2,270 successful Lords amendments to government bills.

There is something fascinating about those amendments. Only 36 of them were forced on the government in a vote. The rest were all moved by a government minister. This is not an anomaly. Research by Meg Russell for the UCL Constitution Unit looked at 12 bills passed between 2005 and 2012. She found that 88 per cent of the 498 amendments made to the bills in the Lords were from the government itself. One hundred and thirty of these had policy significance.

In November 2017, for instance, the government moved an amendment to the Financial Guidance and Claims Bill that would task a finance body with providing advice on the creation of a debt respite scheme. That eventually resulted in the 2020 'Breathing Space' programme, which, among other worthy initiatives, paused any enforcement action from debt recovery firms while someone was receiving treatment for mental health problems. It sounds like a small thing. It is seemingly uncontroversial. But someone, somewhere, right now, is being protected from debt collectors because of what this amendment made possible.

The government was quite clearly using the Lords as part of its drafting process. The errors in the bill when it went before the Commons were being addressed in the Lords Chamber. This was the place where the government was prepared to actually fix the legislation. The stony-faced no-compromise partisan machismo of the Commons was nowhere to be seen.

And yet even that does not reveal the full picture. Something even more unusual was going on.

Many of the changes did not originate with the government. Most had come from their critics in the Lords. Of the 130 significant amendments in Russell's research, 84 could be traced back to members' amendments or recommendations from the Lords' various scrutiny committees. The government wasn't just fixing its legislation. It was actually listening to its critics, then changing its policy in line with what it heard.

This is a baffling state of affairs. A bizarre half-feudal remnant of historical progress is operating at the peak of constitutional efficiency and prompting more rational behaviour from the government in turn.

But the explanation is ultimately quite simple – the Lords is everything the Commons is not.

It has no majority, so the government does not control it. It values expertise and careful deliberation over partisanship. It rejects the culture of political aggression. And, perhaps most importantly of all, it controls its own timetable. 'The real heavy lifting is done in the Lords, where there is genuine expertise,' shadow justice secretary David Lammy says. 'It's why, in our system, it's very unusual to meet lawyers of any political stripe who are overly keen on House of Lords reform. Because lawyers tend to think that constitutionally the House works. Even though we know that democratically it's not great, we're reluctant to make the House of Lords another elected chamber with a bunch of political types who'll do what they're told. You want it to be this house of expertise.'

Not all the lords are experts. As we've seen, many of them are selected for their party loyalty by the prime minister and other party leaders. But the House of Lords Appointments Commission's nomination of crossbench peers means it is also packed with people who have a lifetime of experience at the very top of their field. They include barristers, scientists, business leaders, volunteers and others. Unlike MPs, they are not selected for their campaigning zeal, networking and ambition. They are selected for their achievement. This provides a much higher quality of scrutiny than that found in the Commons. When crossbench peer Lord Anderson, the former Independent Reviewer of Terrorism Legislation, organised opposition to the weak judicial remedies in the Environment Bill 2021, for instance, he found himself allied with Lord Krebs, one of the foremost zoologists in the world, and Baroness Brown, a noted expert in low-carbon technology. 'They provided the moral authority and the environmental knowledge,' he says. 'I produced the legal nuts and bolts.'

New bills that have sailed through all their Commons stages barely being touched suddenly meet the brute force of deep specialist knowledge when they hit the Lords. 'How many MPs can sensibly scrutinise a welfare bill?' a Labour peer says. 'How many MPs actually understand the benefit system? Not many. But when it comes to the Lords, you've got actual benefit experts. When they come out to play, they are really impressive. They will absolutely take the minister apart. They will find holes in it. They will say: "This is not going to work." And at that point, it's almost like that's the first time the government's actually looked at it, so the number of government amendments in the Lords is huge.'

The level of party loyalty in the Lords is surprisingly high. In whipped votes in the 2015–16 session, Labour secured 96 per cent cohesion, the Conservatives 99 per cent and the Liberal Democrats 99.6 per cent. Generally speaking, the parties vote in blocks just like they do in the Commons, albeit without the governing party being able to win on the basis of its majority.

The difference comes from the crossbenchers, who tend to only involve themselves in policy areas they have experience of. That selective application of genuine expertise makes all the difference.

The level of tolerance for political point-scoring, which is the bread and butter of the Commons, is very low even among the party peers. The intellectual culture in the Lords is disdainful of blind partisanship. Anyone standing up in the Chamber to issue the leadership's lines-to-take will be the subject of derision and cringing embarrassment. 'People cannot simply bang on,' a Conservative peer told the anthropologist Emma Crewe. 'The spirit of the Lords is "the enemy of dogma". Party politics is the enemy of debate. It is considered a bit vulgar in this place.'

It's hard to work out why that's the case. After all, most peers have been selected by party leaders, presumably on the basis of loyalty. But the reason again lies with the absence of a majority and the presence of non-party peers. When a government is denied the ability to simply force things through, it must instead make the case of it. When it is faced with independent minds, it must try to convince them of its position.

'In the Commons, it's a culture of assertion,' Tory peer Lord Norton says, 'because the government can proceed by just saying it is our view and we've got the votes to carry it through. In the Lords, it's a culture of justification. Ministers have got to take it seriously if they're going to mobilise a majority. They've got to persuade other groups as much as persuading individuals on their own side.'

That will not be a quick or easy process for them, because, unlike the Commons, the Lords controls its own business. It decides what it wants to talk about and how long for. The Lord Speaker does not select participants for a debate. They do not rule on points of order. They do not even select amendments. There are no standing orders giving government time precedence over other business. There is no programme motion. There are no internal knives.

The amendments that are put down are therefore not grandstanding expressions of rhetorical opposition. They are specific, legally competent proposed improvements to the bill. 'We can influence how long we take to go through a bill,' Lord Anderson says, 'and can choose to do so in bone-aching detail. Ministers have to be prepared to answer questions on every line in every clause. And if they are foolish enough to respond with political fluff, they get skewered.'

Just like select committees, the culture of the Lords Chamber is free of the kind of political machismo you see in the Commons. It does not appeal to those who engage in it, and it does not encourage it in those who attend.

There is also a recognition – unstated but undeniably there – that governments know how poor the state of their legislation is. Counsel certainly does. So the productive suggestions made in the Lords are often taken up, almost as if they were part of the drafting process.

But the Lords offers something else, something it is not in anyone's interest to admit. It offers privacy. No one really cares what happens in it. Journalists rarely write about it. MPs are largely ignorant of how it works or what goes on there. The public has little interest. So the government can graciously accept defeat there without feeling that they are being humiliated by the opposition.

'Amazingly enough, amendment 243 to the Agriculture Bill doesn't get the tabloids exercised,' Lord Norton says. 'And that's the rub of it, you know. The media don't notice it, so the government can make the concessions. It often brings forward its own amendments in light of the discussion, so it's not even apparent there's been a conflict. MPs want to be re-elected, so for them what matters is look-at-me activities. The lords don't need that. We're just getting on with our job. The boring detail – that's what we're here for.'

The Lords amendments are added to the bill, which is then sent back to the Commons. If the Commons agrees with them, the bill gets royal assent and becomes law. If they don't agree, ping-pong is activated.

This is the process where the two chambers try to resolve a disagreement. All bicameral parliaments – those with two chambers – have a system of some sort for this process. Some of them operate by committee, in which representatives from both chambers meet to hash it out. Britain uses a 'shuttle' system, where messages are sent back and forth until agreement is reached.

There are three options open to the Houses. They can reject an amendment outright. They can amend an amendment. Or they can reject an amendment and propose an alternative, which is called 'an amendment in lieu'. There is no limit to how long this process can go on for.

The Prevention of Terrorism Bill, for instance, was sent from the Commons to the Lords in early 2005. It allowed the home secretary to issue 'control orders' for people suspected of terrorism, which could place them under house arrest and restrict their access to phones and computers. It was viewed by civil liberties campaigners as an attack on the ancient English liberty of habeas corpus – the protection against arbitrary detention by the authorities. The Lords demanded that the bill be given a sunset clause, at which point it would cease to operate unless it was renewed, as well as several legal safety nets inserting judges into the decision-making process. In the final frenzied moments of ping-pong over the bill, the Commons sat from Thursday at 11.30 a.m. until Friday at 8 p.m., during which time it went back and forth between the Houses seven times.

'We sent it back to the Commons about 1 a.m.,' Lord Norton says, 'then there was a chance just to nip home and get an hour's sleep before we sat again at 5 a.m. I heard a rumour that the government wanted to meet at 5 a.m. on the grounds that – you know, it's the House of Lords. They're all fairly elderly. They won't be able to get up and be there at 5 a.m. But at 5 a.m. when I went in, the Chamber was crowded. These are people who have fought wars. 5 a.m. is hardly a great challenge.'

If at any point both Houses refuse each other's amendments and do not offer a compromise, the game of ping-pong is over. This is called double insistence. It's not a law or even a standing order. It's just a convention, but one that is followed relatively strictly. At that point, the bill dies.

No one wants that outcome. The government would have to wait a year to pass the bill through the Parliament Act. The Lords would risk a broader political attack from the Commons and possibly another attempt at reform. In truth, it hardly ever gets to that stage, because, as Lord Judge says, the Commons has to win. This constitutional principle has been deeply absorbed by peers. Unless it's a matter of paramount importance, they will back down. Their job is to revise, not kill.

And that defines the limitation of what the Lords can do more generally. In quiet, uncontroversial areas of law, it works as a clearing house – a place away from the Commons bear pit where the government can change course without embarrassment. But on matters of principle, where the government will not back down, the Lords is unable to press the point. It cannot function on its own. It needs the Commons to uphold its end of the bargain. All it can do is send suggestions to the other Chamber and ask them to think again. And that requires MPs who are willing to listen to what the lords are saying and act accordingly.

'The problem is the Commons do not actually examine legislation,' a peer says. 'The standing of members of Parliament is reduced. A lot of them don't even know what the lords do. They don't realise that when we send something back in the form of an amendment, we've actually thought about it.'

On 12 May 2021, the government introduced the Dissolution of Parliament Bill. It was a piece of legislation with significant constitutional consequences. Until 2011, prime ministers had been able to call general elections whenever they liked, but the system was changed by the coalition government. They set them for five-year intervals and gave the Commons the power to agree to an election outside of this time if two thirds of the Chamber voted for it. The legislation didn't really work. Its supposed restrictions were easily sidestepped by Theresa May in 2017 and Boris Johnson in 2019, after which No. 10 decided to repeal it through the Dissolution of Parliament Bill.

But Johnson did so in a very specific way. His bill prevented Parliament from having any role in the calling of an election. Instead, it handed the power exclusively to the prime minister. Its purpose, the explanatory notes said, was to 'enable governments to call a general election at the time of their choosing'.

That carried with it several dangers. With no Commons check on the power, a prime minister could simply call a general election immediately after losing one. Or perhaps they would find themselves challenged by their own MPs and then threaten to call a general election as a way of subduing the rebellion against them. 'Some check is needed to prevent a rogue prime minister abusing the power to call an election for their own personal reasons, over the heads of MPs in their party,' the UCL Constitution Unit warned.

That warning was issued to MPs, but they seemed completely uninterested in it. On 13 September 2021, the bill passed through committee, report and third reading in the Commons in a little over two hours. The fact that the prime minister was being handed such extensive new powers was barely mentioned. It was sent to the Lords unamended.

Before peers had a chance to debate it, something disturbing happened. Reports emerged that several parties had been held in Downing Street when COVID regulations barred people from attending social gatherings. There was a public outcry, which translated into growing signs of rebellion on the Tory benches against the prime minister. And then, in a bid to face them down, Jacob Rees-Mogg, the leader of the House, made precisely the kind of threat the Constitution Unit had warned about. He threatened Conservative MPs with a snap election. 'My view,' he said, 'is a change of leader requires a general election.'

On a constitutional level, this was plainly nonsense. Under first-past-the-post, voters elect MPs, and the leader of the party with a majority in the Commons becomes prime minister. But Rees-Mogg wasn't really speaking constitutionally. He was speaking politically. He was issuing a warning to the party's backbenchers: keep questioning the leadership and we'll call a snap election. The possibility that the powers would be misused was no longer an abstract hypothetical. It was clearly a live tactical option in No. 10.

The Lords demanded the government think again. Lord Judge put down an amendment that introduced a modest additional requirement for an election. The House of Commons would have to pass a motion saying 'that this present parliament be dissolved' before dissolution.

In any normal scenario, this would not be a problem. The prime minister would have a majority, so if they wanted an election, the motion would pass easily. The opposition would presumably support it. The only scenario in which it would be pertinent was that raised by the Constitution Unit: if a prime minister used a public vote to threaten their own backbenchers. Then, under Lord Judge's plan, MPs would have a defensive fallback position. They could use the motion to deny the prime minister the election.

During the debate, Lord Judge all but pleaded with the Commons to stand up for itself. 'We have become habituated, have we not, to the steady, apparently unstoppable accumulation of power in No. 10 Downing Street,' he said. 'And we have done so while simultaneously the authority and weight of Parliament itself, and the House of Commons in particular, have been diminishing. Should not the voice of the elected Chamber be heard? We live in a modern democracy. Why should it not be heard? Why should it be compelled into silence on the very issue of its own existence?'

He repeated the comments from Rees-Mogg. They were an 'astonishing threat', he said, 'that an uncurbed dissolution power might indeed be open to such unexpected misuse.

The threat itself was a misuse, and this unconstrained power should not be restored to the executive.'

The amendment was passed, and the bill returned to the Commons on 14 March 2022. It met a frosty reception. 'With all due respect for the undoubted expertise and value of the House of Lords,' Cabinet Office secretary Michael Ellis said, 'I suggest it is not appropriate for the revising Chamber to ask the elected House to revisit questions, not least when they relate to the process and role of this House, on which this House has already definitively decided.'

Labour MP Chris Bryant made one last desperate appeal for MPs to stand up for themselves. 'What I do not understand is that this is the tiniest, most minimalist check on government that one could imagine,' he said, across the Commons floor. 'Today we have an executive who are more powerful than they have been at any stage since the early seventeenth century, and it is time, occasionally, that the House of Commons said: "You know what? We're a parliamentary democracy. Let's take just a tiny bit of power into our own hands."'

It made no difference. The Lords amendment was defeated by 292 to 217. Not a single Tory MP voted for it.

Then, with depressing predictability, events played out exactly as Lord Judge and the Constitution Unit had feared. On 6 July 2022, less than four months after the Commons had rejected the amendment, Johnson sat down in front of the Liaison Committee, which is composed of the chairs of all the various select committees. Away from the committee room, he was losing control of his MPs. Within 24 hours, he would announce his resignation. But at this stage, he was still fighting for his political life. He hadn't yet given up hope.

The prime minister was asked about reports that he would hold a snap election to force MPs back in line. 'You are asking about something that is not going to happen,' he said. And then, as if it was a throwaway line: 'Unless everybody is so crazy as to try and, you know . . .' He trailed off. 'Unless what?' Tory committee chair Bernard Jenkin asked. There was no answer. He asked again. Johnson hesitated, but then finally he made his intention clear. 'The best way to have a period of stability in government and not to have early elections,' he said, 'is to allow people with mandates to get on.'

And there it was. The warning had come exactly to pass.

In the end, Johnson's authority crumbled too quickly for him to be able to implement his threat. The next morning, after a feverish night of multiple ministerial resignations, he finally fell on his sword. But it was clear from his comments that this was what he intended to do. The emergency lights had been flashing, but MPs had failed to act on them. Even as they could see the executive power grab coming towards them, they did not have the confidence to stand up to it.

'The Lords can't enforce propriety all on their own,' UCL Constitution Unit director Meg Russell says. 'The Lords take the measure of whether there is resistance in the Commons. And if there isn't resistance in the Commons, they generally won't push it. Because what's the point?'

And that really is the nub of it. The Lords operates like a clearing house, solving some of the problems in the system. The tidying-up improvements to a bill, for instance, which in any functioning country would be taking place at committee stage, instead take place in the Upper Chamber. But there is a very firm limit to what that can achieve. You cannot fix a political system in a revision chamber. It requires the participation of elected representatives in the Commons. And yet they are totally unable to fulfil that role.

'How can you expect backbenchers to take anything seriously if what they do is pointless?' Paul Evans says. 'It is really in the government's interest to make everything as pointless as possible. And anything that aids the general air of entropy about debate in the House of Commons is in the government's favour. So many backbenchers just lose all hope. And then the only thing they have to fall back on is saying something they can then tweet for their constituents.'

This is the full cycle of British politics. It ends as it began, because it can only ever produce that which constitutes it.

It starts in a room in a constituency somewhere, behind closed doors, with partisan members selecting partisan candidates for their partisan qualities and without any assessment of their ability to scrutinise legislation. It funnels those candidates into an election system that is designed to give one of the parties a large majority on the basis of a winner-takes-all whitewashing of a pluralist electorate. And then it subordinates them to its will, with no encouragement for independent thought or specialist knowledge.

It establishes around the prime minister a dysfunctional management system that then faces no constitutional restraints, so it is able to broadcast its broken decisions across the country. It hands that prime minister the power to move ministers as often as they like, which they then use at eye-watering speed to consolidate their own position and thereby further discourage effective governance. The ministers are not chosen for their competence or their knowledge, but for the support they provide to the party leader. They are then buried in work, while experiencing strong incentives for short-term tactics over long-term strategy.

It checks those ministers through a Treasury department that is itself compromised by a scrutiny deficiency and cannot therefore do its job properly. And it supports them with civil servants who are moved so quickly they cannot sensibly advise on what is happening, and would be undermined by a spad caste even if they could.

This structure is overseen by a media that is experiencing an advanced stage of financial meltdown, leading it to impose working practices that prevent journalists from doing their job effectively, in the face of a political system that is intent on reducing their coverage to personal power plays rather than policy assessment.

The legislative products of this mangled system are then often imposed through statutory instruments, which sidestep Parliament altogether. And even when they are not, they proceed through a Commons Chamber that has been asphyxiated by the government, so that it is unable to do its job properly.

So then, finally, when the Lords tries to take a stand against government power and poor legislation, it finds that it is doing so alone, without any allies in the place it is trying to strengthen.

This happens because of the way we have allowed our political system to develop. We sat complacently, patting ourselves on the back for the quality of British democracy. And while we did so, it fell apart from underneath us.

Epilogue: Solutions

It doesn't have to be this way. There is nothing uniquely broken about our national dispensation. We are not fated to live under bad government. The current situation is simply the product of circumstance, lethargy and political self-interest. It can be fixed, as soon as we decide that we want to do so. We just have to do less of the things that don't work and more of the things that do.

The bits that work are the select committees and the House of Lords.

These two institutions reject the basic constituent elements of Westminster life: hyper-partisanship, generalism, unnecessary speed, government control, and disdain for expertise. It's not like everyone involved in them is a saint – there are plenty of select committee members and peers who behave obnoxiously and have no idea what they're talking about. But the incentives that operate there encourage the best behaviour rather than the worst. That's partly because of how they work. But really it's bigger and more philosophical than that. It's about what they are. It's about the values they express.

At the heart of the problem with Westminster is machismo. It's a sense, deep at the base of our assumptions, about what politics is about and how we conduct ourselves: that we do not need to seek consensus or compromise, that the winner takes all, evidence can be ignored, the government must get its way, Downing Street should orbit around face time with the prime minister, and the Commons must be subjugated to the executive.

Ironically, it doesn't even make us strong. It makes us weak. It's a brittle form of mock confidence that falls apart in a passing breeze. Without scrutiny, ideas disintegrate when they encounter the outside world. Without expertise, they're built badly and collapse into terminal disrepair. Without compromise, they're not built to last.

Solving British politics doesn't involve some kind of utopian dream of a completely new society. Almost every change we need to make is already a perfectly normal procedure in all sorts of countries around the world, like Germany, the Netherlands and the Nordic states – stable, successful, dynamic places with a better-functioning system than the one we have here.

Below are a few ideas to fix the problems we've seen in this book. They're not comprehensive. They're not even particularly cohesive – implementing a few of the solutions would reduce the need for certain others, while some would likely only be effective if implemented in tandem. But they follow from an assessment of the defects in the system that we've seen over the course of this book.

There are downsides to nearly all of the proposals I make here. That's the way it goes with politics. It's not about absolutes, it's about trade-offs. The biggest downside, which applies to almost all of them, is time – everything would take much longer. That is entirely purposeful. Westminster operates according to a series of arbitrary timetables. Every bit of the system is constantly pressed for time: the prime minister's day, the merry-go-round of a ministerial career, the posting of a civil servant, the deadline of a journalist, the work of parliamentary counsel, the internal knives of report stage. And what for? No one can say. There is no reason for it. It is simply part of the ceaseless chaos of political life, which accomplishes nothing and results in its own negation.

Of course, we need to be able to legislate fast in an emergency. All countries have some avenue to do this. But we have plenty of ways of achieving that already. We need to start thinking about how we can legislate sensibly as well as quickly.

If we were to implement some of these ideas, it would take probably about twice as long to pass legislation. It would create screams of indignation from whips and political leaders. And that would be absolutely fine. More than that: it would be a sign we were going in the right direction. Much of our legislation is a total waste of time, produced for no reason except the desire to create narrative and satisfy departments. Under these plans, governments would still be able to pass something like 100 bills between elections. That's more than enough, if you are going to do it properly.

How likely is any of this to happen? Not very likely at all. The only organisation that can really do it is the government, and any government that comes to power succeeds by virtue of the system operating as it does, so it has little inclination to change it. But we cannot let them control our imagination along with the rest of our political life. We have to be clear about what our ideals are if we are to take the incremental steps towards them. And anyway, political change always seems impossible right until the moment it happens. Each new government comes into power with a two- or three-year period in which it is unusually receptive to new constitutional ideas. The key is to make good use of those periods, whenever they come and no matter who they involve.

The Vote

The quickest and easiest change we can make to the voting system is to open up candidate selection to the public. There is nothing complicated about this – in fact, we've done it before. In 2009, the Conservatives experimented with open primaries, like those that operate in the US, in which all local voters were allowed to vote for the preferred candidate.

It was this process that led to the selection of Sarah Wollaston in Totnes. There was decent participation of around 25 per cent – hardly earth-shattering, but far better than the participation in normal selection processes. More importantly, it fundamentally changed the dynamic. Wollaston campaigned in a non-partisan way, emphasising her experience as a doctor and her hope to work cross-party. Once the electoral pool was expanded outside of membership partisans, that proved attractive to voters. This was then how she operated as an MP – applying her specialist knowledge where she could and being open to cooperating with others. In fact, the experiment was so successful the Conservatives shut it down, which is a very good indication of quite how exceedingly well it worked. It should be the model for all parties.

The single biggest and most important change we can make is to the electoral system.

This is at the heart of many of our problems. It is the origin of the machofication of our political culture and all the inadequacies that flow from that. It fails in two distinct ways. First, it fails on the most basic possible level imaginable by ignoring the majority of voters. Second, it fails by creating a form of government with no need to compromise.

The solution is proportional representation. It means that parties are represented in Parliament roughly in proportion to their support at the ballot box.

Proportional representation will involve enlarging the size of our constituencies so that several MPs can be contained in each one. This means that we can accurately reflect the vote. So if 35 per cent of voters back one party, 30 per cent back a second and 30 per cent back a third, they can all be represented in the Commons, rather than just the winner. The best proportional representation systems involve relatively small constituencies, which vary from between three and seven MPs in each one. These constituencies would not be arbitrary. They would be drawn to reflect real geographic areas. In fact, they would make much more sense to local identity than the ones we have now.

Cornwall, for instance, currently has six constituencies: Camborne and Redruth, North Cornwall, South East Cornwall, St Austell and Newquay, St Ives, and Truro and Falmouth. It could be redrawn into one constituency with six MPs. Or it could be redrawn into two constituencies – West Cornwall and East Cornwall – with three MPs each. There are currently 73 constituencies in London. These could be redrawn into 14. A new constituency of Brent, Camden and Westminster, for instance, would have six MPs. A new constituency of Hounslow, Richmond and Kingston would have five. You would therefore have the same number of MPs per capita as you had before. But the votes would not be wasted. Instead of a winner-takes-all contest, most voters would be represented in Parliament.

Proportional elections can be run under either open or closed lists.

Under closed lists, you simply vote for a party. Behind the scenes, the party organises the priority of candidates.

The more votes they get, the more of their candidates get into the Commons. The problem is that this puts a great deal of power in party hands. If an MP rebels, the party can threaten to put them further down the list, which is akin to political death.

Under an open list system, the voter can see the party list on the ballot paper. They have two options. They can either just put a cross next to the party and accept the list as it stands. Or they can put a cross next to the specific candidate they want. This system is used in countries like Finland, Denmark and Chile. The problem is that it can reward name recognition over ability and encourage candidates to steer resources to particular communities in order to get the preference votes they need to place high on the list. Nevertheless, it is superior overall – it strengthens the candidate against the party, which encourages independent thought, and it makes sure candidates prioritise their public support over internal party networking.

What would happen if we adopted this system? It's hard to tell. Electoral reformers are constantly mapping election results onto alternate voting systems, but it's not a like-for-like comparison. Repeated studies have shown that around one in four voters do not vote for their preferred candidate under first-past-the-post, because they know they are not going to win. Under a system in which they can win, those votes are going to change, typically away from the main two parties and towards smaller ones.

In the medium term, we would probably end up with a radical right party, a centre-right party, one or two centrist parties, a social democrat party, a radical left party and a Green party. Generally speaking, this is the type of pattern we see in countries with proportional representation. And that's because this is how political thought breaks down in a modern advanced industrial economy. Those are people's typical preferences.

The result would very likely be a series of coalition governments close to the median voter. Sometimes it would involve a centre-left coalition and sometimes a centre-right coalition. Occasionally it would involve a grand coalition involving the main parties. We would get better government. Coalitions get rid of the pathological adversarialism of the Westminster system and replace it with constructive adversarialism. Parties must work together to construct a legislative agenda they can all agree on. They encourage a culture of compromise and consensus rather than outright opposition at every step of the legislative process, including committee stage.

They also encourage long-term thinking. They offer the tantalising possibility of governments that are willing to try to address the chronic, perennial problems that beset the UK: social care, productivity, the health service, regional inequality, mitigating and adapting to climate change, poor quality of life in disadvantaged areas. Single-party government struggles to deal with these issues because they involve difficult political decisions that can be easily weaponised against them. The lack of a sustainable funding model for social care, for instance, has scarred countless lives, forcing people to choose between financial hardship and the care of their loved ones. But political movement has been almost non-existent. George Osborne branded Labour's 2010 reforms a 'death tax', before Labour returned the favour by branding Theresa May's 2017 manifesto commitment a 'dementia tax'. And so, for over a decade, the problem was left to stagnate. How many lives were ruined by that level of political failure?

Coalition government forces multiple parties to buy in. It reduces their capacity to attack each other over hard political decisions, because they were involved in them themselves, and instead motivates cooperative adult conversations about what needs to be done. Will it solve everything? Certainly not. Proportional representation is not the panacea for all social ills that its supporters sometimes make it out to be. But it would be a meaningful improvement on what we have now, with a fairer translation of the vote and a more restrained, productive and consensual form of government.

The Members of Parliament

The first way to improve the performance of MPs is to alleviate the workload through a rationalisation of their constituency duties.

MPs do valuable things through their local casework. It allows them to learn about what is happening in the country, for instance with benefits decisions or visa applications. It encourages them to act as a representative of local industry. It gives them access to real-time, real-world focus groups by constantly forcing them into contact with people's lives. It prevents the political class from becoming disconnected from the public. And in certain key cases, especially immigration and welfare, it can prove crucial to protecting members of the public from bad decisions by the authorities: a final emergency valve against bureaucratic misbehaviour.

But the existing constituency casework system has veered completely out of control. The kinds of cases that are brought to MPs are much of the time nothing to do with them. They should be dealt with at a local council level, and sometimes not at all. MPs have proved unable to say no to them, for fear of the electoral consequences. And it therefore has grown to the point where it inhibits their ability to scrutinise legislation.

The solution is to create a body that will take on the casework itself and ease some of the pressure on MPs. There is a version of this in Denmark that works extremely well. It is called, quite simply, the Ombudsman. It can hear any complaint, from any Danish resident or citizen, against any authority. It investigates municipal and regional authorities, state authorities and government departments, boards and councils, hospitals, schools and even day-care facilities.

When a letter from the Ombudsman arrives, it lands with the same smack of gravitas as a letter from an MP. It shocks authorities into action. But the advantage it has over our own system is that it is non-political. It does not rely on the arbitrary relationship of a political figure, but on a statutory agency, operating on an egalitarian basis and approaching matters on their underlying merit.

We also need to increase the institutional support to MPs in Parliament.

One of the main obstacles to effective scrutiny is the inequality of arms between the government on the one hand and everyone else on the other. The former has the entirety of the civil service available to it. The latter has almost nothing.

There are a few disparate resources they can use. The House of Commons Library will conduct research on topics MPs ask it about. The Public Bill Office will help with drafting amendments. Staff on select committees do very useful work. But these provisions are weak and scattered. Instead, there should be a dedicated branch of the civil service, populated by a set cadre of officials, solely for the benefit of backbenchers. It should take the form of a departmental Private Office but be at the service of MPs instead of a minister.

It could take its cue from the Congressional Budget Office in the US, which has a staff of 235, with around 20 in its tax analysis division alone, available to provide non-partisan analysis of tax and spending measures for members of Congress.

It should provide MPs with information, assessments and guidance about how to navigate the system. Rather than being demand-led and simply responding to MP requests, it should have a controlling intelligence that leads it to actively analyse legislation, highlight what is important about it and isolate potential problems. This will be particularly useful in helping parliamentarians scrutinise legislation from the Treasury.

Inevitably some of its resources will be used for constituency work, but it will also help MPs genuinely assess bills in precisely the way that will horrify the whips. And that, in and of itself, is a strong indication that it is worth doing.

Finally, Parliament itself must be simplified. It has turned into an impenetrable fortress of jargon, which is as baffling to most MPs as it is to the public. This state of affairs cannot be justified. Politics should be readily understandable to an interested outsider of average intelligence, but if someone tunes in to a Commons debate in our current system, they will be unable to gain a basic grasp of what is happening.

All institutions and cultures develop their own terminology. It is perfectly natural. But this institution is not like the others. It is the political system of the nation and must therefore be comprehensible to the nation. It should also be easy to navigate for MPs, so that they can operate within it without relying on guidance from the whips, and to journalists as well, so they can improve their assessment of legislation.

Names are a problem. Commons rules state that MPs should refer to each other by their constituency names rather than their actual names. This is supposed to lower the temperature of debate. If so, it has done a very bad job of it. The cost – and it is a considerable one, even if we have grown accustomed to it – is that a member of the public cannot understand who someone is talking to, which when you get down to it is a very basic element of a political debate. The practice should go.

The language of the Chamber in general should be overhauled so that it is understandable to someone in the public gallery. Instead of 'division', we should say 'vote'. Instead of saying that the question is 'as on the order paper', it should be read out so that someone can follow without having to find the order paper.

Keeling schedules should be introduced so that the text of a law that is being amended is printed out as it would be changed, allowing people to understand what is actually being proposed with only one document in front of them. All amendments – including backbench amendments, with the assistance of civil servants – should come with a one-paragraph description, in plain English, of what they are trying to achieve.

The Power

The British government is based in a house. The foolishness of this is immediately obvious as soon as you see it written down, and yet we go about our lives without questioning it.

The argument about the weakness of the centre is not really a constitutional one, it is a practical one. The government is based in a building where it cannot function in a rational way. It consequently fails to plan or implement policy appropriately. And that failure is presented as some sort of institutional debility rather than an organisational one.

There are no genuine arguments against this position. There is just tradition: it must be done this way because it has always been done this way. But this is not an argument, it is entropy garnished with sentimentality. Government is important. Its successes improve the lives of millions and its failures ruin them. It is not the place for nostalgia.

Downing Street's chief value is as a museum, and that is what it should become. That hallowed sense Thatcher spoke of, of being in the room where the decisions were made through history, should be made available to all. It should not be restricted to No. 10 staff nor be allowed to dictate their degree of operational competence.

The Queen Elizabeth II Centre in Westminster is perfectly capable of operating in place of No. 10. Other government departments, like the Foreign and Commonwealth Office, could also be used. Or a new building could be built from scratch, from the ground up, on the basis of modern working practice. But it cannot be a seventeenth-century house in which people are unable to work or communicate together.

That building should be the home of a new Department of the Prime Minister, with an increase in the staff at their disposal, and enough room for a Strategy Unit, a Policy Unit and a Delivery Unit, alongside the Cabinet Office's Economic and Domestic Affairs Secretariat, which contains the PBL.

The units should work largely as they did during New Labour's second term. The Strategy Unit would work long term, thinking about the world five years or ten years from now and planning for the challenges and opportunities ahead. It should communicate extensively with outside experts. This aims to replicate the advantage that oppositions have – of time to think and space to debate. This is what leads them to arrive in Downing Street with a collection of new ideas, before they ossify after years in power.

The Policy Unit should work medium term, predominantly in maintaining communication and coordination between the centre and the departments.

The Delivery Unit should work short term, on the granular level, with key metrics used to ensure the government is meeting its agenda, as it did under Michael Barber.

This structure alone will not fix organisational problems. If a prime minister comes along who does not know what they want to do, or does not have the capacity for sustained attention, or who puts the wrong people in charge, then no organisational structure is going to save them. But it allows for the possibility of effective work. It provides a defensive shield against the constant firefighting of political life, so that long-term thought and short-term practical implementation are still possible.

The Ministers

We need to reimagine the way that ministers work. At the moment, they have too much work and too little control over it, while simultaneously experiencing too little accountability.

If ministers are going to keep their spads, the system needs to be clarified and controlled. Downing Street should lose the ability to fire spads. All appointments should be made publicly, like any other job, rather than through internal party political networks. There should be a published quality threshold for appointments.

A new spad code should outline their responsibilities and the limitations of their role, ruling out any activity that seeks to cocoon the minister or any involvement with policy.

Instead, they should help liaise between Downing Street and the department on the one hand and the minister and the departmental civil service on the other.

We can then try to create the space for outside expertise that Wilson attempted to encourage when he first introduced the spad experiment. Ministers' Private Offices should be expanded with transparently advertised expert policy advisers, whom the minister has a say in selecting, alongside the permanent secretary. Ministerial involvement means these advisers will still come from a given political angle, as Wilson envisaged, but their civil service position means they cannot veer off entirely into party politics.

Secretaries of state should also be put in charge of selecting their own junior ministers, with that power being taken out of the hands of the prime minister. The entire box work system should be scrapped and replaced with a normal working process involving meetings and emails.

The ministerial code should be updated with an expectation that only people with experience and expertise are put in charge of a policy area. Prime ministers should also be encouraged to bring in people from outside Parliament and make them lords, thereby widening the talent pool they can choose from. This will not deal with the problem of ministers' complete lack of awareness of their department's work, but it will help alleviate it, and it will provide a benchmark by which journalists and parliamentarians can hold the prime minister's decision-making to account. With a bit of luck, it might even shift the cultural expectation in Westminster about the need for subject knowledge in the promotion process.

Ministers should be subject to recall to a select committee every two years for the next six consecutive years after they move on to account for their time in a department. We need to introduce the idea that there are consequences for what they do that supersede the short-termism of the ministerial merry-go-round. They need to be given a sense of long-term jeopardy.

The Money

We need to get rid of the Budget. It's an insane way to organise tax policy. Each year, more micro-announcements on tax and spending are added to the pile, leading to ever greater complexity in the system, accompanied by the absurdist theatre of rabbits-out-the-hat and newspaper Budget day specials.

There should instead be a commission established to outline how to implement the Mirrlees review, with tax policy in the short term restricted towards putting its recommendations into action. Clear guiding principles should be published on tax policy, with spending policy reformed to provide a greater focus on long-term growth.

The House of Lords should be given a full role scrutinising Treasury legislation. If it can morally play a role in revising legislation that can remove a citizen's liberty, there is no reason it cannot do so for legislation that can remove a citizen's money. It is the most effective body for assessing what departments do, and its absence from Treasury business is part of the reason that the department has fallen into such a state of disrepair. This should be bolstered with an increase in appointments for those with financial and economic experience.

Two of the other ideas outlined in this chapter will also improve parliamentary scrutiny of the Treasury. The first is the Private Office for MPs as described above; the second is a reform of the public bill committees, as outlined below.

In the case of Treasury legislation, that committee should be particularly well staffed and equipped with a small army of outside specialists.

The Civil Service

The civil service needs to be turned from a generalist organisation to an expert organisation with a managerial overlay. It's quite tiring even writing those words, given how often they've been written over so many decades, but unfortunately it's still necessary.

The current structure entwines two things that should be kept apart: management skill and expertise. The key to fixing the civil service issue is to disentangle them. There should be no policy expertise necessary for a position in management, nor any management position required to reward someone with policy expertise.

Civil servants should be encouraged to anchor their career in a specific area, like education or defence, and develop deep domain knowledge, bolstered by a mix of skills. There should be specific roles for subject matter specialists with a set career structure that rewards them financially for attaining expertise without forcing them to move position. As a first step towards that, there should at least be targeted pay progression for those who acquire extra skills or capabilities now.

Managers can move positions more frequently, although they should still be strongly encouraged to stay until the end of a project.

Permanent secretaries should be made accountable for reducing churn in their departments. This can start with the rudimentary requirement that they collect and publish key workforce data annually. Target levels for the optimal number of personnel changes should be established on an evidence-led basis and used to hold them to account for their performance.

A senior policy official should be given responsibility for the sourcing and retention of domain expertise, and HR departments should be given strategic responsibilities in long-term staffing needs, retention, talent management and corporate culture.

We do not want to stop civil servants moving jobs at all – people can get stale in the same position all their lives. But the expectation should be that they will stay in position for at least three to five years, and certainly until the end of a project. A base-level test should be that they know more than a minister, which at the moment is a very low bar.

A new Civil Service Code should answer, once and for all, the mercurial questions around the split of official and ministerial responsibility. It should clearly establish civil servants' duty to offer ministers objective information and, just as importantly, ministers' obligation to seriously assess it, rather than treat it as a conspiracy by an imaginary enemy.

The Press

Generally speaking, you don't want to start suggesting the government pass laws to interfere with the press, and I won't do so here. But cultural changes can be made to the way media is organised and consumed.

The first is a fund for local journalism. The decline in this area is a profound threat to a functioning democracy. It eradicates the front line, where policy impacts on the public. We need to accept that this is a market failure and it requires public intervention.

In 2017, the BBC created a Local News Partnership Scheme, consisting of a Local Democracy Reporting Service that pays the salaries of 150 journalists working for regional papers under a three-year contract. It has been a tremendous success, publishing 200,000 items in the first four years and breaking stories over issues like a dramatic reduction in bus journeys and failures in criminal background checks by authorities. It should be the model for much more extensive work and aggressive intervention.

Governments should work to bring back the press office as the core element of their communication strategy with the media. In truth, this is in their interest. An informed press officer can add nuance to critical articles and soften their edges if they actually have a working knowledge of what is being discussed. By reducing these offices into email conduits for media spads, governments have actually worsened the coverage they face.

There has recently been a moderate improvement in the media funding model by virtue of increased subscriptions to print brands online. One of the big advantages of this change is that it takes the emphasis away from clicks and towards long-term reader engagement. But this is a double-edged sword. We are creating a world in which the most reliable information is put behind a paywall and the least reliable information is available everywhere for free. A far better alternative is offered by podcasts on the Patreon platform: engaged listeners pay for extra content and to support the team, but the core product still goes out for free.

Readers should be on the lookout for joint bylines in political coverage. This is what we're looking for in an ideal world – two names on the story. It typically means that one of the reporters is in the lobby and the other has some specialism in the subject area. It allows the Westminster coverage to be mediated by someone who understands the policy background. It should be the model for most political articles and treated as a watermark of quality.

The Commons

The first thing we need to do is bring statutory instruments under control.

It's unrealistic to try and get rid of them altogether. Governments need to pass legal changes that are technical, urgent or impossible to formulate in advance due to fast-changing circumstances, without gumming up the floor of the Chamber. The problem is not the existence of the instruments, it is making sure that governments use them responsibly. They have systematically misused them, and this misuse has now reached the point where it constitutes a threat to the basic operation of parliamentary democracy.

We need a complete overhaul of the system, involving new legislation to replace the Statutory Instruments Act 1946. This should be based on the work of the Hansard Society, which has been diligently trying to fix the problem for years.

The Act would be complemented by a new Statutory Instrument Code, which lays out the types of law which governments are entitled to use statutory instruments for, and those which it is not. The latter category would include constitutional matters, retrospective legislation, fees and charges over a certain amount, and criminal offences. It would also include requirements on how narrow ministerial powers must be, based on the work of the Delegated Powers and Regulatory Reform Committee.

Under this new system, a statutory instrument would be sent to a sifting committee in the Commons, which would assess whether it is technical and uncontroversial or not. If it is, it can become law without further ado. This is a generous offer to government, which would allow it to pass genuine statutory instruments with even less hassle than it has now. But if it is not, the sifting committee would have a series of options open to it.

It could send it to a committee of MPs for further debate, with a vote to approve at the end. Or, if it was particularly serious, they could send it to the Commons Chamber. Any statutory instrument in this category would now be subject to amendment and rejection. The amendments do not need to be textual – it would be perfectly fine for MPs to send the statutory instrument back, telling the government to reformulate it to address their concerns. A similar system should operate in the Lords.

This proposed system is fair, democratic, and allows room for sustained scrutiny while still facilitating the speedy passage of technical changes to the law.

The Commons also needs to take back control of the timetable. Outside of electoral reform, there is probably no more urgent constitutional requirement. It is an embarrassment that the government exercises this degree of control, which is more akin to a tinpot dictatorship than a functioning democracy.

The manner in which this would be accomplished is perfectly clear. It was laid out in the Wright committee report, if only the coalition government had had the bravery to see it through. The existing Backbench Business Committee should meet with a newly created Business of the House Committee to agree the fortnightly agenda, then that agenda should be put to the Commons for a free vote. This is a point of principle. Parliament is sovereign. It represents the democratic view of the British public. But it is also practical. Once the Commons regains control over its affairs, it is more likely to act like the Lords, and give matters the time they deserve. It will also help reduce the opaque power of the usual channels, which silences backbenchers while prioritising government proposals and opposition grandstanding.

The Law

Something happens when a bill is published. The moment it becomes public, attitudes harden. Governments become protective and zealous. They start to attach their own sense of virility to its success.

It's therefore useful to see what we can do with legislation before that stage – when it is just a twinkle in a minister's eye. There is an existing process called pre-legislative scrutiny, which is applied to some bills, where they're looked at by a committee. But we can be more radical and inclusive than that.

Sometimes when a government department is considering introducing a new law, it will put together a broad discussion document called a green paper. We should formalise this process. Green papers should be published for all proposed legislation unless the government can show a compelling case for an emergency. The document should then be considered by a citizens' jury – specially convened groups representing the public who would take two weeks to look at the proposals, hear from experts and report back to Parliament on what they make of them.

Citizens' juries aren't particularly helpful for detailed consideration of documents. But they are very interesting when applied at an earlier stage in the process, for the general assessment of problems. Unlike focus groups or opinion polls, they demand that citizens become deeply involved in the subject matter, listen to experts and understand the various trade-offs that are required.

There would be no formal requirement for the government to implement what the jury says. But the final bill would likely be evaluated, inside Parliament and out, by virtue of how closely it stuck to the verdict.

This would also be healthy for the public itself. It would participate meaningfully in politics on the basis of relative advantages, rather than the black-and-white screaming matches often found on TV and social media. And it might shine a moral light on thorny issues like tax reform or the limits of protest that would guide government action.

We also need wholesale reform of committee stage. There is nothing to recommend the current public bill committees and no reason to retain them. They must go. Instead, they should be modelled on the select committee system. They should have a large civil service staff, including outside specialists. Their membership should be elected by MPs. The chairs should be tasked with finding consensus, rather than acting as neutral referees. They should hold extensive witness-testimony and evidence-gathering sessions. And most importantly, they should be permanent, not ad hoc, so that members develop a deep knowledge of the subject matter.

Given that we want to model public bill committees on select committees, it seems logical that we just use the select committees themselves for this purpose. And in some cases, that might work. It could certainly be done for those that shadow departments that produce relatively little legislation, like the Foreign Affairs Committee. But for others, like Home Affairs, it would simply overwhelm them – there is so much legislation that it would take up all their time.

Select committees should be treated like a precious crystal vase. Somehow, by some stroke of luck, we have ended up with a very good system. We should therefore touch it as little as possible. Instead, in the case of most departments, a permanent public bill committee should be established, with the incentives organised in such a way as to create a culture of cooperative work to improve legislation, rather than a tribal shouting match. As with the idea of an MPs' Private Office, this system would be particularly useful for improving the state of Treasury legislation.

We need to reintroduce electronic voting. Combined with Commons control over its timetable, this should serve to fix report stage.

We would expect that report stage would typically take three days, not one. Sometimes it might be more. Sometimes, with a particularly uncontroversial bill, it might be less. But three days is roughly what you'd want.

Electronic voting would then reduce the need to cut down amendments, because each vote would take seconds rather than fifteen minutes. The traditional objection to this argument is that voting in person gives MPs the opportunity to buttonhole a minister and ask them about whatever is bothering them. This is entirely true. It does give that opportunity and we would lose it. But we would also gain something. Firstly, we would gain the time to hold as many votes as the House wants, any number of which might improve the legislation. Secondly, we would reduce the power of the whips. MPs trooping through the lobbies do not just get the chance to make their case to a minister. They are also vulnerable to being bullied by the whips, or even pushed into a particular voting lobby.

It's worth looking closely at the descriptions MPs have given of what it is like to rebel, which most describe as a kind of trauma. The anxiety of going into a different voting lobby from your colleagues. The abuse piled on you by your own allies and the MPs from another party who you plan to vote alongside. That presents a series of emotional demands that most people are unable to undertake. It's this, more than bribery from the whips, that helps explain why MPs are often resistant to crossing the party line. Electronic voting can help alleviate that, in the same way that a secret ballot stopped bullying and intimidation in general elections. It provides a much safer mechanism for MPs to vote according to their judgement rather than social pressure.

Finally, the groups at report stage should be kept to around five or six, with more effort made into making them as specific as possible, so that the debate does not just turn into another vague, disconnected chat. Speakers should be more active in their chairmanship, working to keep debate only on the matter at hand and not allowing it to drift off into generalities. This is the stage of a bill's life that is defined by specificity. It is valuable for precisely that reason.

The Lords

Lords reform is the least pressing issue in this list. Through a bizarre historical accident, it has ended up as one of the best-functioning institutions in Westminster.

But that should not blind us to its deficiencies. It is quite wrong that bishops from the Church of England sit in the legislature. It is also wrong for hereditary peers to still be there. The lords themselves want them gone and so does everyone else. Even more seriously, the patronage power handed to the prime minister for appointments has swung completely out of control. They've used it to stuff the Chamber with party donors, loyalists and morally questionable individuals. These problems are now so severe that they risk completely destroying the Lord's reputation.

Some propose that we make the Lords democratic. But opening it up to the frenzied demands of elections would obliterate the one institution in the Westminster landscape which provides expertise and rebuild it as just another generalist party political body. The idea of the Commons, in its current form, operating without the scrutiny offered by the Lords is frankly terrifying.

Lords reform should have two central goals: preventing any one party having control of the Chamber and giving the expert crossbench peers a decisive vote.

The best way to achieve this is to broadly follow the recommendations in Lord Wakeham's Royal Commission in 2000. It would involve establishing the Appointments Commission in primary legislation and giving it full control over all appointments to the Chamber: both political and crossbench.

Party political appointments aren't a problem in principle. The Lords cannot be completely divorced from party politics. Having high quality former ministers and prime ministers still bringing their experience to bear on our current political debate is an asset. And more importantly, the day-to-day group voting of party political peers keeps the machine chugging along. It gives crossbenchers the freedom to dip in and out of legal debates, only intervening when it is a subject they have expertise in.

But the prime minister must lose their ability to install party political appointees. Instead, the Commission would make the appointments, allocating placements which reflect the share of the votes cast for the parties at the previous general election.

The Commission should also have total control of crossbench appointments, with a view to creating a 50:50 ratio between party political peers and crossbenchers. It would have a duty to maintain contacts with vocational, professional, cultural, sporting and other bodies, to invite nominations from the widest possible range of sources, and to maintain a Chamber with a membership which was representative of the general population in terms of gender, ethnicity and national and regional identity.

All peers, whether party political or crossbench, would be appointed for renewable 15-year terms. This system would clean out the sleaze of the party political process while maintaining the Lords as a Chamber of independent thought and expertise which could restrain and scrutinise the behaviour of the Commons.

Going Back to Basics

The final thing we need to fix is our own approach to politics, which has led us to where we are now.

We're very good at talking about our values. We like to reminisce about the long history of British liberties, or pat ourselves on the back about our national sense of good judgement. But the truth is that we long ago gave up on following these standards in our modern arrangements. We are embarrassingly bad at letting ideas like liberty and good judgement guide our day-to-day behaviour.

People who are truly committed to these ideas celebrate scrutiny, knowledge, the restraint of power and the free exchange of ideas. These are the principles upon which open societies are supposed to function.

People who are not committed to them do something else entirely. They strengthen government at the expense of Parliament. They close themselves off from criticism or challenge. They sideline, ignore and denigrate expertise. They create promotional systems that obstruct specialist knowledge. They prioritise machismo over consensus.

Across the world – from Moscow to Beijing, Tehran to Riyadh – authoritarian regimes act as though they're in the ascendant, as if open societies have neither the self-confidence nor the strength to challenge them. But in fact, they are travelling down an ideological cul-de-sac.

Free societies are not just more open than oppressive ones. They are more efficient. It's by the testing of ideas, the challenging of dogma and the criticism of power that we make progress. This is how we discover questions and improve our answers. It's how we drop that which does not work in favour of that which does. No matter how mighty closed societies might appear in their rare moments of triumph, they never succeed for long, because they lack the ability to spot and act upon their own deficiencies.

Our own current failures stem from the same problem. We might pride ourselves on being an open society, but we've arranged ourselves politically like a closed one. Our constitutional provisions have forsaken our principles, so now we experience the practical difficulties that inevitably follow: an unwillingness to recognise problems and an inability to construct viable solutions.

Words like 'scrutiny' and 'specialism' can sometimes sound respectable or managerial. In fact, they are representations of some of the most radical and liberating concepts in the history of human thought. They are the daily practical application of our values. They show that we believe in free expression and the power of knowledge – not just for their own sake, but because they are the principles that improve life for everyone.

The first step to implementing these reforms is to commit ourselves to the ideals that inform them.

We can fix the problems we've looked at over the course of this book. It might currently feel hopeless, but it isn't. Political change occurs all the time. It takes place every day, all over the world. And that does not happen because of inevitable historical dynamics or predestined social progress. It happens because people agitate for it. It happens because they demand it of politicians as a precondition of their support.

Change will not come from the generosity of those who benefit from the existing state of affairs. It will come from the sustained challenge of those who do not.

Acknowledgements

This book is based on conversations with:

Andrew Adonis, former education policy advisor in Downing Street and secretary of state for transport
David Anderson, crossbench peer and former Independent Reviewer of Terrorism Legislation
Tim Bale, professor of Politics at Queen Mary University
Michael Barber, former head of the Downing Street Delivery Unit
Tania Bassett, national official at the Napo probation trade union
Lewis Baston, former director of research for the Electoral Reform Society
Jason Beattie, assistant editor of the *Daily Mirror*
Margaret Beckett, Labour MP for Derby South and former secretary of state for foreign affairs
John Bercow, former Speaker of the House of Commons
Luciana Berger, former Labour MP for Liverpool Wavertree and shadow minister for mental health
Theo Bertram, former adviser to prime ministers Tony Blair and Gordon Brown
Adam Bienkov, political editor of Byline Times
Peter Bone, Conservative MP for Wellingborough and former deputy leader of the House of Commons

Peter Bottomley, Conservative MP for Worthing West and the father of the House

Ben Bradshaw, Labour MP for Exeter and former secretary of state for culture, media and sport

Michael Braddick, professor of History at the University of Sheffield

George Brock, professor of Journalism at City University

Andy Burnham, Mayor of Greater Manchester and former secretary of state for health

Alastair Campbell, former Downing Street press secretary and director of communications

Christopher Chope, Conservative MP for Christchurch

Nick Clegg, former leader of the Liberal Democrats and deputy prime minister

Damian Collins, Conservative MP for Folkestone and Hythe and former chair of the House of Commons digital, culture, media and sport select committee

Diane Coyle, Bennett professor of Public Policy at the University of Cambridge

Chris Curtis, former political research manager at YouGov

Nikki da Costa, former director of legislative affairs for Theresa May and Boris Johnson

Nick Davies, programme director at the Institute for Government

Gus O'Donnell, former Cabinet secretary

Maria Eagle, Labour MP for Garston and Halewood and former minister of state for justice and equalities

Chris Evans, Labour MP for Islwyn and shadow minister for defence procurement

Nigel Evans, Conservative MP for Ribble Valley and deputy Speaker

Paul Evans, chair of the Study of Parliament Group and former clerk of committees in the House of Commons

Tim Farron, Liberal Democrat MP for Westmorland and Lonsdale and former leader of the Liberal Democrats

Lynne Featherstone, Liberal Democrat peer and former parliamentary under-secretary of state for equalities

Sam Freedman, senior fellow at the Institute for Government and former senior policy adviser on education to Michael Gove

Carl Gardener, professional support lawyer for LexisPSL and former government lawyer

Jess Garland, director of policy and research at the Electoral Reform Society

David Gauke, former chief secretary to the Treasury, secretary of state for work and pensions and secretary of state for justice

Robert Halfon, Conservative MP for Harlow and former chair of the House of Commons education select committee

Holger Hestermeyer, professor of International and EU Law at King's College London

Simon Hix, Stein Rokkan chair in Comparative Politics at the European University Institute

David Howarth, professor of Law and Public Policy at the University of Cambridge and former Liberal Democrat MP for Cambridge

Lindsey Hoyle, Speaker of the House of Commons

James Johnson, founding partner of J.L. Partners polling company and former senior opinion research and strategy adviser to prime minister Theresa May

Jonathan Jones, former head of the Government Legal Service

Ivor Judge, crossbench peer and former Lord Chief Justice of England and Wales

Peter Kellner, former president of YouGov

Neil Kinnock, former Labour MP for Islwyn and leader of the Labour party

Richard Kwiatkowski, professor of Organisational Psychology, Organisational Behaviour and Applied Psychology at the Cranfield School of Management

David Lammy, Labour MP for Tottenham and shadow secretary of state for foreign affairs

Kim Leadbeater, Labour MP for Batley and Spen

Spencer Livermore, former Labour senior advisor for election campaigns and director of strategy to prime minister Gordon Brown

Caroline Lucas, Green party MP for Brighton Pavilion

Polly Mackensie, former chief executive of Demos

Johnny Mercer, Conservative MP for Plymouth Moor View and minister of state for veterans' affairs

Lisa Nandy, Labour MP for Wigan and shadow secretary of state for levelling up, housing and communities

Andrew Neilson, director of campaigns at the Howard League for Penal Reform

Caroline Nokes, Conservative MP for Romsey and Southampton North and former minister of state for immigration

Phillip Norton, Conservative peer and professor of Government at the University of Hull

Jim Pickard, chief political correspondent at the *Financial Times*

Jonathan Portas, professor of Economics and Public Policy at King's College London and former chief economist at the Department for Work and Pensions

Jonathan Powell, former Downing Street chief of staff

Alan Renwick, professor of Democratic Politics at UCL and deputy director of the Constitution Unit

Ed Richards, former senior policy advisor to prime minister Tony Blair

Sienna Rodgers, senior writer at the *House* magazine and former editor of LabourList

Alan Rusbridger, editor of *Prospect* magazine and former editor of the *Guardian*

Meg Russell, professor of British and Comparative Politics at UCL and director of the Constitution Unit

Jill Rutter, senior fellow at the Institute for Government and former civil servant at the Treasury

Dan Sabagh, defence and security editor at the *Guardian* newspaper

Robert Saunders, reader in Modern British History at Queen Mary University

Paula Sheriff, former Labour MP for Dewsbury

Matt Singh, founder of the Number Cruncher Politics polling company

Alyn Smith, SNP MP for Stirling

Anna Soubry, former Conservative MP for Broxtowe and minister of state for small business, industry and enterprise

Rory Stewart, former Conservative MP for Penrith and The Border and secretary of state for international development

Mikael Sundström, senior lecturer at the Department of Political Science at Lund University

Alan Travis, former home affairs editor at the *Guardian*

Dheemanth Vangimalla, researcher at the Hansard Society

Wim Voermans, professor of Constitutional and Administrative law at Leiden University.

Paul Waugh, chief political commentator at the *i* newspaper

Ashley Weinberg, senior lecturer in Psychology at the University of Salford

James Weinberg, lecturer in Political Behaviour at the University of Sheffield
Catherine West, Labour MP for Hornsey and Wood Green
Jo Wolff, Alfred Landecker professor of Values and Public Policy at the Blavatnik School of Government, Oxford.
Julian Zelizer, professor of History and Public Affairs at Princeton University

... and many, many others, in Downing Street, parliament, Whitehall and Fleet Street who chose to not be named.

I'm grateful to every single one of them for taking the time out of their busy schedules to talk to me. And I'm particularly grateful to those who can't be identified here and will receive no recognition for it. They did it because they wanted people to understand how the political world operates and what might be wrong with it. I'm in their debt. I hope I've done something useful with what they told me.

The fact that someone was interviewed for this book does not mean that they agree with its argument, either generally or in specific instances. Several interviewees will disagree with all of it, or at least vast sections of it, and hardly any will agree with all of it. In many instances, they knew this to be the case and spoke to me anyway, out of a sense that people who disagree can maintain cordial relationships and acknowledge shared facts about the world. It's a valuable old fashioned notion which should be more popular than it is.

I'm also incredibly grateful for those who read through sections of this book to see if I was making any mistakes. They were:

Siva Anandaciva, senior analyst at the Kings Fund
Tim Bale, professor of Politics at Queen Mary University

Jasmine Basran, head of Policy and Campaigns at Crisis
Lewis Baston, former director of research for the Electoral Reform Society
Timothy Besley, professor of Economics and Political Science at the LSE
Andrew Blick, professor of Politics and Contemporary History at King's College London
Tom Clougherty, research director and head of Tax at the Centre for Policy Studies
Martin Conboy, emeritus professor of Journalism History at the University of Sheffield
Diane Coyle, Bennett professor of Public Policy at the University of Cambridge
Emma Crewe, professor of Social Anthropology at Soas
Robert Canton, professor in Community and Criminal Justice at De Montfort University
Paul Evans, chair of the Study of Parliament Group and former clerk of committees in the House of Commons
Ruth Fox, director of the Hansard Society,
Ruth Garland, lecturer in Media at Goldsmiths University
Glen Gottfried, associate director at Ipsos UK
Catherine Haddon, senior fellow at the Institute for Government
Chris Hanretty, professor of Politics at Royal Holloway
Holger Hestermeyer, professor of International and EU Law at King's College London
Simon Hix, Stein Rokkan chair in Comparative Politics at the European University Institute
Spencer Livermore, former Labour senior advisor for election campaigns and director of strategy to prime minister Gordon Brown
Phillip Norton, Conservative peer and professor of government at the University of Hull

Tom Peck, political sketch writer at the *Independent*
Gwen Robinson, deputy head of the School of Law at the University of Sheffield
Sienna Rodgers, senior writer at the *House* magazine and former editor of LabourList
Meg Russell, professor of British and Comparative Politics at UCL and director of the Constitution Unit
Jill Rutter, senior fellow at the Institute for Government and former civil servant at the Treasury
Luke Sibieta, research fellow at the Institute for Fiscal Studies
Martin Stanley, former senior civil servant and author of *Understanding the Civil Service*
Gemma Tetlow, chief economist at the Institute for Government
Kevin Theakston, professor of British Government at the University of Leeds
Alex Thomas, programme director at the Institute for Government
Giles Wilks, senior fellow at the Institute for Government
Oliver Wright, policy editor at *The Times*
Tony Yates, former head of monetary policy strategy at the Bank of England

Again, many of them cannot be named, including people who gave up an awful lot of their time to ensure the details were right. In other cases, you'll spot people on both lists, who fact-checked sections of the book while also giving interviews. These guys really were saints, going above and beyond to help. Any mistakes which remain are mine and God knows there must be some left in there. If you spot one, contact me at ianduntmedia@gmail.com and I'll correct it.

Jenny Lord is just an absolutely gold class editor, offering help when it's needed, space when it isn't, and plying me full of booze when neither of the previous two categories applied. She's robustly supported this book from the twinkle-in-the-eye stage right through to what you hold in your hand. None of it would be possible without her, or the incredible team at W&N. Lindsay Terrell has been an extraordinary mixture of generosity and steely determination. Frances Rooney has dealt with all my last-minute changes to the umpteenth proof with the kind of patience which only a true saint could exhibit. My deepest thanks also to Shona Abhyankar at EDPR for delivering the most confident, professional and good-humoured publicity campaign imaginable.

As ever, my agent Lisa Moylett has been by my side through this project, always having my back and offering words of wisdom or advice when they're needed. I'm incredibly fortunate to have stumbled into such a beneficial working relationship. Thanks to her, and the whole team at CMM, including Zoe Apostolides and Jamie Maclean, the first person to ever pay me for a piece of writing. It was absolute filth and I am very grateful to him for commissioning it.

Thanks also to the team at the *i* newspaper, who offered me the time and space to successfully complete the book – in particular Oly Duff, Rupert Hawksley and Heather Saul – and my colleagues at Podmasters, who did the same – including Andrew Harrison, Martin Bojtos, Jacob Jarvis and Jade Bailey. And of course thanks to the podcast gang, without whom the last few years would have been infinitely more dreadful. Dorian, Naomi, Ros and Alex: you guys are the best.

I've discovered while writing books that they will absolutely destroy you in every conceivable way: mentally, spiritually, and physically. So I'm pathetically grateful to the people around me who have made this process more bearable, including the London Clan of Shazia and Farrah, the old school support group of Swinden, Duncan and Westy, and my two wonderful parents, who are the best workable proof of the idea that the world might not be such a bad place after all.

Thanks finally to Menissa Saleem, who is the first person to read whatever I write and whose approval of it is the first sign that it is suitable for wider distribution. You encourage me to see more widely than I ever might do on my own. And you make me laugh, every single day, no matter what is happening or how grim things might look. Thank heavens above that you stumbled into my life.

And last but certainly not least, thanks to Thanos, who sat by feet throughout this thing, rising only occasionally to try to eat my toes, or rub his arse in my face, or eat the electric cable by the TV, or bark at his reflection in the window. He would be a much better trained puppy if I hadn't been writing a book at the same time, and this book would probably have been much better written if I hadn't been cleaning up his piss from the kitchen floor while pursuing it, but I wouldn't change a thing. He's a very good boy.

Glossary

Afghan Relocations and Assistance Policy (ARAP)
Programme designed to help Afghans who worked directly for the UK government during the evacuation in 2021.

amendment
A change made to an existing law.

aye/no lobby
The hallways on either side of the Commons Chamber that MPs pass through in order to vote.

Backbench Business Committee
A committee that decides what is debated during time reserved for backbenchers in the Commons.

backbench rebellion
MPs voting against their party whip.

backbencher
An MP who is not part of their party's front bench team. For a party in government, this refers to anyone who is not a minister or a PPS. For an opposition party, it is anyone who has not been given a shadow ministerial position.

Bank of England
The UK's central bank, tasked with delivering monetary and financial stability. Under Gordon Brown it was made independent, with responsibility for setting interest rates.

bicameralism
A legislature composed of two chambers. In some cases, this is arranged so that one of the chambers can reflect distinct political or social units in the nation, like linguistic groups or local states. In others, it is to provide a sense of restraint and improvement in the legislation produced by the other chamber.

box work
The red box of papers ministers are given to take home so they can work on it overnight or over the weekend.

Brexit
The project to extract Britain from the European Union.

Budget
The annual budget set by the Treasury for the following financial year, usually featuring changes to taxation and spending and a 'rabbit-out-of-the-hat' announcement by the chancellor deployed to secure political advantage.

by-election
A contest in one constituency outside of a general election, typically because of the death or resignation of the sitting MP.

Cabinet
Ostensibly the main body that controls government policy and coordinates the activities of governmental departments, although in recent decades its power has significantly declined.

Cabinet Office
The government department responsible for supporting the prime minister and, to a lesser extent, Cabinet. It can be accessed from No. 10 through a single door that leads to its building in 70 Whitehall.

Cabinet secretary
The most senior civil servant in the British government, working out of the Cabinet Office. This figure used to invariably come from the Treasury, although Theresa May broke with that tradition.

casework
The term for an MP's work in the local constituency.

chair
The term often used for the Speaker in debates.

Chamber
Literally the room of the Commons or the Lords, i.e., Commons Chamber or Lords Chamber.

chancellor
The secretary of state in charge of the Treasury.

chief of staff

A senior adviser to the prime minister. The name was imported from the US under the Blair administration but there is no specific job description.

chief secretary to the Treasury

The second secretary of state at the Treasury, generally tasked with ensuring departmental budget compliance.

civil service

The sector of government composed of non-party political officials. They are officially tasked with serving the Crown, which in practice means serving the elected government of the day.

classified advertising

Adverts typically from an individual or small business in a dedicated section of a newspaper.

clerks

Officials in the Commons and Lords who act as the equivalent to its civil service. The clerk of the House is the most senior figure, equivalent to a permanent secretary.

clickbait

The practice of creating low-quality content online maximised for attention.

coalition government

When two parties govern together because they did not secure enough seats for a government majority on their own. The Conservatives and Liberal Democrats formed a coalition government between 2010 and 2015.

committee stage
The point in a bill's life when it is supposed to be subject to detailed scrutiny, usually by a public bill committee of MPs.

Conservatives
One of the two main parties in the British electoral system, typically taking a centre-right position. It is one of the longest-lasting and most successful political parties in the world.

constituency
The designated local area in which voters elect a representative to the Commons.

consultants
Individuals brought into the civil service from the private sector on a temporary basis, often to assist with a particular project.

crossbenchers
Non-party-political members of the Lords, recommended by the House of Lords Appointments Commission, typically on the basis of exceptional achievement in public life.

delegated legislation committee
Committee of MPs that evaluates statutory instruments.

Delegated Powers and Regulatory Reform Committee
House of Lords committee that provides the nearest thing to jurisprudence on delegated powers.

departmental lawyers
Lawyers working in government departments. Among other tasks, they typically write out a description of a law to parliamentary counsel for them to turn into a bill.

devolved assemblies
The Scottish Parliament, the Welsh Senedd Cymru and the National Assembly in Northern Ireland, where powers have been devolved from Westminster.

disguised legislation
A type of delegated power, often called a tertiary power, that rests on the issuing of guidance or public notices but ultimately has the same effect as law.

display advertising
Typically a business advert placed next to editorial content.

dissolution
The official end of a parliament ahead of a general election.

division
A vote in the Commons.

Downing Street
The street in which the British government is located. The prime minister works from No. 10 and the chancellor from No. 11. Used as a shorthand for government.

emergency debate
Three-hour debate authorised by the Speaker using Standing Order No. 24 on matters the government has failed to make time for.

Erskine May
Parliament's rule book, featuring a collection of hard conventions dictating behaviour in the Chamber.

first-past-the-post
The electoral system used for general elections in the UK, in which voters express their preferences in one-member electoral districts and the candidate with the most votes wins.

first reading
The formal introduction of a bill to Parliament.

Fulton report
Result of a 1968 inquiry into the civil service that criticised it for generalism and lack of specialist knowledge.

grades
The promotional structure of the civil service, going up in a pyramid structure from Grade 7 to Grade 1, which is the permanent secretary.

Greens
A party campaigning for action on climate change. In recent years it has secured one MP, Caroline Lucas, for the constituency of Brighton Pavilion.

government
Otherwise known as the executive. The group of people with the authority to rule the state. In the case of the UK, this is composed of the prime minister and their ministers, as a result of general elections.

government benches
The seats to the right of the Speaker's chair in the Commons Chamber, where the party or parties that form a government sit.

Henry VIII power
A delegated power which allows a minister to change an existing Act of Parliament.

hereditary peers
The 92 members of the House of Lords with a title passed down through their family. Their continued presence in the Lords is a result of a compromise by Tony Blair during his reform of the Upper Chamber in 1999.

House of Commons
The elected Chamber in Parliament, comprising 650 MPs selected through a first-past-the-post voting system in local constituencies. It is tasked with scrutinising the government.

House of Lords
Otherwise known as the Upper Chamber. A revision chamber tasked with improving legislation. The Lords is unelected and composed of life peers, hereditary peers and bishops. It can block legislation, but only for a maximum of 13 months, at which point the government can use the Parliament Act to overrule it.

hustings
A meeting in which candidates address their potential voters. In the case of party selections, this will involve local party members.

Institute for Fiscal Studies (IFS)
Prominent think tank whose pronouncements on the Budget often frame the media narrative.

internal knives
Deadlines for when each group stage of amendments on a bill must come to an end.

King's Speech
A speech made by the monarch at the state opening of Parliament, in which the government's legislative agenda for the year ahead is read out.

Labour
One of the two main parties in the British electoral system, typically taking a centre-left position.

leader of the House of Commons
The minister in charge of organising government business in the House of Commons, including the timetable and the legislative agenda.

leader of the opposition
The leader of the largest party in opposition.

legislation
A law. This can take the form of primary legislation or secondary legislation.

Liberal Democrats
Typically considered the third party in the British electoral system, although it has recently elected fewer MPs than the

Scottish National Party (SNP). It typically adopts a broadly centrist position.

life peers

Members of the House of Lords whose peerage cannot be inherited. This type of peerage was created by prime minister Harold Macmillan. They are either recommended for the House of Lords by the party leaders or by the House of Lords Appointments Commission, which nominates cross-bench peers.

Lobby

The designation for political journalists in the parliamentary estate. They typically work in the building and attend the daily briefings by the prime minister's spokesperson.

majority

In the Commons, this refers to the number of seats the government holds over the 50 per cent mark. There are 650 seats in the Commons, so a government with 326 seats, for instance, would have a majority of one. In a local constituency, the word has a different but related meaning. It is the gap between the winning candidate and the second-placed candidate. If the winning Labour candidate in a local constituency secures 2,000 votes, for instance, and the second-placed Liberal Democrat candidate secures 1,000 votes, Labour is said to have a majority of 1,000.

marginal constituency

A constituency with a thin gap between at least two parties, meaning it could go either way in a general election. Marginal constituencies generally receive the lion's share of attention from political parties during an election.

marginal rate

The tax someone pays on the next £1 they earn.

minister

An MP or lord selected by the prime minister to work in government. Ministers are on the government payroll and are bound by collective responsibility, meaning they must advance the government's agenda regardless of their own personal views.

minority government

A government that failed to secure a majority but managed to govern anyway, usually through a formal or informal support arrangement with another party. Theresa May ran a minority government in the period after the 2017 general election.

Mirrlees review

The product of a two-year inquiry into Britain's tax system, which recommended wide-ranging reform.

MP

A member of Parliament, elected by their local constituency in a first-past-the-post electoral contest. There is no job description for MPs, but they have two core roles: to scrutinise the activity of government and to serve their constituents.

National Audit Office (NAO)

The UK's independent public spending watchdog, responsible for auditing central government departments and others.

National Executive Committee (NEC)

The governing body of the Labour party.

National Insurance
A tax that began as a form of social security but now operates largely as a simple tax on earnings.

No. 10
Shorthand for the prime minister's office in Downing Street, and therefore for government.

Northcote–Trevelyan
The civil service settlement, derived from an 1854 report that constituted the founding document of the service.

Office for Budget Responsibility (OBR)
Independent body set up by George Osborne to provide economic and public finance forecasts.

opposition benches
The seats to the left of the Speaker's chair in the Commons Chamber, where the parties that are not in government sit.

opposition day
A day in which the opposition chooses the subject for debate in the Commons.

parliament
The period of parliamentary time between one general election and the next.

Parliament
The legislative body in the British constitution, composed of the Commons and the Lords. It is tasked with passing laws, representing voters and scrutinising the activity of government. In the UK, Parliament is the sovereign body,

which means it is the source of legitimate political power and stands supreme over all other institutions, including the government and the judiciary.

Parliament Act
Two pieces of legislation, one in 1911 and one in 1949, that reduced the Lords' powers of veto. The end result is that the Lords can only delay legislation, not kill it.

Parliamentary Business and Legislation Committee (PBL)
A key body in the Cabinet Office's Economic and Domestic Affairs Secretariat dedicated to organising the government's legislative agenda and ensuring bills are legally watertight before publication.

parliamentary counsel
The small group of legal figures who write legislation.

parliamentary private secretary (PPS)
A position below that of junior minister, ostensibly aimed as a link between the minister and backbenchers, but in reality used for any number of things, or none at all.

payroll vote
The number of secretaries of state, junior ministers, whips and PPSs who are bound to support the government on the basis of their government salary and can therefore be relied upon in votes. Technically PPSs are not paid a salary, but they are included in this figure anyway.

permanent secretary
The most senior civil servant in a government department, effectively the CEO of the organisation.

pilot
A trial run of a policy, usually in a limited geographical area or a set institution.

ping-pong
The process by which the Commons and Lords attempt to resolve any disagreements over the contents of a bill.

Plaid Cymru
A party campaigning for Welsh independence.

points of order
Complaints raised by MPs ostensibly about procedural irregularities in the Commons, but which are typically party political in nature.

Policy Unit
A group in Downing Street, usually composed of a mixture of spads and civil servants, with an emphasis on the former, which is used in a variety of ways by different prime ministers.

Portcullis House
A large building next to Parliament in which many MPs' offices and cafés are housed.

practice
Ways of doing things in the Commons Chamber that are widely followed.

praying against
An archaic name referring to parliamentarians' communication with the Crown. Most commonly used to protest against statutory instruments.

press
Print journalists, whether for national or local newspapers. Sometimes used colloquially to refer to all journalists, regardless of whether they are broadcast, digital or print.

press office
Government operation that serves to communicate with the media, either in departments or No. 10. Staffed by press officers.

primary legislation
The main laws passed by Parliament. They start as a bill when they are going through the Commons and the Lords, and become an Act when they turn into law. This happens when the bill receives Royal Assent at the end of its legislative journey.

Prime Minister's Questions (PMQs)
A prime minister's version of ministerial question time, which takes place weekly for half an hour.

principal private secretary
Senior civil servant acting as the interface between the minister and their department.

private office
The office of civil servants working for the minister and typically reporting on progress in particular policy areas.

private secretaries
Civil servants working in the private office.

probation
A public service that supervises offenders and attempts to ensure they are rehabilitated. Supervision can apply after the offender has served time in prison or as an alternative to prison.

programme motion
A motion allocating the amount of time to be reserved for debate on a bill.

proportional representation
A broad term that refers to a variety of different voting systems in which most votes cast contribute to the result, providing a representative expression of the electorate's preferences.

prorogation
The ending of a parliamentary session, which triggers a period of inactivity ahead of the state opening of Parliament that begins the next session. Usually a procedural formality, but it was found to be used unlawfully by Boris Johnson in 2019.

Public Accounts Committee
One of the oldest and most senior of all the select committees, tasked with overseeing government expenditure.

question time
A secretary of state's regular session in Parliament in which they and their junior ministers answer questions from MPs.

report stage
The point of a bill's life when it is supposed to be subject to detailed scrutiny by the whole of the House of Commons.

reshuffle
A moment in which the prime minister moves their team around ministerial positions – promoting some, demoting others and bringing in fresh blood.

Royal Assent
The moment a bill becomes law. From this point it will be called an Act.

rulings from the chair
Decisions taken by the Speaker, which form a kind of parliamentary case law.

safe seat
A constituency the incumbent party is considered very unlikely to lose because of the size of its majority.

Salisbury convention
Convention that the Lords will not impede the passage of legislation if it was included in the manifesto of the winning party.

Scottish National Party (SNP)
A party that campaigns for Scottish independence. In recent years it has provided the majority of MPs from Scottish constituencies.

seat
Another term for constituency, on the basis that each one provides a seat in the Commons.

second reading
A general debate on the principles of a bill that has been introduced to Parliament.

secretary of state
A senior minister in charge of a department; for instance, the home secretary at the Home Office, or the foreign secretary at the Foreign Office.

select committee
A cross-party group of MPs tasked with investigating a certain topic. Many of the committees map onto government departments, such as home affairs, while others have a cross-departmental remit, such as government expenditure.

selection
The process of choosing who will stand as the candidate for a political party in the general election. The final decision is typically made following a hustings debate in front of local party members.

selection committee
A committee in the local party that whittles down the list of names of those hoping to be the party's official candidate in the election.

session
A parliamentary year.

shadow minister
An opposition party frontbencher who is in charge of the party's policy in a given area, such as a shadow home secretary.

short campaign
The period between the dissolution of Parliament and the date of the general election.

sitting
The parliamentary day in each Chamber.

skeleton legislation
Legislation with very little content and a great many ministerial powers.

snap election
A sudden general election outside of the normal four- or five-year electoral schedule. There was a snap election in 2017 and again in 2019.

Speaker
The chair of proceedings in the Commons. They sit in the middle of the Chamber, select MPs to speak and rule on points of order.

Speaker's conference
Morning meeting in which the Speaker, their three deputies and the clerk of the House run through the order paper and discuss potential amendments and points of order.

special adviser

Colloquially known as a 'spad'. They are political appointees hired to support ministers and are able to give party political advice and support that would be inappropriate for the civil service to provide.

Special Cases

Programme designed to assist Afghans who had supported UK objectives but were not working directly for Britain during the evacuation.

standing orders

Rules of the House of Commons that have been passed to govern its affairs. Standing Order No. 14 gave government business precedence over any other type, with a few exceptions.

statutory instruments

The most common form of delegated power. The right to make a statutory instrument is set out in primary legislation and usually handed to a minister. They can be negative or affirmative. Generally speaking, they receive far less scrutiny than primary legislation.

surgery

A meeting in which constituents can bring matters concerning them to the local MP.

tearoom

A cafeteria on the parliamentary estate famed as a centre for plotting and gossip.

third reading

Usually a short debate at the end of a bill's passage through Parliament, often a valedictory affair.

trade union

An association of workers to protect and further their interests. Several trade unions have close links with the Labour party, including in their governance structure and candidate selection process.

Transforming Rehabilitation

The official name for Chris Grayling's programme privatising probation services.

Treasury

Otherwise known as HM Treasury or the exchequer. The government department responsible for public finance, departmental budgets and economic policy.

UKIP

A hard-right anti-immigration Eurosceptic party that has historically struggled to secure representation in Parliament but exercised an outsized influence on the right of the Conservative party.

Universal Credit

A social security payment that replaced six existing benefits for working-age households.

urgent question

Request by an MP to ask a question of the relevant minister in the Commons. The urgent question became a key part of the Speaker's toolkit during the Bercow era and remains so today.

usual channels
The informal negotiation arrangement between the government and opposition parties, in which matters pertaining to the day-to-day running of the Commons are agreed.

value-added tax (VAT)
A tax on the price of a product or service.

wet
A term for a moderate under Margaret Thatcher. Such figures were typically removed in favour of more zealous ideological free-market advocates.

whip
The party enforcement mechanism in the Commons and the Lords, which is tasked with ensuring MPs vote as desired by the leadership. The word refers to certain individuals, such as the chief whip, and the instruction. A three-line whip, for instance, is the highest level of demand for loyalty in a vote, with potentially severe repercussions if an MP contravenes it. An MP who 'loses the whip' is still a member of Parliament, but has been expelled from the party.

Whitehall
Shorthand term for the civil service, similar to 'Downing Street' for government or 'Fleet Street' for the press.

Wright committee
A committee established in 2010 to explore avenues for reform of Commons procedure. Its recommendations were only partially implemented.

References and Further Reading

The best single book on the rules, conventions and general way of doing things in Parliament is *How Parliament Works*, by Robert Rogers and Rhodri Walters. It's the definitive account, far more thorough and comprehensive than this one. It is also – and this really isn't their fault – bone dry, long and full of technical detail. But if this book was your first step into understanding Westminster and you're now looking to take on a more substantial journey, that's the next place to go. The references below are to the 8th edition.

There are two books whose shadow falls over this one but that are not referenced or used anywhere in the text. The first is *Perfecting Parliament: Constitutional Reform, Liberalism, and the Rise of Western Democracy*, by Robert D. Congleton. It's a work of astonishing intellectual ambition, encompassing a constitutional history of the UK, Sweden, the Netherlands, Japan, Germany and the US and then applying a new rational choice model to evaluate the causal factors in foundational political change. Along the way, it provides a very good account of the long movement towards parliamentary democracy across the world – why it happened and how others did it differently. It's academic, but very readable.

The second is *Philosophy and the Real World: An Introduction to Karl Popper*, by the former MP Bryan Magee. Magee's interpretation of the liberal philosopher is that open societies are not just more moral than closed ones, they are also more efficient. This is because they are capable of discovering their own problems and formulating a viable response to them. That idea provided my core motivation for writing this book and the basic philosophical framework I used when approaching the problem.

On probation, it's worth reading HM Inspector of Probation's 2019 annual report, available at https://www.justiceinspectorates.gov.uk/hmiprobation/wp-content/uploads/sites/5/2019/03/HMI-Probation-Chief-Inspectors-Report.pdf, on just how challenging it is to improve the lives of people who often have multiple intersecting problems. There's evidence of probation's broadly successful track record before privatisation at https://consult.justice.gov.uk/digital-communications/transforming-rehabilitation/results/transforming-rehabilitation-response.pdf and https://www.gov.uk/government/news/probation-service-wins-excellence-award. For early conclusions on the need for a multi-agency approach to the rehabilitation of offenders, see the 2005 Home Affairs Select Committee report, available here: https://publications.parliament.uk/pa/cm200405/cmselect/cmhaff/193/19303.htm.

You can find information about the pilots Chris Grayling wrapped up in Doncaster and Peterborough here: https://assets.publishing.service.gov.uk/government/uploads/system/uploads/attachment_data/file/449494/hmp-doncaster-pbr-final-evaluation.pdf and here: https://www.russellwebster.com/final-evaluation-of-peterborough-prison-pbr-pilot/. The government's really rather misleading response to the consultation is at https://consult.justice.gov.

uk/digital-communications/transforming-rehabilitation/results/transforming-rehabilitation-response.pdf.

There's a report about the leaked risk register here: https://www.theguardian.com/society/2013/dec/15/probation-reforms-put-public-at-higher-risk, which then led to the quite striking exchange between Grayling and John McDonnell, which you can see at https://publications.parliament.uk/pa/cm201415/cmselect/cmjust/307/131204.htm. The Commons exchanges involving Grayling can be found here: https://publications.parliament.uk/pa/cm201213/cmhansrd/cm130109/debtext/130109-0001.htm#13010946001448, while Toby Perkins' challenge is at https://www.parallelparliament.co.uk/mp/toby-perkins/debate/2013-10-30/commons/commons-chamber/probation-service. Throughout this period, Grayling was relying on Labour's Offender Management Act to sidestep Parliament. You can read that here: https://www.legislation.gov.uk/ukpga/2007/21/section/3. It does exactly what Grayling said it does. He might have been ruinously inept, simple-minded and symbolic of complete national collapse, but he wasn't wrong about the Act.

For a comprehensive and much-needed assessment of the press coverage of the probation reforms, see 'Bad News for Probation? Analysing the Newspaper Coverage of Transforming Rehabilitation', by Carol Hedderman and Alex Murphy, *Probation Journal*, Vol. 62(3) (2015).

There are a series of very good reports on the failing of Grayling's reforms in Westminster by the National Audit Office, the Justice Select Committee and the Public Accounts Committee. Alongside interviews with probation officers, this section of the book leant heavily on the NAO reports Transforming Rehabilitation: https://www.nao.org.uk/wp-content/uploads/2016/04/Transforming-rehabilitation.

pdf; Investigation into Changes to Community Rehabilitation Company Contracts: https://www.nao.org.uk/wp-content/uploads/2017/12/Investigation-into-changes-to-Community-Rehabilitation-Company-contracts.pdf; and Transforming Rehabilitation: Progress Review: https://www.nao.org.uk/wp-content/uploads/2019/02/Transforming-Rehabilitation-Progress-review.pdf. It also used the Public Account Committee's 2018 report Government Contracts for Community Rehabilitation Companies: https://publications.parliament.uk/pa/cm201719/cmselect/cmpubacc/897/897.pdf, as well as the Institute for Government's Outsourcing: What has Worked and What Needs Reform?: https://www.instituteforgovernment.org.uk/sites/default/files/publications/government-outsourcing-reform-WEB_0.pdf, and Better Policy Making: https://www.institutefor government.org.uk/sites/default/files/publications/better-policy-making.pdf.

Many of the damning quotes from senior Ministry of Justice officials came from the transcript to the witness appearance of Sir Richard Heaton and Michael Spurr at the Public Accounts Committee in 2019, which you can find here: https://data.parliament.uk/writtenevidence/committee evidence.svc/evidencedocument/public-accounts-committee/transforming-rehabilitation-progress-review/oral/98065.pdf. That transcript is a uniquely dispiriting experience. It's depressing beyond the mind's capacity for tolerance to listen to senior figures concede nearly every objection to the privatisation experiment years after they were first made, but well after it was too late. Proper head-in-hands stuff.

The impacts of the botched reforms can be seen in the various HM Inspectorate of Probation reports, for instance the one on Dorset, Devon and Cornwall Community

Rehabilitation Company: https://www.justiceinspectorates.gov.uk/hmiprobation/wp-content/uploads/sites/5/2019/02/Dorset-Devon-and-Cornwall-CRC-inspection-report.pdf, or the one on North London: https://www.justiceinspectorates.gov.uk/hmiprobation/media/press-releases/2016/12/northoflondon/, both of which are cited in the book. Official figures on changes in the serious further crimes data are available here: https://assets.publishing.service.gov.uk/government/uploads/system/uploads/attachment_data/file/751113/Annex_B_Serious_Further_Offences.pdf. You can read a news report on the coroner's findings into the murder of Conner Marshall at https://www.theguardian.com/uk-news/2020/jan/17/coroner-supervision-of-conner-marshall-killer-woefully-inadequate, or the full Report to Prevent Further Deaths document by the coroner concerning the murder of Michael Hoolickin at https://www.judiciary.uk/wp-content/uploads/2019/10/Michael-Hoolickin-2019-0292_Redacted.pdf.

In terms of the aftermath of the probation debacle, there's information on the companies going into administration here: https://www.theguardian.com/business/2019/mar/15/interserve-to-go-into-administration-after-shareholders-reject-deal, the civil service award here: https://www.civilserviceworld.com/professions/article/civil-service-awards-2015-the-full-list-of-winners, Antonia Romeo's baffling successful career here: https://www.gov.uk/government/people/antonia-romeo, and Grayling's various inadequacies at the following: https://www.theguardian.com/politics/2019/jan/02/grayling-no-deal-brexit-ferry-contract-company-seaborne-freight-no-ships; https://www.theguardian.com/politics/2019/jan/03/brexit-freight-ferry-firm-appears-all-geared-up-to-deliver-pizzas;

https://www.independent.co.uk/news/uk/politics/chris-grayling-ferry-contracts-blunders-cost-a8803296.html, and https://www.bbc.co.uk/news/uk-politics-54185180. None of it is likely to improve your mood.

The best book on the under-researched topic of the membership of Britain's political parties is *Footsoldiers: Political Party Membership in the 21st Century*, by Tim Bale, Paul Webb and Monica Poletti. Given how crucial these individuals are to the selection of MPs and party leaders, it's extraordinary that there's so little research available on the matter, but this partially makes up for it by being extremely thorough and comprehensive. There's also some information on the membership of political parties from the House of Commons Library report Membership of Political Parties in Great Britain: https://researchbriefings.files.parliament.uk/documents/SN05125/SN05125.pdf. As a side note, the Commons library is an extraordinary resource, staffed by brilliant minds, which provides authoritative reports on all sorts of subjects, all freely available to the general public. Its only weakness is that it can only investigate issues MPs ask it about, so it is restrained by the imagination of politicians. And that, unfortunately, is a very profound limitation indeed.

For more on Labour's National Executive Committee and Keir Starmer's efforts to control it, see https://labour.org.uk/about/how-we-work/national-executive-committee/, https://www.huffingtonpost.co.uk/entry/keir-starmer-labour-corbyn-left_uk_6222078ee4b02186be203a49 and https://labourlist.org/2022/01/local-party-powers-reduced-under-new-labour-guidance-for-selecting-candidates/. Central parties' control over selection during by-elections and snap elections is covered on p.25 of *How Parliament Works*. For more on what central parties have done to improve diversity and representation, see https://salbrinton.co.uk/en/article/2016/1146712/electing-diverse-mps, https://www.theguardian.com/politics/2006/apr/19/uk.conservatives and the House of Commons Library report on all-women shortlists: https://researchbriefings.files.parliament.uk/documents/SN05057/SN05057.pdf.

You can find information about the demographic details of MPs on pp.30–3 of *How Parliament Works*. For the more interesting question of their psychological disposition, read the brilliant *Who Enters Politics and Why? Basic Human Values in the UK Parliament*, by James Weinberg. It's an exceptional piece of work, on another under-researched area – albeit one that is made almost impossible to research because of the reticence of MPs themselves.

For a sense of how brutally first-past-the-post misrepresents people's votes and disenfranchises vast swathes of the electorate, read the IPPR think-tank report Worst of Both Worlds: Why First Past the Post No Longer Works: https://www.ippr.org/files/images/media/files/publication/2011/05/Worst%20of%20Both%20Worlds%20Jan2011_1820.pdf; Peterloo 200: The Path to Proportional Repre-sentation: https://static1.squarespace.com/static/563e2841e4b09a6ae020bd67/t/5d55500c9395e7000197a2c5/1565872177403/Peterloo+200+online+version.pdf; and the Electoral Reform Society briefing on the 2019 general election, Voters Left Voiceless: https://www.electoral-reform.org.uk/latest-news-and-research/publications/the-2019-general-election-voters-left-voiceless/.

There's more information on Britain's safe seats through history at https://www.electoral-reform.org.uk/14-million-voters-are-in-seats-that-havent-changed-hands-since-ww2-heres-why/ and https://www.theguardian.com/politics/2019/dec/02/14million-voters-live-areas-held-same-party-since-second-world-war, as well as the Commons Library report General Election 2019: Marginality, at https://commonslibrary.parliament.uk/general-election-2019-marginality/. There's a useful LSE blog on the way the geographic spread of the first-past-the-post system benefits various different parties over time here: https://blogs.lse.ac.uk/politicsandpolicy/electoral-bias-in-the-uk-after-the-2015-general-election/.

For the grotty little manner in which the towns fund was misused, you can read the whole story in the NAO's Review of the Town Deals Selection Process: https://www.nao.org.uk/wp-content/uploads/2020/07/Review-of-the-Town-Deals-selection-process.pdf, and the Public Accounts Committee report Selecting Towns for the Towns Fund: https://publications.parliament.uk/pa/cm5801/cmselect/cmpubacc/651/651.pdf. Chris Hanretty's revelatory cross-referencing of the data with marginality is available at the LSE: https://blogs.lse.ac.uk/politicsandpolicy/the-pork-barrel-politics-of-the-towns-fund/. To see how and why living in a marginal constituency can save your life, see 'The Impact of Competition on Management Quality: Evidence from Public Hospitals', in *The Review of Economic Studies*, Vol. 82, No. 2 (291), by Nicholas Bloom, Carol Propper, Stephan Seiler and John Van Reenen.

If you want to remind yourself of the Owen Paterson scandal, and then the ensuing scandal over the government's response to it, you can read the report by the Committee on Standards: https://committees.parliament.uk/publications/7644/documents/79907/default/, and then the news report on the ensuing whipping operation: https://news.sky.com/story/owen-paterson-former-minister-saved-from-suspension-as-tory-mps-back-standards-process-overhaul-12458870. Personally, I wouldn't recommend it, although it does have a more satisfying flavour now that we know it started a sequence of events that destroyed the Johnson administration.

There's a good crash course in the basics of the whipping operation on pp.89–90 of *How Parliament Works. Commons and Lords: A Short Anthropology of Parliament*, by Emma Crewe, has a good description of the principal private secretary to the chief whip role on p.16. This seems as good a place as any to praise that work, which I've popped into for quotes and insights throughout this book. It looks at Westminster from a very different angle and is all the more perceptive for it. It's also the source of the striking quote about personal loyalty to a party by Earl Russell, mentioned later in the members of Parliament chapter.

For a good look at Erskine May and the campaign to make it more freely available, see pp.102–4 of *Held in Contempt: What's Wrong with the House of Commons?*, by Hannah White. It's a good book, which deals lightly and effortlessly with all sorts of complex elements of Westminster. You can find Erskine May's rules on MPs accusing each other of lying here: https://erskinemay.parliament.uk/section/4874/language-and-allegations-in-relation-to-other-members-and-members-of-the-house-of-lords/.

The section on how hard it is to read legislation given its reference to amendments in other bits of legislation used the Police, Crime, Sentencing and Courts Act, the relevant section of which is available at https://www.legislation.gov.uk/ukpga/2022/32/part/3/crossheading/public-processions-and-public-assemblies/enacted. Pretty basic example, to be honest. I should have used something more complex and made myself look clever. Caroline Lucas's debate on explanatory notes to amendments is available here: https://hansard.parliament.uk/commons/2013-11-06/debates/13110694000002/AmendmentsToBills

(ExplanatoryStatements), with the depressing final tally of votes here: https://hansard.parliament.uk/Commons/2013-11-06/division/13110694000387/AmendmentsToBills(ExplanatoryStatements)?outputType=Names. You'll notice that Zac Goldsmith acquits himself well in the debate, as he does in the section of the book on the privatisation of the forestry estate. This is frustrating, because he is in general a dreadful and extremely cynical politician. But there we are – he got lucky. I do feel guilty about it, if you were wondering.

The MP job description, or rather an attempt to describe it, is available in the Speaker's Conference (on Parliamentary Representation) Final Report 2010, on p.38: https://publications.parliament.uk/pa/spconf/239/239i.pdf. For the statistics on how MPs spend their time, I used *Why We Get the Wrong Politicians*, by Isabel Hardman, which is generally very good. Despite the title, she is unfailingly kind and generous in her appraisal and yet judicious in her assessments. It's an unusual and admirable mixture of qualities. For more on MPs' constituency work, see p.104 of *How Parliament Works*.

The research on the mental health of MPs comes from 'Governing under Pressure? The Mental Wellbeing of Politicians', by Matthew Flinders, Ashley Weinberg, James Weinberg, Marc Geddes and Richard Kwiatkowski, in *Parliamentary Affairs*, Vol. 73, Issue 2, and 'The Mental Health of Politicians', by Ashley Weinberg in *Palgrave Communications*, Issue 3. You'll notice that Weinberg has the same surname as James Weinberg, who wrote the book on the psychology of MPs. That's because they're father and son, albeit with quite distinct views on the subject they both cover. They are both absolutely delightful, and it's touching to watch them refer so admiringly to the other's work despite disagreeing with much of it.

The section on the constitutional implications, or lack of them, from MP rebellions is taken mostly from pp.336–8 of *The British Constitution*, by Anthony King. It's an exceptional book – witty, charming, knowledgeable, expansive, and highly recommended if you're going to dig deeper on this stuff. His central argument is almost the opposite to mine, but I loved it regardless and got a lot from it. There's more information on backbench rebellions during the coalition era in Philip Cowley's blog, The Most Rebellious Parliament in the Post-War Era: https://www.psa.ac.uk/psa/news/most-rebellious-parliament-post-war-era. You can read up on the Sunday trading issue at https://www.bbc.co.uk/news/uk-politics-35768674 and https://www.theguardian.com/business/2016/mar/09/cameron-defeated-in-commons-over-plans-to-relax-sunday-trading-laws; see Nicola McEwen's assessment of the Internal Market Act at https://twitter.com/McEwen_Nicola/status/1303721735657840640?s=20&t=ThZURV5OoTGnrK-fNVPkfA; and read about the forestry privatisation attempt in the House of Commons Library's The Forestry Commission and the Sale of Public Forests in England https://researchbriefings.files.parliament.uk/documents/SN05734/SN05734.pdf.

The assessments of the comparative size of No. 10 next to international competitors comes mostly from two books – pp.315–20 of the 2014 edition of *The Blunders of Our Governments*, by Anthony King and Ivor Crewe, and p.48 of *No. 10: The Geography of Power at Downing Street*, by Jack Brown. The former is a fine book, looking at a variety of cock-ups under a variety of governments and trying to work out why they happened. If you've got this far in this book, you won't be surprised by the answers. It's perhaps a little scattershot, and some experts are sceptical about the research, but it's generally delightful and perceptive. The latter is a great little history of Downing Street from the first person to ever research it in residence. A lot of the history and the assessment of the spatial layout in this chapter comes from it. The best section on the history is in pp.24–37, and on the spatial arrangement from p.37 onwards.

Gavin Barwell, who worked as chief of staff to Theresa May, wrote the imaginatively titled *Chief of Staff: Notes from Downing Street*, from which I've taken the assessment of a typical prime minister's working week. He also provides his own assessment of the face-time phenomenon on pp.54–9, as does Brown in the pages above. Barwell's book is competently written, and it makes for a useful historical document of a crazed political period, although it is hard to tally its values with the reality of how the May administration operated.

The relationship between various prime ministers and their Cabinets is explored in pp.324–6 of *The British Constitution*, by Anthony King. There's a good assessment of the Downing Street Private Office in pp.56–8 of *No. 10: The Geography of Power at Downing Street* and p.52 of *Chief of Staff: Notes from Downing Street.*

The origin of the Policy Unit is elaborated on p.229 of *The British Constitution* and on pp.17–22 of *Special Advisers: Who They Are, What They Do and Why They Matter*, by Ben Yong and Robert Hazell. This is an excellent and extremely useful book on another under-researched area of British politics. It's perhaps a little too generous to special advisers for my tastes, but as a research document it is impeccable. The expansion of the Downing Street units under Blair is covered in p.316 of *The Blunders of Our Governments*, while the growth of spads in the New Labour period is described on p.230. *Special Advisers: Who They Are, What They Do and Why They Matter* looks at the Policy Unit through the years on pp.21–5. You can read about its decline on p.74 of *No. 10: The Geography of Power at Downing Street* and see the policy impact on A&E waiting times in a King's Fund report at https://www.kingsfund.org.uk/projects/urgent-emergency-care/urgent-and-emergency-care-mythbusters or in media reports such as this one: https://news.sky.com/story/nhs-more-than-1-000-people-waiting-longer-than-12-hours-in-a-e-every-day-figures-reveal-12633551.

There's an excellent description of a reshuffle gone horribly wrong in *Chief of Staff: Notes from Downing Street*, pp.158–66, which serves to demonstrate the knock-on Rubik's Cube effects of the practice. The book also describes the scale of ministerial churn on p.174, which serves as a useful comparison with the relative stability of places like Germany, as described in *The Blunders of Our Governments*, pp.321–2. *Blunders* also has a useful assessment of the consequent increase in legislation on p.344.

The demographic details of spads are described in *Special Advisers: Who They Are, What They Do and Why They Matter*, pp.40–6; their various duties are on pp.65–72; and the extent of No. 10 control over them is on pp.57–8. That's supplemented by an excellent appraisal of how centralised control expanded under the Johnson administration in the Institute for Government report Special Advisers and the Johnson Government: How the Prime Minister and His Team are Changing the Role: https://www.instituteforgovernment.org.uk/sites/default/files/publications/special-advisers-johnson-government.pdf, particularly p.23 and pp.57–8.

The quote about early civil service resistance to spads came from p.130 of *Laying Down the Law: A Discussion of the People, Processes and Problems that Shape Acts of Parliament*, by former parliamentary counsel Daniel Greenberg. You'll notice that his quotes pop up a lot. That is because I fell deeply in love with him while reading the book, which is arguably the most purely enjoyable of all the documents listed here. Greenberg is perhaps eccentric, and not exactly representative of the Office of Parliamentary Counsel, but he is an absolute delight – witty, savage, honest, and ultimately deeply principled in his recognition of what the task of writing law entails. I had to delete at least half his quotes from the first draft of the book, and even now there are probably too many of them. I don't care. He's very amusing indeed.

For the various attempts by No. 10 to batter the Treasury down to size, see *The Chancellors: Steering the British Economy in Crisis Times*, by Howard Davies, pp.162–9. I relied on this book extensively for this section – Davies is a highly experienced Treasury man and brings really sound judgement to the task, even where the results do not cast the Treasury in a good light. He has excellent sections on the independence of the Bank of England on pp.21–5, the Office of Budget Responsibility on p.16, the role of the chief secretary to the Treasury on p.193 and the inadequacy of the Budget process on p.72. For a look at the attempts by the Johnson administration to control the department, see the Institute for Government report Special Advisers and the Johnson Government: How the Prime Minister and His Team are Changing the Role, which I mentioned earlier. For the OBR economic and fiscal outlook that irritated Rishi Sunak by daring to mention Brexit, see https://obr.uk/docs/dlm_uploads/CCS1020397650-001_OBR-November2020-EFO-v2-Web-accessible.pdf; and for the then-chancellor's reaction, see https://www.thetimes.co.uk/article/rishi-sunak-viscerally-hates-office-for-budget-responsibility-mffwtgnvh.

The quote from John Kingman on the intellectually vivacious culture in the Treasury is taken from his speech and Q&A at the Institute for Government, a video of which is available here: https://www.instituteforgovernment.org.uk/events/civil-service-reform-john-kingman. You'll notice that speech popping up rather a lot in the text, because it is very good and worth watching in full.

The best read on the Treasury's spatial failures on investment comes from Diane Coyle and Marianne Sensier (2019): 'The Imperial Treasury: Appraisal Methodology and Regional Economic Performance in the UK', in Regional Studies, Vol. 54, Issue 3. The ensuing Green Book changes are at https://www.gov.uk/government/publications/final-report-of-the-2020-green-book-review. For more on the insanity of the Treasury's refusal to properly spend on school catch-up after the pandemic, see the Royal Society report Balancing the Risks of Pupils Returning to Schools: https://rs-delve.github.io/reports/2020/07/24/balancing-the-risk-of-pupils-returning-to-schools.html#3-learning-loss-from-school-closures; a comment piece by Luke Sibieta for the Institute for Fiscal Studies: https://ifs.org.uk/articles/crisis-lost-learning-calls-massive-national-policy-response; another Institute for Fiscal Studies comment piece by Luke Sibieta and Ben Zaranko: https://ifs.org.uk/articles/hm-treasury-stingy-and-short-sighted-or-prudent-and-practical; and this blog by Robert Slavin, which highlights some of the potential pitfalls of catch-up provision: https://robertslavinsblog.wordpress.com/2021/02/11/avoiding-the-errors-of-supplemental-educational-services-ses/.

On the absurdities of the UK's tax policy, see Better Budgets: Making Tax Policy Better, by the Chartered Institute of Taxation, the Institute for Fiscal Studies and the Institute for Government, which is a proper little troika of gravitas if ever I saw one. It's available at https://www.instituteforgovernment.org.uk/sites/default/files/publications/Better_Budgets_report_WEB.pdf. I'd also strongly recommend Tax Without Design: Recent Developments in UK Tax Policy, by IFS director Paul Johnson: https://ifs.org.uk/sites/default/files/output_url_files/wp201409.pdf. The section on VAT, from which I took the silly examples about things like gingerbread men, is on p.14. There's an excellent section on marginal rates on pp.3–5, which can be read alongside p.12 of the Centre for Policy Studies' Make Work Pay report: https://cps.org.uk/wp-content/uploads/2021/07/181105085949-MakeWorkPay.pdf. And finally there's the Mirrlees review, which is an absolute beast of a thing. Volume one is available at https://ifs.org.uk/sites/default/files/output_url_files/mirrlees_dimensions.pdf and volume two at https://ifs.org.uk/sites/default/files/output_url_files/taxbydesign.pdf. That's around 2,500 pages of tightly argued tax analysis right there. Have fun. See you when you get back.

For a look at the Northcote–Trevelyan settlement for the civil service, check out p.15 of *Special Advisers: Who They Are, What They Do and Why They Matter*. *The British Constitution* has a decent timeline of the increased submissiveness of the service on pp.217–26, while *The Blunders of Our Governments* covers the attack under New Labour on p.335. The various increasingly deranged insults hurled at the civil service during the 2022 Tory leadership campaign can be found at https://www.telegraph.co.uk/politics/2022/08/15/rishi-sunak-plans-combat-civil-service-groupthink-making-staff/; https://www.gbnews.uk/news/penny-mordaunt-claims-whitehall-is-broken-as-she-outlines-plans-for-a-tighter-cabinet/337595; https://www.standard.co.uk/news/politics/brexit-news-suella-braverman-civil-servant-remain-b1009918.html; and https://www.independent.co.uk/news/uk/politics/truss-woke-civil-service-antisemitism-b2143875.html. Daniel Greenberg has some great quotes on this increased reticence from officials on p.57 and p.133 of *Laying Down the Law: A Discussion of the People, Processes and Problems that Shape Acts of Parliament*, which I stitched together in the text.

There's analysis of Thomas Balogh's criticism of the service at https://civilservant.org.uk/csr-fulton_report-background.html, while the Fulton report itself can be found at https://civilservant.org.uk/csr-fulton_report-findings.html. It is still very good and worth reading. Little has changed since it was written.

The various half-hearted attempts to fix the civil service can be found in 'One Step Forward, Two Steps Back? The Rise and Fall of Government's Next Steps Agencies': https://www.civilserviceworld.com/news/article/one-step-forward-two-steps-back-the-rise-and-fall-of-governments-next-steps-agencies; p.13 of the Institute for Government's Better Policy Making report: https://www.instituteforgovernment.org.uk/sites/default/files/publications/better-policy-making.pdf; the public administration select committee Skills for Government report: https://publications.parliament.uk/pa/cm200607/cmselect/cmpubadm/93/93i.pdf; and p.19 and p.42 of the Institute for

Government's Moving On: The Costs of High Staff Turnover in the Civil Service https://www.instituteforgovernment.org.uk/sites/default/files/publications/IfG_staff_turnover_WEB.pdf. For an indication of how ineffective they were after all that, have a read of Michael Gove's speech on the service: https://reaction.life/michael-gove-speech-the-privilege-of-public-service/; or Kate Bingham's: https://www.ox.ac.uk/news/2021-11-24-another-war-coming-kate-bingham-dbe-delivers-romanes-lecture.

There's an account of Lord Freud's experiences at the Universal Credit programme on p.23 of Moving On: The Costs of High Staff Turnover in the Civil Service, which I mentioned above and will do again in a moment. And there's an assessment of what a botched job they did in the Lords economic committee report on it: https://publications.parliament.uk/pa/ld5801/ldselect/ldeconaf/105/10503.htm.

You can read a bit about the civil service grade structure here: https://www.instituteforgovernment.org.uk/explainers/grade-structures-civil-service, and get a sense of pay here: https://www.prospects.ac.uk/job-profiles/civil-service-fast-streamer. The section on pay impacting churn and staff quality comes from John Kingman's speech, mentioned above.

The section on the state of the Treasury civil service during the financial crash comes mostly from Sharon White's Review of HM Treasury's Management Response to the Financial Crisis. The horrific little nugget about the lack of ambassadors who can speak Arabic in the Middle East comes from Rory Stewart and can be found here: https://www.civilserviceworld.com/professions/article/rory-stewart-calls-for-greater-local-expertise-in-national-strategy-and-across-fco.

The success of the Rough Sleeping Unit under New Labour is covered in the Institute for Government's Better Policy

Making report on p.13, while the impact of churn on the government capacity to deal with the problem is documented on p.24 of Moving On: The Costs of High Staff Turnover in the Civil Service. The real-world impact can be found at https://www.ons.gov.uk/peoplepopulationandcommunity/housing/articles/roughsleepingintheuk/2002to2021.

For a general appraisal of the lack of specialist skills in the civil service, and the reasons why it happens, read Moving On: The Costs of High Staff Turnover in the Civil Service, particularly pp.11–14 on churn in the senior positions; the Public Accounts Committee report Specialist Skills in the Civil Service: https://committees.parliament.uk/publications/3932/documents/39375/default/; the NAO's Identifying and Meeting Central Government's Skills Requirements: https://www.nao.org.uk/wp-content/uploads/2011/07/10121276.pdf; and Improving Government's Planning and Spending Framework, also by the NAO: https://www.nao.org.uk/wp-content/uploads/2018/11/Improving-government%E2%80%99s-planning-and-spending-framework.pdf.

The use of consultants in the civil service is documented in the Public Accounts Committee report Building Schools for the Future: Renewing the Secondary School Estate: https://publications.parliament.uk/pa/cm200809/cmselect/cmpubacc/274/274.pdf; the Institute for Government's Managing Consultants: A Guide for Working with Consultants in Government: https://www.instituteforgovernment.org.uk/sites/default/files/publications/managing-consultants_0.pdf; and an absolute cornucopia of NAO reports, including Use of Consultants and Temporary Staff: https://www.nao.org.uk/wp-content/uploads/2016/01/Use-of-consultants-and-temporary-labour.pdf; Commercial Skills for Complex Government Projects: https://www.

nao.org.uk/wp-content/uploads/2009/11/0809962es.pdf; Opinion Pieces on Improving Commercial Skills for Complex Government Projects: https://www.nao.org.uk/wp-content/uploads/2009/11/0809962_opinion_pieces.pdf; and Identifying and Meeting Central Government's Skills Requirements: https://www.nao.org.uk/wp-content/uploads/2011/07/10121276.pdf. There's also a report on the use of consultants during Brexit in particular called Departments' Use of Consultants to Support Preparations for EU Exit: https://www.nao.org.uk/wp-content/uploads/2019/05/Departments-use-of-consultants-to-support-preparations-for-EU-Exit.pdf.

The chapter on the press leant heavily on Mick Temple's brief, dense and authoritative *The Rise and Fall of the British Press*, which is highly recommended for anyone interested in the topic, particularly pp.13–34 on the early history of the press, pp.34–46 on the influence of press barons from Beaverbrook to Murdoch, p.51 on the death of sales, and pp.59–64 on the decline of the local press.

Alan Rusbridger's *Breaking News: The Remaking of Journalism and Why it Matters Now* is an exceptional account of what it's like to edit a national newspaper through this period of technological turmoil, written with a proper sense of moral responsibility and thoughtfulness in the face of extreme market chaos. Pages 69–75 are good on the impact on sales, as are p.124 and pp.166–7, while p.152 is fascinating on the *Guardian*'s penetration of the US market and how little money came from it. For more on the reduced time available to journalists see Nick Davies' book *Flat Earth News*, although the problem has arguably become more severe since then.

The lovely W. T. Stead quote on the influence of the

press can be found here: https://www.attackingthedevil.co.uk/steadworks/gov.php – it's really worth reading the article in full. The strange story of whatever happened to *Mail* editor Geordie Greig can be traced through various news reports, including https://www.dailymail.co.uk/news/article-8441961/Daily-Mail-Britains-biggest-selling-daily-newspaper-time-124-year-history.html; https://www.theguardian.com/media/2021/nov/17/geordie-greig-ousted-as-editor-of-the-daily-mail; https://www.independent.co.uk/news/media/paul-dacre-editor-daily-mail-b1962333.html; and https://www.thetimes.co.uk/article/former-daily-mail-editor-paul-dacre-is-dropped-from-peerages-list-skfcrh0k9. For the government's more formal press operations, see p.70 of *No. 10: The Geography of Power at Downing Street* for the birth of the press office; p.116 of *Special Advisers: Who They Are, What They Do and Why They Matter* for the New Labour attack on official communications; and p.45 of *Chief of Staff: Notes from Downing Street* for the set-up under Theresa May. For an account of government media strategy in the UK read Ruth Garland's 2021 book *Government Communications and the Crisis of Trust: From Political Spin to Post-Truth*.

The chapter on the Afghanistan evacuation is based overwhelmingly on the Foreign Affairs Committee report Missing in Action: UK Leadership and the Withdrawal from Afghanistan: https://committees.parliament.uk/publications/22344/documents/165210/default/. It's arguably the most important select committee report of the last decade, in both the scale of the disaster it is covering and the depth and breadth of the failures it is outlining. Of particular importance are pp.6–7, pp.12–13, p.17 and p.26, which outline the failure of preparation in advance of the Taliban takeover.

There's more on the failure of preparation in these reports, which outline the far superior French response: https://www.politico.com/newsletters/global-translations/2021/08/25/why-did-french-evacuations-go-well-from-the-beginning-494124 and https://www.ft.com/content/fcf46b6d-f650-482b-8a7a-f862cb4f3626. For more on the Taliban advance, see https://www.reuters.com/world/asia-pacific/taliban-claims-control-key-afghan-border-crossing-with-pakistan-2021-07-14/; and https://www.reuters.com/world/asia-pacific/half-all-afghan-district-centers-under-taliban-control-us-general-2021-07-21/. For details of the superior, but still abysmal, ARAP operation, see the testimony of R. R. Davis: https://committees.parliament.uk/writtenevidence/41121/html/. For more on Afghan ethnic groups, see the testimony of the Afghanistan and Central Asian Association: https://committees.parliament.uk/writtenevidence/40550/html/.

The written testimony by Raphael Marshall and Josie Stewart deserves to be read on its own. The first is available at https://committees.parliament.uk/writtenevidence/41257/html/ and the second at https://committees.parliament.uk/writtenevidence/107001/html/. They sacrificed their jobs to provide it. Without it, we wouldn't know what went wrong back then. It's as damning an assessment of British state failure as exists in the modern period.

For the full story of the Nowzad debacle, see both testimonies as well as pp.31–5 of the select committee report, and p.55, which features the conclusion that the prime minister ordered the evacuation. For more about the reprisals that followed the British withdrawal, see the testimony of Shaharzad Akbar, chairperson of the Afghanistan Independent Human Rights Commission, and Shukria Barakzai, a former Afghan MP, which is available at https://committees.parliament.uk/oralevidence/2835/html/.

For a brilliant explainer on the rise of standing orders and how they gave the government so much control over Parliament, read the introduction by Paul Evans to the anthology publication *Essays on the History of Parliamentary Procedure*, entitled 'The Growth of Many Centuries'. Evans is a fierce and extremely knowledgeable defender of Parliament, as he demonstrates in the text of his own work and through quotations in this one. The book in general was much improved by his participation. The standing orders themselves are available here: https://publications.parliament.uk/pa/cm201719/cmstords/1020/body.html.

For a description of how most parliaments around the world decide for themselves how they'll spend their time, see *How Parliament Works*, p.82, and then compare it to how we do it, on p.60. There's more information on that in the Wright committee report, Rebuilding the House, pp.46–7: https://publications.parliament.uk/pa/cm200809/cmselect/cmrefhoc/1117/1117.pdf. It's worth reading the report in full. It's an exceptional piece of work, and its partial implementation remains a tragedy. Its account of its own origin is on p.8, while its recommendations for how the Commons timetable should work are on pp.49–60. *How Parliament Works* has an account of how the Wright reform initiative spluttered out on pp.150–1.

The ancient history of the select committees is in *How Parliament Works*, pp.321–2, as well as in *Commons and Lords: A Short Anthropology of Parliament*, p.37. There's a good obituary of St John-Stevas available at https://www.pressreader.com/uk/daily-mail/20120306/292190921785695. On how the select committees operate, see *How Parliament Works*, pp.322–4, pp.334–7 and p.342. For an account of the psychology of those who sit on the committees and what it does to them, see p.142 of *Who Enters Politics and Why? Basic Human Values in the UK Parliament*; and https://www.democraticaudit.com/2016/07/06/elected-chairs-do-not-seem-to-have-brought-a-new-kind-of-parliamentarian-to-select-committees/. For an account of their influence, see the UCL Constitution Unit's report Selective Influence: The Policy Impact of House of Commons Select Committees, by Meg Russell and Meghan Benton, which is available at https://www.ucl.ac.uk/constitution-unit/sites/constitution-unit/files/153.pdf.

This seems as good a time as any to praise Russell. I've never studied a subject area over which one figures towers so comprehensively. Her work has dominated the study of Parliament for decades. No matter which assessment you read on it, including this one, you'll find her name there. She'll likely disagree with much that's in this book, but it has been hugely improved by the work she has done and her contribution to it. If it weren't for her, our understanding of that building and what on earth is going on it would be immeasurably poorer.

For more on Theresa May's attacks on opposition days, see p.83 of *How Parliament Works* and the relevant Commons Library briefing: https://commonslibrary.parliament.uk/research-briefings/sn06315/.

There are some really key documents out there on statutory instruments, which are doing much of the work of trying to hold these things to account. The first is the Delegated Powers and Regulatory Reform Committee report Democracy Denied? The Urgent Need to Rebalance Power Between Parliament and the Executive, which is available at https://committees.parliament.uk/publications/7960/documents/82286/default/. If you read one thing in this list, probably make it that. The Hansard Society, which – bless them – have been valiantly fighting away on this for some time, have a Compendium of Legislative Standards for Delegating Powers in Primary Legislation, which is available at https://assets.ctfassets.net/n4ncz0i02v4l/29QkqxRDf2k1N4RKN7U5rh/b57e742da52400864d99aec6ae91cef9/Hansard_Society_Legislative_Standards_for_Delegating_Powers_Report_April_2022.pdf. If you'd like to be all after-dinner about it, make a gin and tonic and read the speech by Sir Jonathan Jones, which is available at https://www.ucl.ac.uk/laws/sites/laws/files/statute_law_society_re_secondary_legislation_edited_-_j.jones_27102021.pdf.

Several statutory instruments are mentioned in that section. I'm going to lay out the various reports, mostly from the Lords Delegated Powers and Regulatory Reform Committee, on what they contain. They can all be read by a layman without the original legislation in front of you, and I would strongly recommend you sample at least one or two to get a sense of the scale of the problem. There's one on haulage: https://www.hansardsociety.org.uk/blog/in-it-for-the-long-haul-hgv-driver-shortage-statutory-instruments-show; pornography: https://www.newstatesman.com/politics/2014/12/government-s-new-porn-laws-are-arbitrary-and-sexist; protests: https://publications.parliament.uk/pa/ld5802/ldselect/lddelreg/65/6503.htm; public order: https://committees.parliament.uk/publications/31504/documents/176700/default/; EU withdrawal: https://publications.parliament.uk/pa/ld201719/ldselect/lddelreg/22/2204.htm; schools: https://committees.parliament.uk/publications/22454/documents/165479/default/; immigration detention: https://www.legislation.gov.uk/uksi/2021/962/contents/made; carbon reduction targets: https://www.legislation.

gov.uk/ukdsi/2019/9780111187654; Brexit healthcare provisions: https://publications.parliament.uk/pa/ld201719/ldselect/lddelreg/226/22604.htm, and the Agriculture Bill: https://publications.parliament.uk/pa/ld201719/ldselect/lddelreg/194/19403.htm. There's also, of course, a lot of material on the COVID statutory instruments, which are covered very well in *Held in Contempt: What's Wrong with the House of Commons?*, pp.21–4. You can see the speed with which they were passed by looking at the details around their implementation, such as this: https://www.legislation.gov.uk/uksi/2021/150/pdfs/uksiem_20210150_en.pdf; and this: https://www.legislation.gov.uk/uksi/2020/1103/schedule/1/paragraph/13/made.

The general growth in statutory instruments is outlined in *The Blunders of Our Governments*, p.344, while *Laying Down the Law: A Discussion of the People, Processes and Problems that Shape Acts of Parliament* describes how lawmakers felt as they started to suspect they had become the default form of legislation. A definition of the instruments can be found in *How Parliament Works*, p.238, along with the practicalities of negative versus positive instruments on pp.240–2. There's more on that from the Hansard Society at https://www.hansardsociety.org.uk/blog/living-on-a-prayer-motion-how-do-parliamentarians-debate-made-negative, while the Institute for Government has useful material on just how little time MPs spend scrutinising them at https://www.instituteforgovernment.org.uk/publication/parliamentary-monitor-2020/secondary-legislation.

For a very good explanation of the lawmaking process in the Parliamentary Counsel's office, read – you guessed it – *Laying Down the Law: A Discussion of the People, Processes and Problems that Shape Acts of Parliament*. If your Clive-Barker's-Pinhead level of sadomasochism is so extensive that you want to watch chief whip Mark Spencer trying to convince a Lords committee on how effective the PBL is, you can watch it here: https://www.parliamentlive.tv/Event/Index/cd967995-32b6-4c51-a3af-4be5dc12b929. If, on the other hand, you want evidence of how it works in practice, you can see the effects in Priti Patel's late-stage additions to the policing bill at https://inews.co.uk/opinion/priti-patel-anti-protest-powers-stuffed-policing-bill-1316830, and the subsequent hammering it received in the Lords at https://twitter.com/ConUnit_UCL/status/1483458121607622659?s=20&t=uXNhRm4gV-ZLsdHKvEotHA. You can find out more about what they were trying and then failing to do with education policy at https://committees.parliament.uk/publications/22454/documents/165479/default/ and https://www.theguardian.com/education/2022/jun/30/government-announces-u-turn-on-schools-bill-after-criticism.

There's useful material on the first reading stage of a bill on p.193 of *How Parliament Works* and on the second reading on p.194. Committee stage is dealt with in pp.196–205 and p.371. *The Blunders of Our Governments* has a useful section on pp.370–2 listing the faults of the system and the various ways in which it's done much better in other countries, particularly Germany. There's very good material on report stage on p.90 of the Wright committee report, available here: https://publications.parliament.uk/pa/cm200809/cmselect/cmrefhoc/1117/1117.pdf; and on p.207 of *How Parliament Works*.

Programme motions are dealt with on p.187 of *How Parliament Works*. The usual channels are dealt with on p.90, as well as on p.50 of the Wright committee report. Third reading is on p.207 of *How Parliament Works*.

There's a very good history of various efforts at Lords reform from 1911 to Robin Cook in pp.298–303 of *The British Constitution*. A technical account of how the Parliament Act works, along with the Salisbury Convention, can be found on pp.223–5 of *How Parliament Works*. You can see the composition of the Lords by party and peerage type at https://members.parliament.uk/parties/lords/by-peerage. And to put a more dispiriting angle on it, there's information about some of Boris Johnson's more egregious appointments at https://www.bbc.co.uk/news/uk-politics-60765665 and https://www.gov.uk/government/news/political-peerages-2020.

You can see the extent of government defeats in the Lords and, more importantly, accepted amendments, in *The British Constitution*, p.307, and *How Parliament Works*, pp.226–7. For an example, you can read about the 'breathing space' debt respite system at https://bills.parliament.uk/bills/1990/stages/9993/amendments/7933 and https://www.gov.uk/government/publications/debt-respite-scheme-breathing-space-guidance/debt-respite-scheme-breathing-space-guidance-for-creditors. The extent of whip cohesion in the Lords is on p.41 of *How Parliament Works*, while the Chamber's hatred of dogma is outlined on p.2 of *Commons and Lords: A Short Anthropology of Parliament*.

For ping-pong, see p.230 of *How Parliament Works*, p.306 of *The British Constitution*, and the excellent Hansard Society blog by Paul Evans called Ping-Pong and Packaging: https://www.hansardsociety.org.uk/blog/ping-pong-and-packaging. As an example, the epic battle over the Prevention of Terrorism Bill is documented at https://monthlyreview.org/2005/11/01/the-end-of-habeas-corpus-in-great-britain/; https://www.hrw.org/legacy/

backgrounder/eca/uk0305/; https://www.theguardian.com/politics/2005/mar/10/uk.september111; and on p.230 of *How Parliament Works*.

The fight over the Dissolution of Parliament Bill is outlined in the Commons Library research briefing on the topic, which is available at https://researchbriefings.files.parliament.uk/documents/CBP-9308/CBP-9308.pdf. The Constitution Unit's warning is at https://constitution-unit.com/2022/03/09/the-house-of-lords-amendment-to-the-dissolution-and-calling-of-parliament-bill-returns-appropriate-power-to-mps-they-should-accept-it/. Jacob Rees-Mogg's threat of a snap election is at https://twitter.com/gov2uk/status/158306 9395060166656?lang=en. The Lord Judge amendment is at https://votes.parliament.uk/votes/lords/division/2683. The Lords debate, together with that very striking speech by Lord Judge, is at https://hansard.parliament.uk/lords/2022-02-09/debates/B64A4892-4F08-4DDD-AEF9-101093D87DDB/DissolutionAndCallingOfParliamentBill#contribution-01E537E5-2542-499F-A027-FB918DD1D707. The ensuing, predictably disappointing, Commons debate is at https://hansard.parliament.uk/commons/2022-03-14/debates/885EE1A2-32C5-44EE-B3F0-4A6F2824C743/DissolutionAndCallingOfParliamentBill. The even more disappointing Commons vote is at https://hansard.parliament.uk/Commons/2022-03-14/division/DB526832-B94C-4D26-BE35-703B2B53C735/DissolutionAndCallingOfParliamentBill?outputType=Party. And then, even more predictably, Johnson's final snap election threat is at https://www.youtube.com/watch?v=0fMYh8AAHxg.

The outline of how constituencies might work in a proportional system is taken from work by the late, great Ron Johnston, Britain's foremost political geographer, which was then updated by Kevin Cunningham. There's a piece by Jack Blumenau and Simon Hix for the LSE on what the House of Commons might look like if the election were held under a more proportionate voting system, which is available here: https://blogs.lse.ac.uk/politicsandpolicy/what-would-the-election-look-like-under-pr-2/.

And if you've read all that, I would recommend a long sit-down in a darkened room with that gin and tonic, to have a good hard think about what you're doing with your life. That was certainly my approach to the experience.

Index